Collins

Student Support
Materials for
AQA A2 Psychology

Unit 4
Psychopathology

Author: Alison Lee
Series editors: Mike Cardwell and Alison Wadeley

Published by Collins Education
An imprint of HarperCollins*Publishers*
77–85 Fulham Palace Road
Hammersmith
London
W6 8JB

Browse the complete Collins Education catalogue at www.collinseducation.com

ISBN 978-0-00-741841-1

British Library Cataloguing in Publication Data.
A catalogue record for this publication is available from the British Library.

Commissioned by Charlie Evans and Andrew Campbell
Project managed by Shirley Wakley
Editorial: Hugh Hillyard-Parker
Design and typesetting by G Brasnett, Cambridge
Cover Design by Angela English
Production by Simon Moore
Printed and bound by L.E.G.O. S.p.A. Italy
Indexed by Christine Boylan

Acknowledgements
Every effort has been made to contact the holders of copyright material, but if
any have been inadvertently overlooked the publishers will be pleased to make
the necessary arrangements at the first opportunity.

Credits and Permissions
p.8 (Table 1), McGuffin, P., Farmer, A., and Gottesman, I.I., (1987), 'Is there
really a split in schizophrenia? The genetic evidence', *The British Journal of
Psychiatry*, 150, 581–92, Royal College of Psychiatrists; p.40 (Fig. 2), adapted
from Beck, A. T. (1976), *Cognitive therapy and emotional disorders*, New York:
International Universities Press; p.52 (Fig. 5), Ellis, A. (2001), Overcoming
Destructive Beliefs, Feeling, and Behaviors: New Directions for Rational
Emotive Behavior Therapy, Promotheus Books; p.57 (Study), Office for
National Statistics.

Illustrations and photographs
Cover and p.1, © Greg Hargreaves/gettyimages.co.uk; p.50, © Manchan/
gettyimages.co.uk; p.54, © Gina Sanders/shutterstock.com.

Contents

Clinical characteristics

Schizophrenia is a psychiatric disorder characterized by a lack of contact with reality. It is one of the major **psychoses**. Someone diagnosed with schizophrenia would characteristically experience delusions (a belief in something that is not true) and hallucinations (experiencing stimuli that are not present), both of which severely disrupt normal cognitive functioning. The delusions, in particular, would be most characteristic of madness or insanity. The schizophrenic would seem as though they were having difficulty telling reality from fantasy. Schizophrenia is a very serious condition and can be disabling especially in an acute phase.

Emil Kraepelin first described schizophrenia at the end of the 19th century. He was one of the first people to try to make sense of insanity by grouping together the common **symptoms** (behavioural characteristics) he saw in his patients. Eugen Bleuler refined Kraepelin's early description of schizophrenia in 1911, and this was then further refined by Kurt Schneider in 1959. Schneider divided the symptoms of schizophrenia into two groups, positive symptoms and negative symptoms:

- Positive symptoms reflect behaviours the patient is experiencing that they should not be if they were well.
- Negative symptoms are behaviours the patient should be showing but is not, such as having conversations.

Positive symptoms are the more characteristic of schizophrenia, as they are the most disturbing. There are many possible symptoms of schizophrenia, but not every patient displays all the symptoms.

Positive symptoms of schizophrenia

Positive symptoms include different types of hallucination and delusion.

Hallucinations
The most common hallucinations are auditory hallucinations, when the person with schizophrenia hears something, normally an unknown voice, saying things when there is really no one there. However, the person can also see things that are not there (visual hallucination) and feel as though someone is touching them (tactile hallucination). More rare are hallucinations involving the other senses of taste and smell. When people first experience hallucinations, they may think these are real, but often with experience they can learn to tell when they are hallucinating. Nevertheless, hallucinations must be frightening experiences.

Delusions
Delusions frequently involve the person losing control of their thoughts. For example, **thought broadcasting** is the belief that an external force is broadcasting what the individual is thinking to others (on radio or television). **Thought insertion** is when an external force makes the individual think something that is distasteful or unwelcome in some way. This can lead to delusions of control when the individual feels as though they are not in control of their thoughts or actions.

Essential notes

Schizophrenia can be thought of as a collection of behavioural symptoms. For a diagnosis of schizophrenia, the person must show several different kinds of abnormal behaviour.

Other kinds of delusions are:

- **delusions of belief** – when the person experiencing schizophrenia may think they have special powers or that people around them have special powers
- **paranoid** or **persecutory delusions** – the belief that the individual is being followed by spies or other people who want to harm them.

Although these beliefs may seem silly, when you are the person experiencing them, you are convinced they are real. Someone telling you not to be silly will only feed into the delusion ('well they would say that, as they are against me too'). This has led some psychiatrists to say that the positive signs of schizophrenia reflect a **reality-monitoring deficit** – a problem telling what is real from what is not.

Incoherent or irrelevant speech

The other positive symptoms of schizophrenia are incoherent or irrelevant speech, where speech can be rambling and sparking off in all directions (known as **knight's move thinking**). It can be very difficult to follow the speech of someone experiencing schizophrenia, something that can only add to their sense of isolation.

Catatonic behaviour

A final positive symptom of schizophrenia is **catatonic behaviour**, where the individual makes characteristic movements that are repetitive or purposeless. Someone with catatonia may twist their bodies into strange positions or sometimes not move at all.

Negative symptoms of schizophrenia

Negative symptoms include a **flatness of affect**, meaning the individual seems apathetic and talks without emotion. Sometimes someone with schizophrenia can answer questions with a meaningless phrase. This is known as **poverty of speech**. A final negative symptom is **anhedonia**, which is defined as the inability to react to pleasure or enjoyable experiences.

Diagnosis of schizophrenia

Because not all people will show all the symptoms described above, psychiatrists have to be careful about making a diagnosis of schizophrenia. Diagnostic manuals, such as the **ICD** (see p. 6), stress the minimum number of symptoms that a patient needs to show for a set period of time. The ICD views thought control, delusions of control, hearing hallucinatory voices and other delusions as the most important symptoms. The patient needs to have been experiencing one of these for at least a month. The less important symptoms are persistent hallucinations of any kind, the negative symptoms, catatonia and speech problems. The patient needs to be experiencing at least two of these over a month to be diagnosed as schizophrenic.

Essential notes

These types of reality monitoring deficits make it difficult for the person to seek help, or even to be aware that they need help. This makes it difficult to diagnose schizophrenia. Similarly, treatment is often distrusted because it feeds into the delusion the person is experiencing.

Examiners' notes

You will never be asked to distinguish between positive and negative symptoms in an exam question. In fact, you will never be asked about symptoms at all! Questions will use the term 'clinical characteristics', for which detailing the symptoms is the most obvious response. You can select positive or negative symptoms or both.

Essential notes

It is more typical for people to think of the positive symptoms of schizophrenia rather than the negative ones. It is easier to identify the presence of certain behaviours than the absence of others. This bias is also reflected in the way the diagnostic manuals describe schizophrenic behaviour; hence a person is more likely to be diagnosed as a result of positive symptoms than of negative ones.

Issues in classification and diagnosis

There are no diagnostic tests for schizophrenia; a doctor cannot tell if someone has the condition by looking at their blood or scanning their brain. For a diagnosis, the individual affected would have to tell a psychiatrist of their current feelings, or have their behaviour described by those closest to them. Because this is the only way of establishing the individual's mental condition, it has proven difficult to diagnose schizophrenia both reliably and validly.

Reliability

A **reliable** diagnosis is making sure that every person showing the behaviour outlined on the previous pages gets the diagnosis of schizophrenia and not some other psychiatric disorder. In the past, it has proven difficult to make the diagnosis reliable for various reasons.

Different countries have different classification systems

The ICD, mentioned in the previous section, was devised by the World Health Organization. In the United States of America, however, a different classification system is used, called the Diagnostic and Statistical Manual of Psychiatric Disorders or the **DSM**. Currently, American psychiatrists (and some psychiatrists in Europe) are using DSM-IV-TR.

Although these classification systems are similar, they place a different emphasis on which symptoms are important. Because of this, it is possible that a person diagnosed with schizophrenic behaviour in the USA might not be diagnosed with schizophrenia in Europe. The ICD lists two types of schizophrenia not listed as schizophrenia in the DSM ('simple schizophrenia' and 'post-schizophrenic depression'). The effect of this is that different types of behaviour may be labelled schizophrenic depending on which classification system is used.

The skill of the clinician is influential

Although diagnostic systems make misdiagnosis less likely, they are not perfect. The success of the system relies on how well they are interpreted by the person making the diagnosis. This is very different to medicine, where, for example, someone is diagnosed with diabetes when their blood-glucose level is consistently over a certain point. One solution to the reliability problem that is currently being investigated is changing the concept of schizophrenia into one of the **schizophrenic spectrum**. This would encompass a wider range of behaviour and less reliance on the presence of certain symptoms for certain lengths of time. It would also make the idea of subtypes of schizophrenia unnecessary. This would make the diagnosis more reliable.

Validity

The **validity** of schizophrenia refers to whether the condition actually exists or not. This issue is important because various people have developed the concept of schizophrenia over time. It is a label that covers a broad range of different symptoms. There are even some psychiatrists who are not convinced that schizophrenia exists at all.

Rosenhan's 'On being sane in insane places' study

Rosenhan (1973) and several collaborators (pseudopatients) showed how easily schizophrenia can be misdiagnosed. They approached psychiatric hospitals saying they could hear voices saying 'empty', 'hollow' and 'thud'. This one symptom was enough for them to be admitted with a diagnosis of schizophrenia. Thereafter, Rosenhan and the pseudopatients behaved normally, yet once the schizophrenia label was given, it stuck such that even normal behaviour was seen as schizophrenic; for example, waiting outside the dining room for a meal was said to be 'characteristic of the oral-acquisitive nature' of schizophrenia. Also, on their eventual release, most pseudopatients were given a diagnosis of 'schizophrenia in remission'.

This controversial study led psychiatrists (particularly in the USA) to refine the diagnostic process, to include longer-lasting symptoms. However, the use of deception was unethical. The diagnostic process was clearly flawed, but responsible psychiatrists would not expect healthy people to invent psychiatric symptoms and risk hospital admission; nor would they turn away someone apparently in need.

A diagnostic straitjacket?

The diagnosis of schizophrenia is so specific that some people who show schizophrenic-like behaviour, but do not quite meet all the diagnostic criteria, are therefore not diagnosed as schizophrenic. These people are often given a diagnosis considered to be less serious, such as that of **schizoid personality disorder**. A criticism of the validity of schizophrenia could therefore be: 'How do we know we have set the right criteria?' This question is not easy to answer because a psychiatric diagnosis relies upon the psychiatrist's experience rather than on physical test results.

The schizophrenic spectrum

Use of the schizophrenic spectrum would be one way of solving the problem of validity. It would have the effect of turning schizophrenia from a categorical disorder to a dimensional one. This means that instead of looking for the presence of symptoms, the psychiatrist would look at the severity of the symptoms the patient is experiencing.

Differential diagnosis

Another validity problem with schizophrenia is the overlap with conditions that have an element of **mania**, such as **bipolar disorder**, making it difficult to distinguish between them. People with a diagnosis of bipolar disorder also experience delusions and hallucinations. For schizophrenia really to be a valid diagnosis, you would expect to see it as the *only* disorder with these symptoms.

Categorical vs smaller diagnoses

The problems with schizophrenia as a diagnostic category are summarized best by Richard Bentall (1993), who feels there is more evidence for the disorder to be broken down into smaller diagnoses with each symptom becoming a separate disorder.

Biological explanations: genetics

Schizophrenia is a complicated condition, with many different combinations of symptoms. In fact, because delusions and hallucinations can have individual significance to the person experiencing schizophrenia, it is possible to say that every person has a different version of schizophrenia. When you add this to the information on pages 6–7 regarding some of the problems with reliability and validity, you can appreciate that this condition does not have a simple cause. The development of schizophrenia relies upon multiple factors, including the environment in which the individual lives. Some of these factors are biological, including genetic explanations.

A schizophrenic gene?

There is no **gene** for schizophrenia; the best we can say is that several genes may contribute to the onset of this condition. Most of the evidence we have for the genetic explanation of schizophrenia comes from studying the incidence of the disorder in families.

Concordance rates

We share more of our genetic material with closer relatives, so the closer the relationship between the person experiencing schizophrenia and the family member, the higher the incidence of schizophrenia should be. This is known as the **concordance rate** (the probability of someone in the family also developing schizophrenia).

Twins are important in the study of schizophrenia because identical twins share the same genes, whereas non-identical (fraternal) twins have only 50 per cent of their genes in common. Fraternal twins result from two fertilized ova (eggs), and identical twins result from one fertilized ovum, which then divides into two. The pair of chromosomes below each individual represents genetic material inherited from the parents. If schizophrenia has a strong genetic component, then if one identical twin has schizophrenia, we would expect the other twin also to have it.

Concordance studies study the closeness of the genetic link between the person diagnosed with schizophrenia and family members. Table 1 below shows Gottesman *et al.*'s (1987) findings that the closer the genetic relationship, the higher the chance that that family member will also be diagnosed with the condition. This compares to a 1 per cent incidence rate in the general population.

Examiners' notes

Don't spend too much time detailing background information on genetics, although a distinction between fraternal and identical twins is a useful one to make and should receive credit in the context of questions on the genetic influences on schizophrenia because it helps to explain much of the research in this area.

Essential notes

Genetic linkage analysis (e.g. Holmans *et al.* 2009) is a recently developed system for comparing the tendency of certain genes to be inherited together so, for example, we can look for a genetic link between handedness and schizophrenia. It is early days, but there is evidence that certain genes might be involved in, but not cause, schizophrenia. The best we can say is that genes contribute to the development of schizophrenia in conjunction with other factors.

Table 1
The link between genetic relationship and diagnosis of schizophrenia

Family member	% diagnosed with schizophrenia
Brothers/sisters	7.3
Fraternal twin (dizygotic, DZ)	12.1
Identical twin (monozygotic, MZ)	44.3

Source: Gottesman *et al.* (1987)

Twins separated at birth

A way of getting around the effects of a shared family environment is to look at pairs of twins separated at birth. The best known of the studies to do this is probably that of Kety *et al.* (1994). They found that twins separated at birth who went on to experience psychosis were around 21 per cent more likely to have biological relatives with a schizophrenia spectrum disorder than their adopted family for which the rate was around 5 per cent.

Recent advances in technology have allowed us to take a closer look at the actual genes involved in schizophrenia-type behaviour. One technique is called genetic linkage analysis (e.g. Holmans *et al.* 2009). Genetic linkage is a system that compares the tendency of certain genes to be inherited together. So, for example, studies can look for a genetic link between handedness and schizophrenia. Although it is relatively early days for this type of study, they have found evidence that certain genes might be involved in schizophrenia. However, there is no gene that causes schizophrenia. It seems as though the best we can say is that genes contribute to the development of schizophrenia in conjunction with other factors.

Adoption studies

Another way to assess the contribution of environment and genetics to schizophrenia is to compare concordance rates between adopted children and their biological or adoptive parents. In a longitudinal study begun in 1969, Tienari followed Finnish people who had been adopted before the age of 4. Of those whose biological mothers had schizophrenia, the concordance rate in the children was 7 per cent compared with 1.5 per cent where there was no history of maternal schizophrenia. This study showed how the effect of genetics persisted even when a child's environment had changed.

Evaluation of genetic concordance studies

- If the cause of schizophrenia were entirely genetic, then the concordance rate between MZ twins would be 100 per cent (and between DZ twins 50 per cent, reflecting the amount of genetic material they share). This does not happen, which clearly shows that other factors must be involved in the onset of schizophrenia.

- It is impossible to isolate totally the effects of genes (nature) from nurture (a shared environment and experiences) when studying human behaviour. Therefore, studies that indicate the concordance rates for schizophrenia must be treated with caution.

- A problem with studies that are retrospective (look back) or prospective (follow participants forward) is that the diagnostic criteria for schizophrenia change over time. This means that we are not necessarily comparing the same symptoms in parents and offspring, and this could distort the concordance rate.

Examiners' notes

There is no need to reproduce exact percentages in an exam answer, but you should try to be at least in the same ball park!

Essential notes

It is important that you ask exactly what a study is telling us. Placing an emphasis on percentages probably shows that there are only small numbers of participants involved. Kety and colleagues are basing their conclusions on only 34 people out of the many thousands diagnosed with schizophrenia in Denmark.

Examiners' notes

It would be a good idea to use adoption studies as an evaluation point and talk about *how* they attempt to differentiate between the role of the environment and biology.

Biological explanations: biochemistry

The dopamine hypothesis

Essential notes

Dopamine has been known about since the early part of the 20th century, and it was classified as a neurotransmitter in 1958. There are several dopamine pathways in the human brain (see Fig. 1), and schizophrenia is thought to involve abnormalities in at least two of these. Both of these pathways originate in the midbrain, one of them going to the cortex and the other going to the cortex by way of the limbic system.

Essential notes

An agonist is a chemical that works in the same way as a naturally occurring neurochemical. An antagonist is a chemical that blocks a naturally occurring neurochemical.

The main biochemical theory of schizophrenia since the 1950s is the **dopamine hypothesis**. This theory suggests that schizophrenia is caused by an overactivity of the neurotransmitter dopamine in certain parts of the brain.

Evidence to support the dopamine hypothesis

The evidence for the involvement of dopamine comes from two sources:

- Drugs such as amphetamine and LSD (when taken by people without psychiatric disorder) cause behaviour that resembles the positive symptoms of schizophrenia.

- People with Parkinson's disease (a disorder caused by too little dopamine in another dopamine pathway) can develop a mild psychosis when given too much medication. Levodopa is the primary treatment for Parkinson's disease and it is a dopamine **agonist**.

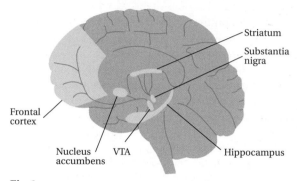

Fig. 1
Dopamine pathways in the human brain

The other source of evidence for the dopamine hypothesis of schizophrenia is that the medications for schizophrenia (called neuroleptics or antipsychotics) are dopamine **antagonists**. These drugs reduce the amount of dopamine available in the brain by blocking the synapse.

Criticisms of the dopamine hypothesis

Complications of medication

Critics of the dopamine hypothesis have said that there is little direct evidence for the involvement of the neurotransmitter in schizophrenia. For example, while there is evidence from postmortem studies to show that those with schizophrenia have an increased number of dopamine-receiving cells in parts of the limbic system (e.g. Bird *et al.* 1979), these fail to take into account whether the patient has ever received treatment for the condition. If they have, then the excess dopamine cells could be the result of the medication rather than the cause of the schizophrenic behaviour (see next point).

The problem of cause and effect

When we are looking at the brains of people showing schizophrenic behaviour, we can never really be sure that any changes we see are the *cause* of schizophrenia rather than the *result* of it. This cause-and-effect problem is one of the largest problems with the dopamine hypothesis, and it is very difficult to overcome it. A potential solution would be continually to scan people at risk for developing schizophrenia, but this would be expensive and unethical. It seems as though we cannot discover the exact relationship between dopamine and schizophrenia until we are better at identifying the early stages of schizophrenia.

Dopamine cannot be the sole cause of schizophrenia

Another note for caution with the dopamine hypothesis is that the drugs developed to treat schizophrenia do not work for everyone. Some patients (approximately 25 per cent) do not respond well to the medication at all, which is puzzling if too much dopamine is the sole cause of the disorder.

Studying these patients led to the discovery of the different types of dopamine (at least five subtypes called D_1, D_2, etc.). It was found that most of these patients responded better to the subsequent wave of second-generation drugs that targeted dopamine in a different way to the earlier drugs. However, there are still people who do not respond to antipsychotics at all. This suggests that an excess of dopamine cannot be the sole cause of schizophrenia. The fact that different subtypes of dopamine seem to be affected in different people also casts some doubt on there being only one dopamine theory. It seems something more subtle is happening in the brains of people with schizophrenia.

Negative symptoms and glutamate

Problems with other neurotransmitters are also reported as the cause of schizophrenia. There is a suggestion that giving someone with schizophrenia amphetamine will reduce the presence of negative symptoms. This would not make sense if only dopamine were involved in the condition. The negative symptoms of schizophrenia seem instead to involve a type of **glutamate** receptor called NMDA receptors. NMDA is the neurotransmitter involved when people take ketamine or PCP (phencyclidine or angel-dust). People who take ketamine/PCP once experience disrupted emotions and social withdrawal. They are also impaired on the same sort of neuropsychological tests that people with the negative symptoms of schizophrenia find difficult. Repeated abuse of PCP causes the onset of positive schizophrenic symptoms. This tells us that the relationship between dopamine and glutamate is crucial in the development of schizophrenia. The dopamine hypothesis as it currently stands is only the beginning of a process that we still do not fully understand.

Essential notes

We are still discovering how the brain works, and this means that understanding the biochemistry of schizophrenia is also a work in progress. It seems, however, that the dopamine hypothesis is too simplistic and reductivist.

Examiners' notes

If you were responding to a question that asked for biological explanations of schizophrenia, you could use material drawn from both this and the previous spread on genetics (pp. 8–9). This would also be the case if you were asked to discuss two biological explanations of schizophrenia, so together they could constitute 'the' biological explanation of schizophrenia, or separately they could constitute 'two' biological explanations.

Psychological explanations: behavioural

The major perspectives of psychology have all offered explanations for schizophrenia, some of them more successfully than others. The behaviourist explanation for schizophrenia relies upon conditioning. Central to this is the idea that the frequency of different kinds of behaviour can be altered by their consequences:

- Behaviour that is followed by pleasant consequences (reward or reinforcement) tends to increase in frequency.

- Behaviour that is followed by unpleasant consequences (punishment) or none at all is likely to decrease in frequency.

The idea is that, because those experiencing schizophrenia are rewarded for their odd behaviour by the medical profession, they are unwittingly encouraged to keep behaving in this fashion. However, the behaviourist approach cannot explain what caused the behaviour to occur in the first place. It is also highly unlikely that encouragement alone could cause hallucinations, so underneath the behaviourist explanation is the unpalatable assumption that the person is making up their schizophrenic experiences. However, the use of behaviourist therapy can successfully treat some of the behavioural problems associated with schizophrenia, as we will see later.

Conditioning and schizophrenia

There is some evidence to show that conditioning can account for the continuation of the symptoms of schizophrenia. Cognitive-behavioural therapy can be used successfully to treat some of the symptoms of schizophrenia (discussed later on pp. 28–9), and so it seems logical that behaviourism can explain the maintenance of such symptoms. Both of the following studies show how altering the consequences of behaviour can change its frequency.

Support for the role of conditioning in maintaining schizophrenic symptoms

- *Reducing delusional speech* – Some recent work has been carried out to look at the bizarre vocalizations and speech patterns that some people with schizophrenia experience. This work is based on a study by Ayllon and Haughton (1964). They trained hospital staff to ignore an inpatient's delusional remarks. The staff were told to give no positive feedback at all when the patient made remarks about her delusion that she was the Queen, but to respond normally to non-delusional speech. This resulted in a massive reduction in delusional speech.

- *Reducing bizarre statements* – Other studies have built on this work, including Wilder *et al.* (2001), who treated a patient who constantly made statements unrelated to the topic in hand. Every time the patient made one of these bizarre statements, the therapist would say something like, 'You shouldn't talk about X so much. This may be too stressful, let's take a break', and then looked away for 30 seconds before resuming. The only time the therapist spoke during this time was to answer appropriate (non-delusional) questions or statements. These sessions lasted for 10 minutes, and there were two or three sessions a day. The patient's bizarre vocalizations reduced dramatically over 30 sessions.

Problems with identifying cause and effect

This raises an interesting question about the symptoms of schizophrenia. Do the bizarre vocalizations reflect something else occurring in the brain, or are these just learned behaviours that have the effect of making the person doing them seem 'crazy'? This is not an easy question to answer for many reasons. One of those reasons is that we are not sure of any biological cause of these symptoms, so a psychological trigger seems likely. However, *why* the person is making the bizarre comments and talking about their delusions is much harder to explain. Perhaps someone who is not very good at communicating with others might enjoy the positive feedback that a bizarre utterance might cause. However, this approach cannot provide an answer as to how it could have appeared the first time.

Changing conversational behaviour using conditioning

The fact that failing to reinforce some kinds of behaviour helps to rid a patient of certain symptoms of schizophrenia is positive, although neither Allyon and Haughton (1964) nor Wilder *et al.* (2001) talk about what happened to their patients next. A study that does do this is Mace and Lalli (1991), who offered their patient training in conversation skills by both initiating conversations and manipulating the consequences of his behaviour in various ways. For example:

- The therapists withdrew attention for making bizarre statements.
- The therapists responded to appropriate vocalizations with attention and made attempts to continue the conversation.

This was very successful in reducing bizarre vocalizations and increasing appropriate ones. This is a clear indication that some of the bizarre conversational interjections by those with schizophrenia serve to draw attention to themselves; they talk like this because they have nothing (no skills) to initiate and maintain conversation. Bizarre statements, however, lead to attention (but from clinicians and psychiatrists, not friends), and so they continue them. Training in how to make conversations reduces the bizarre behaviour. Work such as this leads to the tentative suggestion that some symptoms of schizophrenia are the result of poor social skills. This idea is further expanded in the psychological therapies section of this chapter (pp. 24–9).

(pp. 24–9)

Examiners' notes

Remember that there is no *requirement* in Unit 4 to include material linked to 'Issues, debates and approaches' (as in the Unit 3 paper). However, any such material would receive AO2 credit *provided* that it forms an integral (and appropriate) part of any evaluation of behavioural explanations.

Essential notes

Behaviourism has suggested that some of the bizarre symptoms seen in schizophrenia could be caused as a cover for poor social skills. When you consider that the mean age of onset (slightly lower in boys than girls) is the late teens when children start to become independent, this seems to be a clue for the causes of the disorder. However, the approach cannot really answer the question of how the more complex and disturbing symptoms of schizophrenia, such as visual and auditory hallucinations, begin.

Psychological explanations: cognitive

Schizophrenia has several symptoms that feature disrupted cognition, and, in fact, cognitive psychology has also provided explanations for hallucinations and delusions. Although cognitive psychology cannot provide any real insight into the cause of schizophrenia, the models it offers are useful when it comes to the treatment of the condition.

Early cognitive models

Problems with attentional features

Some early cognitive models of schizophrenia focus on the concept that the attentional filters are not working adequately. We use filters to lessen the number of stimuli in the world that are irrelevant to us. If those with schizophrenia lack these filters, then the world would be both unpredictable and noisy. One of the ways a healthy person uses the filters is to decide whether a stimulus is worth processing. For example, there can be nothing more annoying than the ticking of a loud clock, but attentional filters allow you to ignore the ticking (until someone draws your attention to it).

These ideas have been tested with the Stroop test (identifying the colour of ink a colour word is written in). People experiencing schizophrenia tend to be very slow when the colour name and ink colour don't match and make more errors (e.g. Barch *et al.* 1999).

Failure to understand context

Frith (1993) talks of schizophrenia as a failure to appreciate the context of a situation. This, for example, would make it very difficult to work out the beliefs and intentions of those around you. If, for example, someone stood to offer you a seat on the bus, you might think they had done so because you were carrying a lot of shopping. Someone with schizophrenia, on the other hand, might interpret the gesture with suspicion or even with paranoia:

- Frith believes that this behaviour is caused by underactivity of the frontal lobes of the brain, which handle motivation and action (among other behaviours).

- Although there is some evidence that the frontal lobes of those with schizophrenia are underactive, it is hard to establish whether this is the cause of schizophrenia or an effect of schizophrenia.

There are also studies that demonstrate that participants with schizophrenia perform better if you pay them for correct responses in tests of neuropsychological functioning such as the Wisconsin Card Sorting Test (Summerfelt *et al.* 1991). Money would act, perhaps, as a form of unambiguous context adding motivation. Therefore, this finding does not falsify Frith's hypothesis, but rather offers support.

Examiners' notes

Pages 14–19 cover several psychological explanations of schizophrenia. In exam questions that ask for 'explanations' or 'theories' in the plural, it is often more effective to cover just two explanations or theories. Trying to cover too many explanations can make your description and evaluation less detailed than it should be for the higher mark bands.

Examiners' notes

Although you may find yourself précising this material to fit it in with other information you have about cognitive explanations about schizophrenia, remember that higher marks are awarded for material that is detailed.

Essential notes

Summerfelt *et al.*'s experiment offers insight into the world of schizophrenia and also shows how difficult it is to design experiments around people with schizophrenia. It is difficult to whip up enthusiasm for an abstract cognitive experiment when you are feeling unwell and in hospital. Offering money, on the other hand, adds context; it is tangible even within hospital where you could buy treats. You should always try to look beyond experimental results and try to work out why the psychologists might have achieved the results they did.

Failure to utilize schemas

Hemsley (1993) offers a similar cognitive theory. He also talks about the importance of context, but links it to the idea of someone with schizophrenia failing to utilize schemas. Schemas are cognitive shortcuts that we develop on the basis of past experiences; they are about learning how to act in certain situations. Hemsley suggests that people with schizophrenia do not use schemas and so treat each situation as novel, which must be overwhelming, exhausting and confusing.

Evaluation of cognitive theories

Limited scope of cognitive testing
Both Frith and Hemsley's theories have led to exhaustive cognitive testing. They both try to match the disorganized thought processes characteristic of schizophrenia to tried-and-tested cognitive theories. They have each had some success, but neither really gets to grips with the full range of behaviours experienced in the disorder.

Differences between Frith and Hemsley's theories
Hemsley's theory is perhaps more able to deal with the subtle differences in behaviour that one person with schizophrenia might show to someone else. Whereas Frith's theories can explain disrupted cognition, Hemsley's offer an explanation for symptoms such as hallucinations too. For example, if you hear a voice when there is no one around you, you might try to add context to explain it (e.g. 'It's a hot day, I have my window open. Perhaps that is someone outside talking or someone's radio'), whereas someone with schizophrenia will immediately feel the voice is talking to them and will interpret it as such.

Reductionist, but valuable
Although cognitive neuropsychological theories can be seen as reductionist and simplistic, they do offer explanations of schizophrenic behaviour. Both the biological and the cognitive approach focus only on one aspect of functioning at the expense of understanding the complexity of the whole person. However, such approaches have immense value when it comes to devising treatments for schizophrenia.

Essential notes

Understanding what is going on in schizophrenia by relating it to healthy behavioural processes is undeniably reductionist, but sometimes reductionism helps psychology to devise treatment strategies for conditions like schizophrenia. They are not really intended to provide exhaustive explanations for why these symptoms exist, but they do offer some kind of insight into what it might feel like to experience schizophrenia.

Examiners' notes

If you decide to include other explanations by way of evaluation you need to do more than just *describe* them. For example, you might say something like: 'Cognitive explanations may only describe how some symptoms occur, rather than showing us the cause of schizophrenia. An explanation that does that better is the dopamine hypothesis, which sees the basis of schizophrenia as a biochemical imbalance that may, therefore, contribute to the cognitive dysfunction found in schizophrenics'.

Psychological explanations: psychodynamic

Examiners' notes

If you answer a question on psychodynamic explanations of schizophrenia, do *not* get drawn into a long description of Freudian theory, which would add very little (if anything) to your essay.

Psychodynamic therapy was developed by Sigmund Freud, primarily to deal with anxiety and neuroses. Freud's original ideas focused upon psychosexual development and how children came to terms with their own sexuality. This original emphasis makes it hard to apply this approach to schizophrenia. Although Freud is not the only psychodynamic therapist, he is the most influential, and such therapists, even if they play down the psychosexual element of the theory, still focus on childhood problems as the start of a process that will result in schizophrenia.

Family life

Psychodynamic theory also offered the idea of a **schizophrenogenic** family: a family with high emotional tension, shifting alliances and disrupted and illogical conversations between some members and not others. This idea has largely been ignored since the 1970s, but out of it came the idea that disrupted communication within a family may be a contributing factor to the disorder. This theory is best encapsulated by the idea of the **double-bind hypothesis** (Bateson *et al.* 1956). This suggests that the children received confusing, and sometimes contradictory, messages from their parents with respect to love and praise. This confusion could lead to self-doubt and withdrawal:

Essential notes

An example of a double bind might be when a parent asks their child for a hug but wears an expression of distaste. Whatever the child decides to do, this is a no-win situation.

- The biggest criticism of this idea is simply that self-doubt and withdrawal are clearly not sufficient to lead to schizophrenia.
- The idea of disrupted communication styles and fractured family life in schizophrenia was researched for a number of years before being rejected as an individual cause of the disorder.

However, the types of communication problems experienced by someone with schizophrenia would not help family tensions. This idea was taken further in the concept of a **diathesis-stress model** of schizophrenia. Although having nothing directly to do with the psychodynamic approach, this model incorporates the ideas that came from this approach, as well as other, less specific hypotheses.

Diathesis stress and schizophrenia

Diathesis-stress models place importance on the interaction between the person and their environment. The biological predisposition to schizophrenia (talked about in this chapter) is dormant until stress in the environment makes it active. The source of stress could be the schizophrenogenic family, or perhaps disrupted and inconsistent parenting and communication within the family. Other sources of stress could also be major life events – for example, the stress involved in moving country or experiencing bereavement could be enough to trigger schizophrenia in susceptible persons.

Studies into the development of schizophrenia that focus on family life, such as Tienari *et al.* (1987), have looked at how childrearing skills affected those at risk from schizophrenia spectrum disorders. They found that high genetic risk children adopted into homes with 'healthy' rearing patterns were at less risk of developing schizophrenia than those integrated into families with 'adverse' parenting. Children classified as at lower genetic risk did not develop schizophrenia in this adverse group. Again, this shows that schizophrenia is developed in response to a number of factors. None of the factors we have discussed so far is sufficient on its own to lead to the development of schizophrenia.

Evaluation of family life factors and schizophrenia

Expressed emotion
It does seem that communication between family members can affect the course of schizophrenia. When those with schizophrenia improve enough to return home from a period of hospitalization, their family might treat them differently from how they treated them before. This can be in the form of being excessively concerned, as well as showing more negative emotions such as hostility or resentment. Research into **expressed emotions** (EE) such as these (e.g. Butzlaff and Hooley 1998) has shown that high levels of emotion within a family can shorten the time to a relapse, so although expressed emotion is no clue as to the *cause* of schizophrenia, it can reliably help to explain why so many people relapse into schizophrenic experience after a period of remission.

Projective identification
Expressed emotion is a link to the psychodynamic concept of **projective identification**. This is when the person without schizophrenia projects emotions onto the person with schizophrenia. They tell the person with schizophrenia how they should be feeling, despite the fact that the person with schizophrenia cannot experience that particular emotion, something that contributed to the development of their schizophrenia. So, in some families, the pressure caused by the diagnosis of psychiatric illness on the people around the patient can lead them to act in a way that perpetuates the schizophrenic behaviour. This can force a relapse and prevent recovery. As stated above, there is evidence that patients released into families with high EE do relapse sooner, but whether the psychodynamic explanation is supported by this observation is open to debate.

A limited range of explanation
Psychodynamic theory struggles to provide a cogent explanation for schizophrenia. Early ideas focused on children regressing to an earlier stage of development as a means of coping with the demands of the **superego**. This does fit in with the observation that schizophrenia can onset for the first time during teenage years, when children are becoming more independent. However, the theory cannot explain the variety of symptoms caused by schizophrenia.

Psychological explanations: sociocultural

It is unlikely that any one strand of explanation of schizophrenia is sufficient on its own. However, some psychological theories have tried to combine the biological with the social, with reasonable success. Sociocultural explanations tend to use **epidemiological studies** (studies looking at the incidence and distribution of diseases) to look for characteristics that people with schizophrenia have in common.

Factors affecting the development of schizophrenia

Within the population of people with schizophrenia, several characteristics emerge.

Birth in the winter months

The first characteristic is a birth in the winter months. A recent systematic review of season of birth studies found that there was a small, but positive, increase in risk for developing schizophrenia for a winter/spring birth for people born in the Northern Hemisphere (Davies *et al.* 2003). This finding fits well with another that proposes that schizophrenia is more likely to occur when the mother experienced a virus during pregnancy. As viral infections are more common during the winter, this seems to make some sense. Fuller Torrey (1988, 1996) has done most of the work in this area, but really it is difficult to form a causal link between a virus and a psychiatric disorder appearing decades later. Many people experience viruses such as flu and yet do not go on to develop schizophrenia.

Birth trauma and handedness

Another epidemiological factor that correlates with schizophrenia is birth trauma. Again, this relies on retrospective memory to form a link between a distant event that the person with schizophrenia cannot remember and the onset of a psychiatric condition. However, the birth trauma idea does fit in with the idea that people who are left-handed or ambidextrous have a susceptibility for developing schizophrenia. Handedness has long been associated with schizophrenia (e.g. Green *et al.* 1989), and left-handedness can be associated with birth trauma. Tim Crow (1990) used the idea of abnormal brain development as a factor in schizophrenia. His suggestion is that language, which is normally lateralized to the left hemisphere, is present in both hemispheres in those experiencing schizophrenia. This offers an explanation for auditory hallucinations as the patient hearing language coming from a usually mute hemisphere. Other researchers have used this as an explanation for the higher incidence of schizophrenia in those who are left-handed or ambidextrous. However, there is very little evidence for this theory, and there is nothing to differentiate cause and effect for the higher incidence of schizophrenia in left-handers.

It seems as though switched cerebral dominance may be a factor in the development of schizophrenia, although not a direct one, as not every switched-dominance person has the symptoms of the disorder.

Examiners' notes

It is a useful exercise to plan how you would respond to all the different combinations of questions that might include the requirement of 'sociocultural' approaches. These might include full essay questions worth 24 marks (25 marks prior to 2012) or parted questions. This is a good thing to do as a group.

Essential notes

Most people are left-hemisphere dominant, which reflects the fact that their language functions are located within this hemisphere. Around 30 per cent of left-handed people have switched dominance (compared to 5 per cent of right-handed people), with the language in the right hemisphere.

Cannabis use and schizophrenia

A third recent factor in the development of schizophrenia is a correlation between cannabis abuse and psychosis. One of the neurochemical changes in the brain caused by cannabis use is increased activity of dopamine synapses. If someone abusing cannabis also had a susceptibility for schizophrenia, this could well be a factor in the onset of the disorder.

There are also problems with these studies, however. It could be that people experiencing the early symptoms of psychosis use cannabis as self-treatment. As discussed earlier, the problem of cause and effect is a hard one to research. However, there is enough evidence here for the link between cannabis abuse and schizophrenia to be further explored.

Urbanicity

There are studies which suggest that living in densely populated areas is correlated with schizophrenia – or perhaps, those at risk from the development of schizophrenia move into densely populated areas. Population density is an aspect of **urbanicity** (characteristic of a town or city). These findings explain the studies that claim that there are cultural and socioeconomic differences in schizophrenia. This ties in with studies that found that minority ethnic immigrants are more at risk of developing psychosis. The Aetiology and Ethnicity of Schizophrenia and Other Psychoses (AESOP) study, which compared the incidence of schizophrenia in south-east London, Bristol and Nottingham, found an elevated risk for people from an Afro-Caribbean background living in south-east London. This was also the most densely populated region of the three investigated. The AESOP study concluded that this was nothing to do with ethnicity, but instead to do with the social cohesion problems that go hand in hand with high populations. In other words, people might find it hard to integrate in an area where they are different from the rest of the population, and this risk is intensified as the population increases.

Essential notes

The AESOP study shows how it is important to look beyond the simple facts of any correlation. By studying the epidemiology of schizophrenia across different regions of the UK, a clearer picture emerged than if they had chosen to study only one. This reflects both the complexity of schizophrenia and the importance of being rigorous when designing investigations. It also shows that you have to be careful when interpreting data. Although there are cultural differences to be found, they are explained by living conditions rather than anything specifically about culture.

Evaluation of factors associated with schizophrenia

- Studies into season of birth, birth trauma and handedness are sometimes complicated by being retrospective. The findings are only reliable if the records kept of maternal health and the nature of a birth are accurate and detailed. Prospective studies, which follow up individuals over time, could help to clarify any causal pathways but are ethically and practically difficult to do.

- All the factors described above have been suggested as having a causal role in the development of schizophrenia, although none of them alone is sufficient to cause the disorder. It seems as though schizophrenia is a complex disorder reflecting problems with genetics and birth, as well as with more general problems living in a busy society. However, such factors do feed into the diathesis-stress model described on page 16.

Examiners' notes

When answering exam questions in this area (and all other A2 areas in psychology), it is essential that you remember the 8/16 mark split (9/16 prior to 2012) and provide the corresponding division of material to match this. This means almost twice as much AO2 material as AO1 material.

Biological therapies: psychosurgery and ECT

Early biological treatments for schizophrenia included **psychosurgery** and **electroconvulsive therapy (ECT)**.

Psychosurgery

Psychosurgery is defined as any operation performed on the brain with the aim of alleviating the symptoms of mental illness.

The prefrontal leucotomy

The most famous example of psychosurgery is the frontal lobotomy (more properly called the prefrontal leucotomy), devised by Egas Moniz in 1936. Moniz discovered that destroying the frontal lobes of someone with schizophrenia had a calming effect. He performed this operation by injecting surgical alcohol (which kills brain tissue) directly into the front part of the brain, and then disrupting this tissue with a small hooked instrument called a leucotome. Nothing is actually removed in this procedure.

Moniz discovered that his patients experiencing a florid schizophrenic episode, when positive symptoms flare up, became much calmer and less paranoid after the operation.

Evaluation of Moniz's work

- *A 'child of its time'* – The work of Moniz has to be evaluated as part of the era in which it occurred. Most people with schizophrenia were committed to hospitals, as there was no medical treatment at that time. The operation had noticeable results, but not all of these were positive. Patients showed fewer negative emotions, but they also showed fewer positive ones too. They were calmer, but they were also less active.

- *Continued use and modern alternatives* – Although the procedure of leucotomy continued for several years after Moniz first demonstrated it, it was discontinued as therapy for schizophrenia when alternative treatment became available. Egas Moniz won the Nobel Prize for Medicine in 1949 as a result of this work, although some people who survived the surgery have asked for it to be revoked. Leucotomies continue to be carried out to this day, mainly in the cases of violent criminals and occasionally people with violent mood swings. Leucotomy is very rarely used in the case of schizophrenia, although the development both of scanning and of more accurate placement of electrodes ensures a less dramatic operation.

Essential notes

Techniques such as prefrontal leucotomy cause much anger when people explore the archives and see what changes were made to people who experienced it. This operation was performed on naughty children and young people with mood swings, and these surgeries were undeniably unethical. However, these primitive neurosurgeries led on to more refined techniques, possibly allowing useful techniques such as deep brain stimulation today. This is no justification for this radical treatment, but it does show how quickly science moves on.

Electroconvulsive therapy

A more successful form of therapy – although one with an equally negative treatment in the media (e.g. in the film *One Flew over the Cuckoo's Nest*) – is electroconvulsive therapy (ECT). ECT is a form of treatment whereby an electric shock, applied through electrodes on the scalp, causes a seizure with the purpose of alleviating the symptoms of schizophrenia. Nowadays, patients undergoing ECT are anaesthetized and given a drug to make their muscles relax during the procedure. Electrodes can be placed at one or both temples and an electric shock is applied for a second or less. The resulting seizure will take around a minute and the patient wakes up after this.

- There is significant evidence that such therapy works for patients for whom antipsychotic medicine does not.

- There is even limited evidence that antipsychotics begin to work in such patients when ECT is added to their treatment (e.g. Fink and Sackheim 1996).

Evaluation of ECT

- *Most effective in certain patients* – Electroconvulsive therapy seems to work best for patients showing catatonia or those experiencing emotional problems. It is also a good form of therapy for those suffering from profound depression.

- *Limits in use of ECT* – However, it is still believed that ECT should only be considered in patients who are unresponsive to medication or severely affected. The government body that oversees types of treatment in the UK (NICE – the National Institute of Clinical Excellence) says this treatment should not be used in the general management of schizophrenia, but as a short-term fix only.

- *Side effects* – The suggested restrictions on use of ECT are only partly because the treatment has such a bad press; another important reason is that its results tend to be short-lived. Patients have been left with long-term memory problems as a result of a course of ECT treatment.

Essential notes

Both psychosurgery and ECT have been portrayed negatively in the media and this shapes the way we feel about them now. ECT is a useful short-term therapy, but seems to be more effective when given alongside traditional medicinal treatments. Both of these treatments show how the history of treatment of conditions such as schizophrenia is a relatively short one and reflect the lengths that medics are prepared to go to in the search for a cure.

Biological therapies: drug treatments

The most common treatment for schizophrenia is drug therapy. The class of drugs given to those with schizophrenia is called neuroleptics or antipsychotics. The main action of antipsychotics is to reduce the amount of dopamine in the brain, although some of the more recent drugs work on other neurotransmitters as well.

Early antipsychotics

The first antipsychotic drugs were found when looking for a treatment for malaria. They were not effective for this condition, but it was noted that they had a strong sedating effect. One of these drugs, called chlorpromazine, was found to be effective in treating patients during a psychotic episode. By the mid 1950s, the drug was being used by huge numbers of patients. A second drug, haloperidol, was licensed by the end of the 1950s.

Evaluation of the use of early antipsychotics

- *Effectiveness of early antipsychotics* – The early antipsychotic drugs were not perfect as they only seemed to work for around 75 per cent of people diagnosed with schizophrenia, but it is important to realize that they offered hope where previously there had been none. Many psychiatric patients were able to leave hospital and attempt to resume their normal lives. The medication had reduced the positive symptoms of schizophrenia.

- *Side effects of drug treatments* – A number of problems emerged with the use of these drugs, especially in the form of undesirable side effects. Those for whom the drug worked reported feeling apathetic (that they had no enthusiasm for anything), and that they were experiencing dry mouth and gastrointestinal problems. It was also discovered that long-term use of these medications increased the risk of the patient experiencing depression.

- *Long-term, serious side effects* – After two years of continuous therapy with the antipsychotics, some patients began to experience more dramatic side effects. These were extreme motor problems called **extrapyramidal problems**. For some, this was only stiffness and tremors, but for around 30 per cent of patients, it started a problem called **tardive dyskinesia**, characterized by repetitive and pointless movements, including lip-smacking and other facial tics.

Links to Parkinson's disease

A better understanding of how to treat schizophrenia with drugs has grown from incorporating knowledge about Parkinson's disease, a motor disorder caused by too little dopamine in part of the brain. The side effects of the drugs just described were similar to symptoms seen in this disease. It seemed the drugs were working too well and were affecting a dopamine pathway called the nigrostriatal pathway, which is not generally involved in schizophrenia. As a result, people stopped taking the drugs, and the positive symptoms returned. It is now established that people taking these first-generation antipsychotics should also take preventative medication usually given to patients with Parkinson's disease.

Another and perhaps more ethical solution to the problems caused by tardive dyskinesia is to prevent people with schizophrenia taking the first-generation antipsychotics for prolonged periods. The longer the medication is used, the more likely the patient is to develop this serious movement disorder. After 25 years of constant medication, tardive dyskinesia would be found in an estimated 68 per cent of all users (Glenmullen 2000). This is certainly one argument against the use of compulsory therapy for those experiencing schizophrenia.

Second-generation antipsychotics

The problems with first-generation drugs encouraged the pharmaceutical companies to develop a second generation of drugs, called the atypical antipsychotics. One of these drugs is clozapine, which works by blocking both dopamine and serotonin receptors; there are no extrapyramidal problems caused by this drug.

Evaluation of second-generation antipsychotics

The atypical antipsychotics seemed to be more effective at treating the negative symptoms of schizophrenia, as well as the positive symptoms. They were also reported as being more successful treating the 25 per cent of patients who weren't helped by the first generation. However, there are a number of problems.

- Other than clozapine, the second-general antipsycotics also lead to the same extrapyramidal motor problems that the first generation of drugs caused.

- Clozapine is also not ideal, as it causes a potentially fatal problem by suppressing the immune system. This has to be monitored in patients with a weekly blood test, which is both invasive and impractical.

- All of these drugs seem to induce weight gain in patients, which also impacts upon their quality of life.

Psychological therapies: psychodynamic and family-centred

One of the advantages of the antipsychotic medicine calming those with schizophrenia is that it gives an opportunity to treat the most florid symptoms with psychological therapy. This is becoming increasingly successful as more therapists attempt it. The majority of current psychological interventions in schizophrenia involve cognitive-behavioural therapy, although other techniques have also been attempted.

Psychodynamic therapy

As detailed on pages 16–17, there is no obvious link between psychodynamic psychology and schizophrenia. This means that psychodynamic therapy has to focus on childhood memories and unconscious motivations as the root of schizophrenia. Although there is evidence that many of those experiencing schizophrenia had difficult childhoods, psychodynamic therapists are challenged by the communication difficulties caused by schizophrenia. However, there are several studies that have explored the uses of psychodynamic therapy in schizophrenia.

Freud believed that psychoanalysis would not be a useful therapy in schizophrenia, although he made this declaration before the advent of pharmaceutical intervention. Since this time, there have been many studies about the use of psychodynamic therapy in bettering the life of those with schizophrenia. Psychodynamic therapy characteristically takes a long time to complete. As such, many of the studies found that patients would withdraw without completing the process.

Evaluation of psychodynamic therapy

- There are examples of psychodynamic therapy being more successful than antipsychotic treatment (e.g. Karon and VandenBos 1975), especially in dealing with positive symptoms. However, this study is alone among many that say that psychodynamic therapy is not effective. Stone (1986) followed 72 patients who had received a year's intensive therapy and found that more than half were severely dysfunctional.

- Even more distressing are the studies that talk about how psychodynamic therapy made patients worse (Strupp *et al.* 1977). This is because psychodynamic therapy relies on the ability to build interpersonal relationships between therapist and patient, and it also requires patients to be capable of insight, something many with schizophrenia find difficult.

Exploratory, insight-orientated therapy

One type of psychodynamic therapy is called exploratory, insight-orientated (EIO) therapy, in which the therapist explores the patient's feelings about certain situations, such as starting a new job. The therapist expects the patient to imagine what might happen in such situations and how they might feel about these events. They encourage the patients to relate these perceptions to similar events in their past, with the aim of forging connections between events in order to add context to a situation. This type of therapy, however, is not very successful at creating a meaningful change in the life of the schizophrenic (Gunderson *et al.* 1984).

Family interventions

Interventions into the family life of those experiencing schizophrenia are designed to run alongside other treatments. Most interventions offer education into the effects of schizophrenia, as well as offering problem-solving advice and support. Interventions can take place in the patient's home, and these sessions do not necessarily need to have the patient present.

The concept of expressed emotion (EE) was mentioned on p. 17, and it is an important part of family intervention therapy. The EE scores are established by giving each family member a structured interview. A high EE could lead to hostility to the family member with schizophrenia, but it can also relate to overinvolvement, i.e. trying to help too much. Patients returning from hospital to families with high EE ratings are more prone to relapse. Family intervention helps to delay that relapse significantly (Dixon and Lehman 1995) and might sometimes prevent a relapse occurring. If the intervention is repeated every few years, then it is possible that it might contribute to a successful treatment for schizophrenia, as long as the patient is in close contact with their family.

Evaluation of family interventions

- *The importance of a study's duration* – Although the data shows that family intervention delays relapse, it is also important to ask how long the study period was. Patients with schizophrenia relapse at different times, and some patients do not relapse at all. The longer the period that the patient is followed increases the validity of the investigation.

- *Differences in how relapse is defined* – It is also important to ask how relapse is defined: is it time between hospital stays or is it when symptoms suddenly worsen? There is no clinical difference between these two measures, but it might make a difference to the data. In some countries, a patient might not be readmitted because symptoms are worse. Instead a doctor might adjust medication. Is this defined as a relapse?

- *What does family intervention actually achieve?* – Another question that needs to be asked is whether family intervention makes the schizophrenia less intrusive or is simply educating the family to live with a schizophrenic. If it is the latter, then this is not really a way of treating the effects of schizophrenia; it is just making it easier to live with. This is not a bad thing, but it is not a treatment.

Essential notes

Freud believed that psychodynamic therapy was not suitable for use in schizophrenia, and studies that have attempted the use of these techniques seem to support his opinion. Patients are not able to use insight into their behaviour as a means to change that behaviour, nor are some able to develop a successful therapeutic relationship.

Essential notes

Family intervention seems to be a way of intervening in families with high EE to educate the other members of the family about what to expect. It is not a treatment for schizophrenia, but it seems as though it does help the person with schizophrenia avoid a relapse. This is probably because the reduction in EE lessens the amount of stress the patient experiences. Although you should evaluate the measures these studies use, family intervention seems to be a valuable part of our existing therapies.

Psychological therapies: behavioural

Behavioural therapy focuses upon the relationship between learning and behaviour, and how breaking a learned link between a stimulus and response can improve or change behaviour. Behavioural therapy has struggled to find a link between a stimulus and schizophrenic behaviour. Schizophrenia is a disparate condition, and its causes are complex. How behavioural therapy can help, however, is to provide the person with schizophrenia with skills to make the effects of that condition less apparent. So, for example, behavioural therapy can improve the social isolation schizophrenics feel by teaching social skills to make them better fit in with those without the condition.

Social skills training

Social skills training comprises a set of interventions designed to train the person with schizophrenia in interpersonal skills. So, for example, if the patient is unwilling to leave the house to meet other people, a therapist will first break that behaviour down into several smaller steps (e.g. looking at the cause of the anxiety). Each of these steps will then be treated using established behavioural techniques such as:

- modelling, in which desirable behaviour is demonstrated to the patient
- role-play, in which the client acts out appropriate behaviour, modelled or otherwise
- shaping behaviour by controlling its consequences, usually using reinforcement or ignoring and, less often, punishment (see p. 12 for an explanation and examples)
- rehearsal and feedback, in which the patient practises desirable behaviour and receives supportive feedback on how they are doing.

One of the reasons why such training is important is because there is a link between the social skills of the patient before their first schizophrenic episode and their eventual recovery (Strauss and Carpenter 1974). Many schizophrenic patients, especially those without a supportive family life, are socially isolated and lacking in the skills to reintegrate themselves back into a social life.

There are two types of therapies here: the token economy and personal effectiveness training.

The token economy

The token economy was the first attempt at social skills training among people hospitalized during schizophrenic episodes. It utilizes the principles of operant conditioning. The token refers to a reward offered as a reinforcer whenever the patient does something well or does a task in a particular way. The tokens are given for performing self-care or basic social interaction, or working at something within the hospital. Once enough tokens have been accumulated, they can be exchanged for a larger reward or privilege. It is important to have this second level of reinforcement,

Examiners' notes

If you read the specification, you will notice that behavioural therapies are only included as *examples* of appropriate psychological therapy. This is important because it means that you can't specifically be asked about behavioural therapies in the treatment of schizophrenia. You should, however, be able to describe and evaluate two types of behavioural therapy, so the choice is yours whether you choose this particular therapy as one of them.

Essential notes

Token economies are in use in the treatment of many different psychological and behavioural disorders, but it is essential that you restrict your discussion to just their use in the treatment of schizophrenia.

because it teaches the patients to appreciate the gap between effort and reward in the real world – for example, most jobs pay fortnightly or monthly, and so knowing that there is a delay between successful behaviour and reward is important.

Evaluation of the token economy

- *An effective method* – Most studies found a significant benefit for the token economies. They seem particularly useful in treating patients with negative symptoms (e.g. McMonagle and Sultana 2003). The usefulness of the token economy in a hospital or residential setting seems well established.

- *How long do the benefits last?* – However, less research has been done into whether the benefits of the token training continue after discharge and the end of the programme. The patients traditionally used in such studies have all been hospitalized for some time and so may benefit more from training. Would such programmes work in people who have only just begun to experience schizophrenia?

Personal effectiveness training

Being personally effective refers to situations where you can express yourself confidently, whether positively and negatively, in situations with others. To do this, it is important to be sensitive to the way the other person is feeling. Sometimes, this can mean assertiveness training – simply, learning the ability to be confident in any social setting.

The methods used in personal effectiveness training include role-playing, where the patient is asked to act out a situation with either a trainer or another patient. The trainer then reviews the patient's performance, reinforcing correct behaviours and offering tips about how better to play the situation. The process is then repeated until the trainer is happy with the performance. The trainer is looking for the patient to maintain things such as eye contact, smiling when appropriate, and conversing properly. Sometimes, those with schizophrenia have to be taught to listen to the other side of the conversation and how to select an appropriate response to what the other person is saying. They can be given homework in the 'real world' to reinforce what they have learned in training.

Evaluation of personal effectiveness training

- *Addressing gaps in social behaviour* – Schizophrenia is a socially isolating disorder, and this type of training offers the opportunity to refresh the social skills needed to develop friends. This type of therapy acts to add something missing from the patient's behaviour.

- *Limited transferability of skills* – The evidence suggests that personal effectiveness training can be successful, but only for situations the patient had been trained in; novel situations were more difficult (Frederiksen *et al.* 1976).

- *Anxiety reduction* – The training is particularly effective at reducing anxiety about experiencing certain situations and should be a part of the treatment for schizophrenia.

Essential notes

The programmes provide an interesting look into the treatment of patients who require long-term treatment. However, research into other types of patient are lacking. We also have to ask if it is ethical to offer or withhold 'treats' to people as a part of their care. Token economies seem to be a useful addition to current treatment options, but more up-to-date research needs to be done to evaluate them for current times.

Essential notes

This type of therapy provides skills that might be missing from someone with schizophrenia. It offers them context: something with which to compare their post-schizophrenia episode experiences. The skills seem useful, but it is impossible to prepare the patient for every experience they might have in their life. There is little evidence to suggest that this is a treatment for schizophrenia, but it might be something to improve quality of life, and so is worth offering.

Psychological therapies: cognitive-behavioural

Cognitive-behavioural therapy (CBT) links behavioural therapy with the cognitive approach. This means that the emphasis within CBT is on the cognitive causes of the abnormal behaviour. CBT is used most frequently to treat conditions such as phobias and depression. It is a successful form of therapy not least because it requires the clients to do homework assignments to improve their behaviours. This makes a client confront their own problems rather than passively allowing a therapist to sort them out. The value of CBT in treating schizophrenia is only now being seriously evaluated, and although it is early days, this form of therapy seems to be very useful in dealing with some of the symptoms of schizophrenia.

Cognitive-behavioural therapy

One of the major symptoms of schizophrenia is cognitive disorganization. It makes sense then that CBT should be used, as part of a treatment programme, to deal with this disorganization.

- CBT makes connections between a patient's feelings and thought patterns that reinforce their illness, and makes the patient aware of these.

- CBT challenges the patient's interpretation of events, and helps them to change their habit of thinking about things in a pathological way so, if a patient has the delusion that MI5 are following them, a CBT therapist would ask them to discuss the 'evidence' for this belief and encourage the patient to come up with new explanations for that evidence.

This not only helps with symptoms of hallucinations and delusions, but it also allows the patient to become better at problem-solving and coping with their illness because the therapy lets the patient do the hard work of challenging their own perceptions.

Evaluation of CBT

A positive contribution to treatment options

The use of CBT alongside traditional medication is the first large step forward to be taken in the treatment of schizophrenia in 60 years. As of yet, the number of studies is small; more studies need to be done in order to evaluate the worth of CBT properly. Although CBT does not seem to prevent a schizophrenic episode developing, it does seem to reduce the time the patient spends in hospital as a result of that episode. This is because the positive symptoms seem to be less serious in those who have had CBT. A criticism of this result could be that the patients who received CBT were not as severely affected by the disorder as the other group. It is hard to assess the worth of this because the severity of a schizophrenic episode is hard to quantify.

A palliative but not a cure

CBT is a promising addition to the available treatment options for schizophrenia. It is not a cure, but it seems to have long-term benefits for those with schizophrenia (e.g. Tarrier *et al.* 2004). We are not yet sure whether these improvements occur simply because someone is just talking to the patients about the strange and scary things they are experiencing or whether the cognitive remodelling makes the difference.

Success in changing cognitions about hallucinatory voices

Benjamin (1989) was one of the first to document the usefulness of CBT in schizophrenia.

Benjamin found that patients had meaningful relationships with their hallucinatory voices. A patient would say that the voice liked them, even though it would say negative or hostile things to them. Benjamin wrote that he believed the content of the voice is directly responsible for the actions of the patient's schizophrenic behaviour. As most people with schizophrenia developed their abnormal beliefs by normal thought processes, it should be possible to get rid of those abnormal beliefs by normal thinking. Chadwick and Birchwood (1994) were among the first clinicians to simply ask patients what they thought about the voices using the techniques above. They found that the amount of time patients spent hallucinating fell considerably. Chadwick and Birchwood were surprised that CBT was as successful as it was and suggested that the therapy had decreased the patient's acute stressful response to the hallucinations. Once the stress response is combated, the patient's 'reason' to generate the voices goes away too.

The importance of the therapeutic relationship

We now know that the patient's relationship with the therapist is important (Day *et al.* 2005); there has to be trust. It is also important that the therapist uses the same kinds of language that the patient uses (Birchwood *et al.* 2000). Patients' delusions, hallucinations and anxiety are all very real to them, and this has to be addressed if the patient is to improve. This means spending time talking to the patient rather than emphasizing that this is treatment.

Early intervention

Another finding shows that CBT during the patient's first episode of schizophrenia (Lewis *et al.* 2002) shortens the length of that episode. Eighteen months later these patients suffered the same relapse rate as patients who did not have CBT, but were still less negatively affected by their symptoms.

Breadth of application

CBT also seems to be effective at treating the negative, as well as the positive, symptoms of schizophrenia (Sensky *et al.* 2000), although it seems this is characteristic of longer terms of therapy.

Examiners' notes

CBT tends to be used in conjunction with other forms of treatment (usually drug treatments). It is a useful exercise to do your own Internet research on this (via your favourite search engine), and track down a study that has examined the effectiveness of CBT when combined with other treatments against CBT alone. This can then be used as evaluation *and*, because it is something you discovered yourself, will be more memorable.

Essential notes

Although it is relatively early days, CBT seems to be a useful addition to the range of treatment offered for schizophrenia. It seems that the success of CBT relies on the therapist's ability to talk normally to the patient. As we have spent over 100 years of treating schizophrenia as something strange and the patients as people who need to be withdrawn from society, this is a step forward. Newer studies evaluating a combination of medication, CBT and family therapy are currently underway. The results have the potential to change the way we treat those experiencing schizophrenia.

Clinical characteristics

What is depression?

Depression is an **affective disorder** or mood disorder that is characterized by sadness. At its worst, it can cause an overwhelming lack of interest in the self or the world and a sense of futility of trying to do anything. Moods vary throughout everyone's life in reaction to the things experienced, and this is perfectly normal. However, **clinical depression** is very different, as it is the extreme end of a spectrum of moods; the other end of the spectrum is mania, characterized by euphoria, excitement and overactivity. Most people with a mood disorder suffer only from depression, therefore they are considered to be suffering from **unipolar disorder**. Others experience alternating states of depression and mania, therefore they are considered to be suffering from **bipolar disorder**.

The incidence of depression

According to the World Health Organization, depression is the fourth leading cause of 'disability and disease'. They also calculate that 121 million people worldwide are affected by depression at any one time. Paykel *et al.* (2005) estimate that this equates to 5 per cent of the European population. The lifetime risk for clinical depression is approximately 10 per cent (Andrews *et al.* 2005). Women are more than twice as likely to experience episodes of severe depression (Nolen-Hoeksema 2002) than men – or, at least, are twice as likely to seek treatment for depression.

The condition typically onsets in young adulthood, with the median age of onset being 24 years. Depression can happen to anyone, at any time in their life.

The symptoms of depression

The two major diagnostic manuals for psychiatric disorders, the **DSM**-IV-TR and the **ICD**-10, both specify similar symptoms for depression. These are:
- sad depressed mood
- loss of interest in usual activities
- low self-esteem
- feelings of excessive guilt for something the patient had no control over
- **suicidal ideation**
- inability to concentrate or make decisions
- either sleeping too much or inability to sleep
- either weight gain or lack of interest in food leading to weight loss
- either agitation or lethargy.

For a diagnosis of major depressive disorder, the individual must have either of the first two symptoms in the above list. These symptoms should be present all or most of the time and should have persisted for longer than two weeks (see opposite).

The last few symptoms in the list might seem a little vague, but this is because of a condition called **atypical depression**, where the patient will overeat and oversleep instead. This type of depression is experienced by as many as 40 per cent of the total number of those with a diagnosis of clinical depression (Nierenberg *et al.* 1998). The typical pattern is difficulty sleeping (characteristically waking early in the morning) and undereating causing weight loss.

Most of these symptoms are assessed either by self-report (as answers to a series of questions) or after conversation with the family and or friends of the person with the depression. It is important that the person making the diagnosis rules out the chance that the depression is a secondary symptom of a much larger medical problem, or that the depression is a side effect of other medications or substances such as alcohol. They should also establish whether the depression is the reaction to a stressful life event, such as a bereavement. This kind of **reactive depression** should not be medicated initially, although this might alter in the next version of the DSM.

Types of depression

The two major classification manuals each classify depression slightly differently.

DSM-IV-TR classification
The USA's DSM (see p. 6) includes:
- major depressive episode (MDE) – for a single depression episode
- major depressive disorder (MDD) – classified as a relatively short-lived depression of at least two weeks.

The depression can either be severe, moderate or mild. If the patient experiences the symptoms of psychosis (hallucinations and delusions), they are diagnosed with **psychotic** depression. If they experience manic episodes, the diagnosis becomes bipolar disorder.

ICD-10 classification
The World Health Organization's ICD (see p. 6) places more emphasis on the severity of the depression, but otherwise has similar categories. The ICD also makes the distinction between a depressive episode (one event) and recurrent depression (many episodes over time) more important in the diagnostic context.

Other mood disorders
Depression is only one of a range of mood disorders, including conditions such as **dysthymic disorder** (or dysthymia), which is characterized as a milder but longer-lasting depression. The category of mood disorders ranges from mania and euphoria to severe depression, and establishing where on this continuum the patient falls takes great skill.

Essential notes

The clinician has to listen closely to the patient to perform an accurate diagnosis and to estimate the severity of the episode. This is one of the problems with the non-specific nature of current diagnostic criteria. Identifying the severity of the episode is very important as that determines whether medication is prescribed or not. Trying to get this information from someone who is depressed and has a lack of interest in the proceedings must be very difficult.

Issues in classification and diagnosis

A diagnosis of depression is only as good as the criteria the clinician uses to make the diagnosis, so there are problems of reliability and validity. Any diagnosis ultimately rests on someone's clinical judgment, and this means that some mistakes are inevitable.

The skill with which clinicians make these decisions will affect:
- how appropriate (valid) the diagnosis is
- how consistent (reliable) it is across similar cases and between different clinicians.

However, depression is especially problematic to diagnose, because there are rarely grand psychiatric signs (such as hallucinations and delusions in schizophrenia) to signpost to a particular condition. Instead, the clinician has to establish whether the patient's mood is low enough to justify a psychiatric diagnosis. To do this, the clinician has to make several decisions, as outlined below.

Establishing the cause of symptoms

A clinician assessing someone who may be depressed has to consider both what the symptoms are and, crucially, what might be causing them. There are several important issues here.

Psychological or physical cause?
Several of the symptoms of depression are physical (referred to as somatic symptoms by the ICD) – for example, losing weight and experiencing problems with sleeping. This means the doctor has to make sure that these symptoms are not the symptoms of an organic illness, such as a dysfunction of the brain caused by injury, a disease affecting brain tissues, or chemical or hormonal abnormalities. For example, the symptoms of anaemia (iron deficiency) include fatigue and decreased energy that could resemble apathy. A verbal description of the way anaemia makes you feel could be interpreted as depression, so it is important that a doctor establishes an accurate clinical picture.

Role of psychoactive drugs
There is the chance that the symptoms of depression occur as a secondary symptom to the use of **psychoactive drugs**. Alcohol, for example, is a depressant; it slows down the rate at which the brain works. If enough alcohol is drunk for over a prolonged period, it becomes hard to separate the effects of the alcoholism from those of the depression.

This picture is made more complex as depressed people sometimes use alcohol as self-medication. This tends not to help someone with depression, as any improvement of mood is only temporary. It is important that the clinician establish whether the depression is caused by alcohol or not, as this affects treatment options.

Reactive or endogenous depression?
Depression that occurs as a result of environmental stressors (such as grief), called reactive depression, is not considered to be the same as a

Examiners' notes

Exam questions in this area will not ask specifically about reliability and validity, but about 'issues in the classification and/or diagnosis'. Reliability and validity are the most obvious choices to answer such a question.

clinical or **endogenous depression**. Reactive depression is usually short-lived and will remit on its own. It does not require medication, although there is a possibility that it will develop into a more severe depression.

Comorbidity

Depression can occur alongside (i.e. be **comorbid** with) another psychiatric condition (e.g. an eating disorder). There is a tradition within psychiatry that clinicians should begin by treating the condition that occurred first. However, establishing which came first can be very difficult. As depression can be so serious, this probably does not matter, as long as both conditions receive treatment.

Is it major depression?

The first decision the clinician has to make is whether the patient is clinically depressed or whether they are showing a normal sadness in response to some event. Everyone experiences sadness from time to time, and these low moods will usually lighten spontaneously. The decision about whether the low mood is indicative of a more serious problem should be for a clinician to make. There are so many variations of mood disorder that patients should ideally see a psychiatrist or mental health professional when seeking treatment. In the UK, however, the busy nature of the NHS means that diagnosis is frequently left to a GP, who, as a non-specialist, might not reach the right decision. Mitchell *et al.* (2009) report that, in general practice, depression is misidentified more frequently than it is missed, and this is probably the result of the ambiguous criteria.

Differential diagnoses

A second decision to be made by a clinician is whether the patient has shown evidence of mania in the past, as this possibly indicates bipolar (previously manic-depression) disorder. It is not advisable to give someone with bipolar disorder antidepressants, and it increases the rate of the moods cycling. The two conditions have very different medications.

Another condition that can seem similar to depression is anxiety. An anxious person will also withdraw from their life and may present as someone depressed. Anxiety and depression go hand in hand, and they may require separate treatments for the patient to recover.

Gender differences?

As mentioned earlier, depression seems more common in women. One reason for this could be hormonal variations, but it could just be that women are more inclined to seek help rather than suffer in silence. For men, admitting depression could be seen as a weakness, which could make some men less likely to go to a doctor. If this were the case, then gender differences in depression are not *real* differences, but merely differences in men and women's *responses* to feelings of low mood. Failure to acknowledge this affects both the validity and reliability of depression diagnosis in men and women. See p. 45 for more on depression and gender.

See p. 45 for more on depression and gender.

Essential notes

As already mentioned, the lack of reliable clinical signs is a real problem for the reliability of diagnosing MDD. It also means that general practitioners have a difficult job when it comes to making a diagnosis. There is no easy solution to any of these problems. However, we need to continue to search for solutions because of the implications of giving people medications they might not need.

Examiners' notes

There is a need to match your material to the specific demands of the question set in your examination. So, if you are answering a 24-mark question (25-mark prior to 2012) that is specifically on issues relating to the classification and diagnosis of depression, you could include *any* of the material on these two pages. If you are answering a 10-mark AO2 question, you require about 250 words, so select the material from these two pages that you think constitutes a good critical review of the these issues.

Essential notes

The diagnosis of depression is not straightforward. Establishing the diagnosis has problems of reliability and validity. It is hard to see this situation changing unless we can establish a reliable biological marker to give reliable test results. Sociocultural background and cultural differences may also play a part in diagnosis of depression. See p. 45 for further explanation.

See p. 45 for further explanation.

Essential notes

The role of nature and nurture in determining behaviour is very difficult to unravel as they interact in very complex ways.

Examiners' notes

There are many different types of depression, and many different terms for it, including 'major depression', 'major depressive disorder' and 'clinical depression'. You can refer to all these simply as 'depression'. However, other forms of depression (e.g. premenstrual dysphoric disorder and seasonal affective disorder) have different causes and aetiology, and so if you *do* decide to write about these (note that this isn't necessary), you would need to consider them separately.

Essential notes

The nature–nurture problem is especially complex when studying a disorder such as major depression. The fact that everyone has low moods indicates that life-factors must play a major role in mood. However, the observation that only *some* people go on to develop MDD suggests that there is something different about these people. We are struggling to discover reliable ways to establish the role of the nature part of the equation.

Biological explanations: genetics

Depression seems to run in families. This could either be because there are genes responsible for depression or because there is a predisposition for depression in certain families. Another argument is that depression is entirely sociocultural, and a predisposition within families merely reflects the environmental causes of the condition experienced by members of the same family. Together, these arguments are a good example of the **nature–nurture debate**. There is no doubt, however, that environment plays a role in the onset and course of depression. This is shown by the observation that depression becomes more prevalent as economic circumstances worsen (Lorant *et al.* 2007).

Evidence from family studies

Family studies look for incidence of certain conditions within a family and then compare the results to the incidence for the same condition among the general population. This gives an idea of how heritable the condition is. First-degree relatives (parents, siblings and offspring) share about 50 per cent of their genetic material. As the relationship between family members gets more distant, this percentage decreases. Cousins share, at most, 25 per cent of their genetic material.

When we look at the heritability for mood disorders, it is clear that there is an inheritable component, especially for bipolar disorder (Gershon 1990). For major depressive disorder (MDD), the risk factor for developing depression among children who have a parent with depression is two to three times greater than the risk in the general population. When the **proband** (the original patient in a genetic study) developed the disorder as a child or adolescent, the risk factor for subsequent children increases dramatically (Weissman *et al.* 1984). In addition, anxiety disorders and substance abuse disorders are more common in the children of depressive parents (Weissman 1987).

Evaluation of family studies

The increase in risk of developing some kind of psychiatric disorder when a parent has a diagnosis of MDD might still not be down entirely to genetics. It could still all be the result of a shared environment, with children learning their depressed mood from observation of parents, or, more probably, an interaction between that and genetic pre-disposition.

Evidence from twin studies

Slightly stronger data comes from twin studies. Monozygotic (identical) twins have nearly identical genetic material (Fraga *et al.* 2005). Twin studies are useful because twins experience similar environments, or at least, they are expected to have more in common than non-twins. An example of a methodologically sound twin study is that of Kendler *et al.* (2006). They studied over 15 000 twins using the Swedish Twin Registry and assessed their medical history using a diagnostic interview. Of these, 8378 twins met the criteria for major depression. On the basis of these data, Kendler and colleagues estimated that the heritability of major depression is 38 per cent. For women, the risk rises to 42 per cent; for men, the risk decreases to 29 per cent. This is broadly in line with other studies.

Evaluation of twin studies

Despite the convincing nature of these studies, they are still not able to separate the effects of the environment from that of genetics. If anything, the situation is more confused by use of twins in this instance. Twins share an environment and are subject to the same influences. A better population to test would people who are related but exposed to different environments because they have been individually adopted. That allows us to look at the influence of genetics without the confusion of environment.

Evidence from adoption studies

Adoption studies are perhaps the best way of addressing the nature–nurture problem in depression. However, there are methodological problems with studies of this type. For example, to assess the heredity level, researchers would have to contact the adoptees' biological and adopted parents, and only use those whose adopted parents showed no mood disorders. Doing this would isolate the potential influence of genetics from the potential complication of learning depressive tendencies from adoptive parents.

An example of an adoption study

The largest adoption study looking at the causes of depression was by Wender et al. (1986). They interviewed people who had been adopted and found that they were seven times more likely to experience depression if their biological parents were depressed. This study found little evidence for depression being behaviour that is learned. However, Wender got his information about the biological relatives from hospital records only; he did not interview these people at first hand, and so the results have to be treated with some caution.

Other genetic studies

We are starting to see new genetic studies made possible with the advance of technology. Genetic linkage studies look for common genes among those with a diagnosis of the disorder. These are still quite rare, and they are not yet indicating any specific genes that are solely responsible for depression (Boomsma et al. 2008). However, they are well worth pursuing because they offer the best hope for developing more successful medication. Current studies are focused on investigating the genes responsible for the transmitting of neurochemicals – in particular, monoamine neurotransmitters (e.g. serotonin, dopamine, noradrenaline – see pp. 36–7) – as finding problems here would be the easiest route to generating new types of medication.

Examiners' notes

Research evidence can be used as part of your AO2 evaluation by building it into a critical argument. For example you might say something like: 'The role of genetics in the onset of depression is supported by a study by Kendler et al. (2006), who studied over 15 000 twins using the Swedish Twin Registry and assessed their medical history using a diagnostic interview. They estimated that the heritability of major depression was 38 per cent, suggesting that genetics pays an important causal role in the onset of this disorder.'

Essential notes

Attempts to add to the nature–nurture debate regarding depression are hampered by methodological problems. As such we must be cautious when drawing conclusions from family-based studies.

Biological explanations: biochemistry

Monoamines

Biochemical evidence is very important for depression because this evidence is used to establish pharmaceutical treatments. Depression seems to involve several neurochemicals in the brain. These chemicals are called the monoamines, and include dopamine, serotonin and noradrenaline. All of these chemicals are involved in the functioning of the **limbic system**, which is a part of the brain involved in the control of emotions.

The monoamine hypothesis of depression suggests that a reduction of one or more of these three neurochemicals is the reason for depression. The evidence in support of this hypothesis comes from the simple observation that current medication for depression seems to work for some people. Antidepressants all affect the amount of monoamines in the brain. They do this principally by affecting the way serotonin works, as the levels of serotonin in the brain will affect the levels of other monoamines. It is hypothesized that a low level of serotonin disrupts other monoamine systems, which leads to depression.

Evaluating the evidence for the monoamine theory

Antidepressants seem to work for around 50 per cent of the people who take them, and this is the major piece of evidence in favour of the monoamine hypothesis. However:

- We aren't really sure why these medications work.
- We are not sure why they take six to eight weeks before patients report feeling better, when **brain imaging** suggests medications are having an immediate effect.

Although there are changes evident in the brains of the depressed, there are two reasons why we should be cautious about this evidence:

- The most noticeable changes occur in people with a history of depression in the family (Drevets 2000), rather than those with a spontaneous onset. The changes seen in people without family history are similar to those seen in people with low mood or who are stressed or anxious.
- Perhaps most importantly, we are not certain whether these changes are the *cause* of depression or the *result* of depression. This is important, because if the change is the result of depression, then treating with drugs affecting monoamine levels will not address the underlying problem. This could be one reason why antidepressants only work in some people.

Serotonin function and suicide

There is some evidence from the brains of suicide victims showing that there is a change in serotonin function in the prefrontal cortex of these individuals (Arango *et al.* 2002). However, any conclusions drawn from such sources need to be treated with a great deal of caution because:

- not all people experiencing a major depressive episode commit suicide
- not all suicides were experiencing major depression.

Using suicide data, therefore, involves making generalizations from a very specific sample of the population.

In summary, there is some evidence for the monoamine theory, but it is not conclusive. Therefore, this theory should be treated with caution.

Hormonal factors in depression

Premenstrual dysphoric disorder

The fact that more women than men report major depressive episodes suggests that hormones play some role in the onset and/or continuation of depressive episodes. This has been recognized in **premenstrual dysphoric disorder**, a depression that has its onset in the week prior to menstruation. Hormones fluctuate to a great extent in women, and an imbalance in hormones caused by these fluctuations is thought to affect 25 per cent of women. However, this depression is not at the same level of severity as MDD and doesn't require treatment in most women.

Cortisol

A more likely candidate for hormonal involvement in depression is cortisol, which is increased in those suffering from depression. Cortisol is raised as a result of exposure to stress, and it seems as though a similar response occurs in the severely depressed (Brouwer *et al.* 2005). This implicates the hypothalamic-pituitary-adrenal (HPA) cortex system and again underlines the relationship between anxiety and depression.

Clinical trials are currently underway to test the success of medications that reduce the release of cortisol in MDD. These results will be interesting because they could suggest a new way of treating depression. They might also answer the questions of why more women than men are affected (because women's hormones fluctuate more) and why antidepressants do not work quickly or for all patients (because they are treating one symptom rather than the whole condition).

Evaluating the cortisol explanation

Strickland *et al.* (2002) found no evidence of raised cortisol levels in a large group of women with depression. This posed problems for a cortisol explanation for depression. However, they did find elevated cortisol levels in some of the women who had experienced stressful life events yet had not developed depression. This suggests that stressful life events can result in increased cortisol levels but this does not necessarily lead to depression.

Examiners' notes

One of the joys of studying psychology is that there is always new research to enlighten our understanding of a particular area. So, a useful way of adding valuable AO2 material that 'supports' the role of hormonal factors in depression is to hunt out your own research on this topic. Research has suggested a connection between cortisol levels and depression, and although studies tend to contradict each other, each adds to our complete understanding of this association. Beware of getting carried away with your 'project' though!

Essential notes

Recent research is moving away from the monoamine theory of depression because it seems that, although these systems are involved in depression, they are not causal factors. Instead, new research is focusing on hormonal factors, especially those involved in the HPA-axis, that seem to underpin the monoamine changes in certain people. However, it is very early days for this sort of research. Hormonal changes that occur in women alone seem unlikely to be a significant factor in major depressive disorder.

Psychological explanations: behavioural

The previous section (pp. 34–7) discussed the biological changes that occur in depression. However, the problem of cause or effect was raised. How do we know that the biological changes observed in depressed people are the cause, rather than the effects, of suffering from depression? What if depression is primarily caused by psychological factors, which then lead to biological changes in the brain?

Lewinsohn's behavioural theory of depression

Lewinsohn and Libet (1972) suggested that depression is the consequence of a reduction in pleasant events (to use traditional terms of behaviourism – a reduction in **positive reinforcement**) or an increase in adverse events (**punishment**, in behaviourist terms). So for example, when a person suffers an environmental stressor (such as losing a job) at the same time as experiencing a decrease in pleasurable events (e.g. having to move away from family and friends to find work), they become particularly vulnerable to depression. The reduction of positive reinforcement associated with having fun with family and friends can induce depressive behaviour. Similarly, increased rates of punishment (e.g. not being able to go out because you know no one in your new surroundings) can also lead to depression.

Testing Lewinsohn's theory

Lewinsohn *et al.* (1981) tested his theory by questioning a sample of 998 people using various tests of **cognitive style**. Interviews included a psychiatric diagnostic interview to identify those people who were currently experiencing depression. He retested a sample of these people around eight to nine months later to see what, if anything, had changed. The people retested were:

1. those who scored highly on a depression inventory or highly on other psychiatric symptoms (such as irrational beliefs)
2. those who had changed their marital status
3. a random selection from everyone else.

This gave them 698 people to re-interview.

The most important thing they found was that those with a history of depression scored approximately the same on the tests as people who had never been depressed, so, their experience of depression had not made them more prone to thinking like a depressed person when recovered. Secondly, people who became depressed *during* the study were indistinguishable at the time of their first interview from people who did not become depressed at all. This supports Lewinsohn's claim that depression occurs as a consequence to negative events, and that there is nothing about a person to indicate that they are prone to depression. It is the reaction to experiencing bad events, or not experiencing positive events, that is the major contributing factor to depression.

Learned helplessness

A similar idea was developed at the same time by Seligman (1975). He found that dogs that had been placed in stressful and inescapable situations were less likely to attempt escape from subsequent stressful situations. Seligman called this **learned helplessness** and compared it to when people cannot control or influence events. Eventually, some people lose motivation and stop trying to change the hopeless situation they are in. Seligman tested his ideas on people (using similar methods as he did with the dogs) and found that some humans exhibited learned helplessness too.

Evaluation of behavioural theories

Behavioural theorists stress that the circumstances an individual is experiencing are important contributors to the onset of depression. Neither of the theories outlined here makes any claim about the personality or biology of the depressed person. Although this is somewhat reassuring (if the cause is simple, perhaps the treatment will be too), it is also a little misleading for several reasons.

Lewinsohn: methodological problems

The Lewinsohn study used many participants, which is always a good thing because it makes generalization to a larger population more reliable. However, they recruited their sample of participants by sending out 20 000 letters to residents in a specific US location. The people who wrote back because they were happy to take part are self-selecting – in other words, Lewinsohn and colleagues only tested people who *wanted* to take part. This means that those people who might have been severely depressed may have lacked the motivation to take part in the study. The Lewinsohn study would have carried more weight if the sample they used had been selected randomly.

Seligman: methodological problems

Seligman's theory equates stress with depression (an analogue experiment, where you assume one behaviour is similar to another). However, we have little evidence to suggest that the experience of too much stress is the same thing as the experience of depression. In his experiment, Seligman induced stress in humans by playing loud noises and giving mild electric shocks. Can we say that this is equivalent to depression? We cannot be sure of the answer to this question, which means that we have to treat the theory of learned helplessness with some caution.

Role of other factors

Not all people who experience bad events go on to develop depression. There must be other factors in play rather than just these behavioural ones. These factors could be individual differences in vulnerability to depression based on genetics or biochemistry.

Examiners' notes

Remember that for every 24-mark question (25-mark prior to 2012), the AO2 component is twice as important (in terms of marks awarded) than the AO1 component. AO2 marks are also dependent on the level of elaboration in your answers, so when revising from the critical points on this page, make sure that you incorporate a sufficient level of elaboration. (See p. 101 for more about how to elaborate points in your answers.)

Essential notes

Lewinsohn's and Seligman's theories are useful because they show that the environment plays a causal role in depression. However, they cannot explain why some people do not develop depression when they experience negative events. Both theories presented here have methodological problems, and this suggests that they are not conclusive.

Psychological explanations: cognitive

Both of the types of theory described so far (Lewinsohn's behavioural theory and Seligman's learned helplessness) ignore the *cognitive* inputs to depression. Depression appears to involve cognition because symptoms of rumination (thinking deeply about something) and apathy (not caring about anything) both involve active states of mind. The addition of cognitive factors to the existing theories stresses the concept of **agency**; it involves the person and their individual responses to situations. In other words, cognitive factors might explain why people respond to the same stimuli in different ways.

Essential notes

Cognitive-behavioural theories of depression (such as Aaron Beck's theory described here) offer a more complete theory of depression. This is because they stress the interplay of person and their environment as causal factors in the onset of depression.

Aaron Beck's cognitive theory of depression

Beck's (e.g. 1972) cognitive theory of depression is perhaps the most famous theory of depression, not least because it offers an eventual means of treatment. Beck theorized that depression is caused by negative thinking, especially about oneself. Negative thinking involves ruminating and catastrophizing (thinking the worst about things). He believes this type of thinking causes **cognitive errors** (a belief in something that is not true). In Beck's theory, negative thinking comes before the development of depression.

The negative cognitive triad of depression

Beck hypothesized that depression has three components, shown in Fig. 2. These negative views interfere with normal cognitive processing, such as memory and problem-solving. Each one also feeds into the other. So the idea 'I'm not going to get a job' (negative view of oneself) feeds into 'I will never be able to buy my own home' (negative view of the future), which feeds into 'Everybody is against me' (negative view of the world). This forms an unending, intrusive cycle of depressive thoughts that cannot be controlled by the thinker.

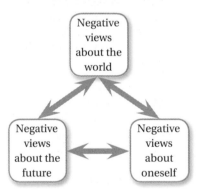

Fig. 2
Beck's cognitive triad of depression

Self-schemas

Beck believes that people develop **schemas** about themselves, which makes them think in this negative way. These early schemas come from problems with rejection by parents or friends in the form of criticism and ostracism, or perhaps by the loss of a close family member. This part of his theory is tied to his training as a psychoanalyst, which grounds depression in events that occur in childhood. Such negative events mould the person's concept of themselves as unwanted or unloved. This then filters all subsequent experiences.

Evaluation of Beck's theory: positives

Since it was first published, Beck's theory has been a staple part of theories *about* depression and treatments *for* it. Beck developed a brief questionnaire called the 'Beck Depression Inventory', which has become a common way of assessing and diagnosing depression. This theory is a very simple and effective one, although Beck has added to it over the past 40 years. For example, he added work on personality, as well as looking at the biological mechanisms of depression. This theory has been tested many times and used in particular clinical settings (e.g. treatment for alcoholism).

Evaluation of Beck's theory: negatives

Although studies have shown that depressed people have negative self-schemas, many fail to support the idea that the negative self-schema is the way people think about themselves *before* the development of depression (e.g. Segal 1988). It is hard to gain a snapshot of people before they develop an illness, because they do not present themselves for study! One study that did manage to do this, however, was Evans *et al.* (2005), using a questionnaire study of pregnant women. They found that women with a high negative self-schema were subsequently more likely to become depressed than those with a low negative self-schema. This type of study is rare, and again relied upon a self-selecting sample, but it does provide support for Beck's theories. However, more confirmatory studies like this one are needed before all aspects of Beck's theory become accepted.

Hopelessness theory

Seligman's theory of learned helplessness was reformulated by Abramson *et al.* (1978) into the hopelessness theory. This theory suggests that when people experience failure, they try to attribute it to a cause. Table 2 below gives an example of this.

Table 2
Attributional styles: 'hopeless' and 'hopeful'

Hopeless	Hopeful
Internal ('It's me')	External ('Someone made a mistake')
Stable ('This always happens to me')	Unstable ('That was unlucky')
Global ('I am so stupid')	Specific ('I need to do more to succeed')

The people more prone to depression tend to attribute the cause of a bad event to internal, stable and global factors. Seligman (1974) tested this idea on college students when exam results appeared, and his findings supported the theory. People who failed and made internal, stable and global attributions remained depressed. Those who had failed and made external, unstable and specific attributions had recovered.

Evaluation of the hopelessness theory

Seligman supported his theory, but he did not use depressed people to test it. Instead he used college students in a very specific situation. Failing exams can make you very upset, but it is not the same thing as experiencing clinical depression. Seligman would need to show the same findings with a depressed population for the theory to be accepted.

Examiners' notes

Although we have included positives and negatives about Beck's theory, there is no need to provide both when constructing an evaluative response. Both are equally relevant in this respect. Remember that supporting research can also be a positive critical point, but you need to make an explicit statement about which aspect of the theory is actually supported by the study being discussed.

Essential notes

Beck began the idea of cognitive-behavioural therapy (CBT) in depression, which is still used with success today. However, his *theory* is not as universally accepted. Like the other theories, this theory adds to the overall picture of depression, but it does not tell the entire story.

Examiners' notes

Tables are a good way of illustrating a theory and giving examples to make your revision easier, but there is no need to reproduce these in an examination. Continuous prose (i.e. writing in proper sentences) is always better.

Essential notes

Cognitive theories are important because they offer a relatively simple way of treating depression: namely, altering a negative ('hopeless') attributional style so as to consider other explanations when bad things happen.

Psychological explanations: psychodynamic

Freudian explanations of depression

Sigmund Freud developed the first psychodynamic theory of depression, and he tied it to grief and loss. Freud believed that depression was the result of an 'excessive and irrational grief', as the individual fails to come to terms with the loss. Freud believed that two of the stages of grief, those of sadness and anger, become internalized, i.e. turned towards the self. He made several parallels between the symptoms of depression and what occurs in grief (e.g. loss of appetite, trouble sleeping). Freud believed that the grief stems from the feelings (or imagined feelings) about losing the person on whom the individual depended upon when a child.

Grief and loss

It is important to realize that Freud is not just talking about the loss of a person; grief can apply to the loss of anything held precious (e.g. becoming blind in adulthood). He called this concept **symbolic loss**. Symbolic loss is as powerful as grief because the individual will use the same thought processes as they would if they had lost someone dear to them. Thinking about this loss before it has happened will, in addition, make the individual feel guilty, and this can make the resulting depression worse.

Parent–child relationships

Freud and subsequent psychodynamic theorists also considered those people who perhaps had unhappy childhoods or did not have successful relationships with their parents. In this case, the guilt from not having those 'normal' feelings and relationships will also lead to guilt and self-directed hostility. Psychodynamic theory believes that children who have been abused or neglected repress the feelings such things cause, but that this repression will eventually resurface in the form of depression and anxiety.

Evaluation: evidence against Freudian explanations of depression

- Freud's ideas in general are notoriously difficult to test scientifically. For example, concepts such as 'the unconscious' or 'inward direction of hostility' cannot be directly observed, which causes practical problems in testing them empirically.

- Grief and depression do resemble each other in some ways, but in other ways they are quite different. It is established that bereavement causes a deep sorrow, but, if depression results, it is likely to be a reactive depression (relatively short-term) rather than a clinical depression, and should, therefore, be treated differently.

- Freud emphasizes the importance of self-hostility, yet depressed people are more likely to be apathetic than hostile.

- Although depression may be punishing, depressed people tend not to use terms of self-hostility when explaining how they feel.

- A further problem with Freud's ideas is also evident in other theories – that is, that not everyone who is depressed has had a bad childhood or has experienced any significant loss, symbolic or otherwise. The theory simply does not explain depression in many cases.

Evaluation: evidence in favour of Freudian explanations of depression

- Shah and Waller (2000) found that many people who have suffered from depression described their parents as 'affectionless', thus supporting Freud's concept of loss through withdrawal of affection.

- The best support Freud has for the close relationship between loss and depression comes from studies of the elderly who have lost a spouse or close friend. Some of the bereaved elderly show something called **complicated grief**, which can include anger and suspicion (e.g. Prigerson *et al.* 1995). However, this does not seem to have its origins in childhood experiences.

Essential notes

Freud's ideas stress the importance of loss and guilt, which may indeed be causal factors in depression. However, this theory is too specific to provide a universal explanation of depression.

Bowlby and attachment

John Bowlby explored Freud's work by looking at the quality of the mother–child attachment. He wrote a book called *Loss: Sadness and Depression* (Bowlby 1980) as part of his work on attachment. Bowlby believed that the early loss of a mother results in the child losing their safe platform to explore the world. This leads to a tentative and anxious child becoming a tentative and anxious adult, believed to be a precursor to depression.

Evaluation: evidence in favour of Bowlby's explanation of depression

There is some support for the idea of insecure attachment being a causal factor in depression. For example, Pettem *et al.* (1992) found that an insecure and anxious attachment was a characteristic of adult depression. They gave the Reciprocal Attachment Questionnaire (RAQ) to a group of depressed and non-depressed people. The RAQ assesses the quality of a current relationship that has been shared for at least six months. They found that the depressed patients compulsively sought care and attention in a relationship. This accords with Hodges and Tizard's (1989) finding that temporarily institutionalized, insecurely attached children, who were later adopted or restored to their families, tended to be more attention- and approval-seeking than controls.

Examiners' notes

Make sure, when describing either Freud's or Bowlby's explanations, that you only include material that is *specifically* relevant to depression. You would not get credit for material that is more general concerning these theories (e.g. Freud's ideas of id, ego and superego, or a lengthy description of Bowlby's work with maternally deprived children).

Evaluation: evidence against Bowlby's explanation of depression

It is hard for proponents of Bowlby's ideas to show that the depression in people who have lost attachment figures are suffering from these factors alone. A child who loses a parent may experience other problems than purely grief. For example, they might suffer financially. There are many factors that can impact upon an adult life other than attachment problems. For example, Follan and Minnis (2010) claimed that the key to insecure attachment was maltreatment in childhood rather than separation alone. In addition, Rutter (2006) suggested that individual differences in 'resilience' might explain why some people can resist the adverse effects of the loss of an attachment figure and others cannot.

Essential notes

Bowlby's idea has some support, but again the theory can only account for a limited number of people who experience depression.

Psychological explanations: sociocultural

Each of the theories discussed so far in this chapter has been able to explain the depression seen in *some*, but *not all* people. In fact, it is probably likely there are many different causes for the range of behaviours that we call depression – considering all the symptoms of both typical and atypical depression, it would seem unlikely should there just be one cause. Perhaps depression has several causal factors, and different people have different combinations of those factors. A successful unifying theory, such as the one illustrated in Fig. 3, would allow for this event.

The diathesis-stress model of depression

The diathesis-stress model brings together these disparate causal factors into a unified model of depression. The flexibility of the model is that individual differences can account for various contributing factors of depression. This means that the model can explain most instances of depression.

Fig. 3
The diathesis-stress model – different factors included in a unifying theory of depression

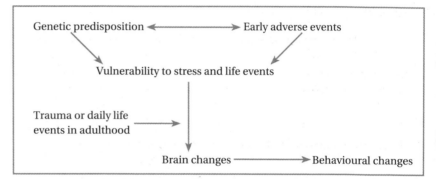

Examiners' notes

Should you draw a diagram in the exam? Diagrams can sometimes help you in that they clarify your understanding and make it easier for you to describe a particular model or concept. They will get some credit if they add something to your answer. However, you should not *replace* your description with a diagram and leave the examiner to expand it for you!

Diathesis-stress has its origins in a book called *The Social Origins of Depression*, written by Brown and Harris (1978). They identified two factors that were essential for the development of depression:

- severe life events (such as physical and sexual abuse when a child)
- long-term difficulties (such as money worries) causing severe stress.

When the individual experiences additional problems, referred to as *vulnerability factors* (e.g. losing a job, lack of adequate childcare options) on top of the long-term worries, then depression may result.

Diathesis

A diathesis is a vulnerability, a predisposition that gives the potential for conditions such as depression and anxiety to arise. The vulnerability for depression would be the biological factors discussed on pp. 34–7. It could also include the cognitive factors discussed on pp. 40–1. In some ways, the diathesis can be thought of as a time-bomb waiting for the right combination of circumstances before it takes effect. The vulnerability might never be expressed, but it is always there.

Stress

There are many different types of stress. It can be caused by:

- ongoing and significant life events, which are interpreted by the individual as undesirable.

- a myriad of everyday hassles
- things such as low socioeconomic status (and problems associated with that such as poverty or unemployment).

There have been many studies, for example, that have investigated the impact of membership of an ethnic minority (e.g. Luther and Zigler 1991). Different things are stressful for different people. Some people thrive on deadlines and others cannot cope with the idea of an impending deadline. We can summarize all of these things by saying that stress is something that affects the normal balance of life, whether physiologically or psychologically. This is a very broad definition to cover a very wide concept.

Evaluation of the diathesis-stress model of depression

- *An account of gender differences* – The diathesis-stress model can explain why more women than men experience depression. Women appear to handle stress differently from men, due to different cognitive styles. For example women are:
  - more likely to attribute failures to their own incompetence and stupidity and to attribute their successes externally (e.g. to luck) than are men
  - more prone to rumination (almost compulsive deep thinking) than are men (Nolen-Hoeksema 1990)
  - prone to ruminate more when feeling down than men do.

  Women also have the additional situation of fluctuating hormone levels, especially after childbirth (when postnatal depression can occur) and menopause. All of these factors are likely to contribute to the higher incidence of a diagnosis of clinical depression in women.

- *Sociocultural background and diagnosis* – Members of social minorities tend to have a higher level of mental health problems compared to majority groups. The reason for this is unclear, but the diathesis-stress model does serve to alert physicians to take extra care. There is a possibility that they could fail to detect depression or even misdiagnose or over-diagnose it in groups they do not belong to and who express their distress in unfamiliar ways.

- *Cultural differences in symptoms* – The diathesis-stress model also alerts physicians to differences between cultural groups that may affect how mental health problems are expressed. For example, Kua *et al.* (1993) found that 72 per cent of Chinese people who presented with chest and abdominal pains actually had a mental health problem that they had masked physically – this may be because there is a cultural stigma attached to showing psychological weakness.

- *Breadth of application* – The diathesis-stress model is a good explanation for depression. This is partly because it is so wide-ranging and flexible that it is hard to fault. There is also a wide range of supporting evidence, perhaps the most persuasive of which comes from **prospective studies** that have found that people with early-life adversity are more likely to develop depression (e.g. Bifulco *et al.* 1998).

Essential notes

Reactions to stressful events seems to be a matter of individual differences, and it is likely that how we respond to stress is something that is genetically determined. It is also dependent on whether we have experienced an easy, relaxed childhood or a more disruptive one. It seems that these factors make us susceptible to depression.

Examiners' notes

Gender differences can be used as AO2 evaluation if you make something of this point beyond merely pointing out that they exist. For example, gender differences indicate that a particular explanation does not apply equally to both genders, i.e. it is not *universal*.

Essential notes

Of course, there is no such thing as a perfect theory. It is a problem that the diathesis-stress model of depression is hard to fault, because there may yet be a better explanation of depression. For this reason, it is important to keep collecting data on people's perceived cause of their depression. However, this is the dominant theory because it gathers together the disparate strands of other approaches.

Biological therapies: drug treatments

In the medical model of depression, symptoms are seen as manifestations of pathological physiological processes, which are diagnosed and then treated with whatever methods are considered appropriate.

The medical model

The medical model of depression is responsible for the medications currently used for the treatment of depression. These drugs aim to correct a neurotransmitter imbalance. However, antidepressants are not the only biologically based treatment. There are other interventions, such as electroconvulsive therapy (ECT – see pp. 21 and 48) and psychotherapy, the use of which is growing rapidly, either in conjunction with medication or even as a sole treatment.

The main types of antidepressant drugs are:
- the first generation of antidepressants, i.e. the monoamine oxidase inhibitors (MAOIs) and tricylics (TCAs)
- the second-generation drugs, such as selective serotonin reuptake inhibitors (SSRIs) and selective noradrenaline reuptake inhibitors (SNRIs).

Monoamine Oxidase Inhibitors (MAOIs)

MAOIs were discovered in the 1950s. The medication was supposed to be a treatment for tuberculosis, but physicians noticed that it also made the patients happier (Sandler 1990), and it was found to have the same effect on depressed patients. The drug was discovered to slow down the body's production of monoamine oxidase (MAO). MAO is an enzyme that speeds the breakdown of the monoamine class of neurotransmitters, specifically noradrenaline. MAOIs block this effect, which means more noradrenaline is available for action.

Evaluation of the use of MAOIs

MAOIs are an effective antidepressant; however, the early versions had an unpleasant side effect in that they caused a dangerous rise in blood pressure if the patient ate foods containing the chemical tyramine (cheese, wines, beers) so they also had to accept a rigid diet. Newer versions of MAOIs do not cause this problem, and the drugs experienced a renaissance in the 1990s. MAOIs work relatively quickly and seem to be effective in atypical depression and depressions resistant to other medications (Krishnan 2007).

Tricyclic antidepressants (TCAs)

The first TCAs were discovered when pharmacology was looking for a treatment for schizophrenia. The first TCA was called imipramine and was found to be successful in relieving depression. TCAs block the reuptake of noradrenaline and serotonin. (Reuptake is when the neurotransmitter is drawn back from the **synaptic cleft** into the neuron. Blocking this process leaves the serotonin effective and available for longer.) TCAs are moderately effective, with most review articles claiming that TCAs are successful for the majority of patients (e.g. Rogers and Clay 1975).

Evaluation of the use of TCAs

A recent meta-analysis of the effectiveness of tricyclics (Moncrieff *et al.* 2004) has reported that these drugs work no better than active placebos (a drug that gives the same side effects as the real drug). When TCAs are compared to active placebos, there is very little difference between the two drugs. Moncrieff and colleagues suggest that the primary benefit of TCAs is that they are also a sedative and allow patients to sleep relatively normally. This has the beneficial side effect of lightening depression.

Such results, coupled with the finding that patients may slip back into depression if they stop the course of TCAs too soon after the symptoms of depression disappear, makes the drugs unattractive compared to the second generation of drugs, the SSRIs and SNRIs.

Selective Serotonin Reuptake Inhibitors (SSRIs)

SSRIs can be thought of as more refined TCAs. They were the first drugs to focus purely on serotonin, and the best known of these drugs is probably Prozac (fluoxetine), which blocks the reuptake of serotonin from the synaptic cleft. SSRIs seem to enhance energy, primarily treating the apathy that is characteristic of depression. It was thought that Prozac had fewer side effects than either the TCAs or MAOIs.

Evaluation of the use of SSRIs

The backlash against SSRIs started almost as soon as the drugs came on the market, for several reasons:

- There is no evidence that serotonin levels are abnormal in depressed people (e.g. Moncrieff 2009).
- There have also been several studies associating SSRIs with a higher risk of suicide in children and adults (e.g. Hetrick *et al.* 2007).
- Stopping SSRIs can lead to **discontinuation syndrome**, which means the drugs have to be stopped very gradually.

All of these findings mean that SSRIs were not the 'wonder drugs' they first appeared to be, and pharmacologists returned to noradrenaline as the problematic chemical in depression.

Selective Noradrenaline Reuptake Inhibitors (SNRIs)

Newer drugs – the SNRIs – inhibit the reuptake of noradrenaline and serotonin, but have a different action compared to TCAs. Evidence suggests that they are slightly more successful, with fewer side effects than SSRIs (Papakostas *et al.* 2007).

Evaluation of the use of SNRIs

It is relatively early days to evaluate the success of this type of medication in depression, although recent reports are not promising for one drug (Eyding *et al.* 2010). They also carry the same problems of withdrawal as with the other medications. People have to be weaned off such medication; it should not be suddenly stopped.

Essential notes

Using active placebos means that neither the patient nor the people caring for them know which drug is being taken. This is known as a double blind procedure and guards against both participant reactivity and experimenter effect.

Essential notes

Prozac was hailed as a miracle drug when it first appeared in the 1980s, and was almost certainly overprescribed, especially in the USA.

Examiners' notes

Being aware of the latest developments in drug treatments for depression is not required, but would certainly impress an examiner and could contribute to the 'stretch and challenge' requirement of questions.

Essential notes

It is fair to say that medication for depression is not as successful as would have been hoped. It is proving difficult to untangle the effects of the drugs from the placebo effect, and there is very little evidence for a chemical imbalance as either the cause or effect of depression. However, there are many people who have been successfully treated using these drugs, and this is something that cannot be ignored in its evaluation.

Biological therapies: other

St John's Wort

A popular remedy for depression is St John's Wort (*Hypericum perforatum*). This is thought to be a natural serotonin reuptake inhibitor, although there is some evidence that it also limits the reuptake of dopamine and noradrenaline (Butterweck 2003).

Many studies have systematically reviewed the effectiveness of St John's Wort (e.g. Williams *et al.* 2000) and found that it is comparable with some antidepressants in mild to moderate depression. It also tends to perform better than placebo in mild and moderate depression (Linde *et al.* 2005). However, St John's Wort is not successful in the treatment of major depression compared to a placebo.

Evaluation of St John's Wort

St John's Wort has fewer side effects than the other medications for depression, and so perhaps people might be prepared to try the medication for longer than they would other medications. Despite this, there are still some side effects. The drug can interfere with the effectiveness of some contraceptives and can make people more sensitive to the sun. There is also the important warning that people should not take St John's Wort at the same time as regular antidepressants, as the patient can experience 'serotonin syndrome', where the central nervous system cannot cope with the amount of serotonin in the system. This leads to a variety of symptoms, including fast heart beat, hallucinations and increased body temperature. Untreated serotonin syndrome can be deadly.

Electroconvulsive therapy (ECT)

A much more useful, but contentious, therapy is ECT (see p. 21 for a description of this treament). At first, this treatment received a bad press because of films such as *One Flew Over the Cuckoo's Nest*. The technique caused side effects such as memory loss and speech problems. However, it has subsequently become much less dangerous, as patients are given muscle-relaxants and short-acting anaesthetics when receiving treatment. Modern techniques deliver the current to only one half of the brain, which seems to make ECT less damaging.

Evaluation of ECT

- *An effective last resort* – ECT is very effective at relieving severe depression, especially when other treatments have failed. Richards and Lyness (2006) report a success rate of 60 to 70 per cent. The treatment is not permanent, it has to be repeated occasionally, but it affords hope where there previously was none.

- *Invasive and unexplained* – The action of ECT is unknown, but it is unlikely that the treatment works in the same way as the traditional medications. It is invasive and there is always a risk with administering a general anaesthetic; however, it does seem to work.

(see p. 21 for a description of this treament).

Essential notes

The biological approach (and behavioural and cognitive approaches) are considered to be scientific and most amenable to testing by experimentation. They can all be criticized, however, for being deterministic and reductionist, i.e. they marginalize self-determination and the complexity of the whole person.

Essential notes

St John's Wort seems to be a natural mood lightener; however, it does not work in severe depression. Perhaps this indicates that we need to think about the level at which we treat major depression, possibly leaving the SSRIs like Prozac for those with severe symptoms.

A promising similar treatment is transcranial magnetic stimulation (TMS) where the brain is stimulated using magnets. It is early days for evaluation of TMS as a treatment for depression and more long-term studies are needed, but this treatment does also seem to be effective (Janicak *et al.* in press).

Psychosurgery

The last resort in terms of treating depression is psychosurgery (brain surgery). Brain surgery must always be considered a last resort because, once damaged, the brain will not recover.

One modern psychosurgery is called a subcaudate tractotomy, targeting an area (the caudate nucleus, see Fig. 4) known to be involved in negative emotions. This surgery is also effective in combating the obsessional part of obsessive-compulsive disorder.

Evaluation of psychosurgery

- *Effective but drastic* – This surgery is drastic, not least because the circuitry of emotion within the human brain is not fully understood. Psychosurgery can be effective, but other less invasive methods should perhaps be considered first.

Deep brain stimulation (DBS)

Recent work (e.g. Mayberg *et al.* 2005) places electrodes deep within the brain in an operational technique called deep brain stimulation (DBS). Although the action of the electrodes stimulates the brain tissue, the net result is a decrease in the hyperactivity of the region. When the electrodes are switched on, patients report feeling calm and experiencing a sudden interest in what is happening, where previously there had been no interest. Mayberg and colleagues report patients experiencing a brightening of the room and increased intensity of colours. Switching off the electrodes immediately returns patients to the same state as before.

The best region for DBS for depression seems to be the subgenual cingulate region, part of the limbic-cortical network. This area is important in emotions, and the subgenual cingulate seems to modulate negative mood states. When people take traditional antidepressants, or experience ECT or TMS, this area becomes less active. DBS has the same effect, but is more permanent.

Evaluation of DBS

- *Long-term improvement* – Two-thirds of patients who had experienced this operation showed long-term positive behavioural changes at the end of six months. All of these patients had previously reported no benefits from antidepressants, so this is a dramatic alteration.
- *Brain surgery is serious* – BDS is brain surgery and should not be considered lightly, as the mechanisms being operated upon are not yet fully understood. However, it seems to work and it is a promising area for further investigation.

Fig. 4
Location of the caudate nucleus in the brain

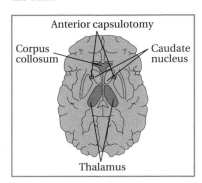

Anterior capsulotomy

Corpus collosum

Caudate nucleus

Thalamus

Essential notes

Any treatment that permanently affects the brain needs to be taken very seriously. However, when all else has failed, these more drastic treatments need to be considered. It is important that the patient is in the right mental state to give proper informed consent for such invasive procedures.

Psychological therapies: behavioural

Lewinsohn and positive reinforcement

Lewinsohn (1974) developed a behavioural treatment strategy that placed emphasis on patients trying to resume the activities that used to give them pleasure, as this would provide positive reinforcement. As many depressed people are lonely or awkward in company, Lewinsohn also advocated giving patients social skills training, thereby giving them the skills needed to meet other people more comfortably. This, in turn, enables them to become less lonely and find more activities to give them positive reinforcement.

Early studies into **behavioural activation** therapy advocate observing the patient in their home setting, as a means of identifying exactly what the individual's problem areas are. This enables the therapist to develop a programme specifically tailored for that patient.

Lewinsohn's idea in group therapy

Lewinsohn *et al.* (1970) tried these ideas out within a group setting. The group setting helped the patient meet new people; in fact, simply realizing that the other people were suffering from similar problems could be thought of as an added benefit. The primary benefit of this type of therapy, however, is that the therapist could actually see how the patient interacted with other people, as opposed to either interviewing the patient in clinic or in their home. The other depressed people who were part of the group acted as a peer group within which the patient can try out their new social skills. The therapists running the group specifically looked for and rewarded examples of reciprocal interaction between the group members. In other words, a normal conversation with give and take between the participants was rewarded.

Examiners' notes

When describing these treatments, it is a good idea to concentrate on the underlying psychology, demonstrating *why* a particular aspect of therapy is effective in the treatment of depression. For example, pointing out that 'this enables them to become less lonely and find more activities to give them positive reinforcement'.

Group therapy has been found to be very successful, not least in giving a setting for practising social skills

Evaluation of group therapy

- *Multiple benefits* – Group therapy was extremely time intensive but, at the same time, very successful. The group members started to initiate conversation, instead of just waiting for someone to talk to them. The social skills training did not just improve social interaction, but also started to ease depression.

- *An adjunct to drug treatment* – This first attempt at group therapy was a three-month session. As drug therapies normally take some time to begin to work, this type of therapy could be a useful additional treatment.

Other behavioural therapies

Another type of group behaviour therapy for depression was offered by Rehm *et al.* (1987). They also rewarded examples of positive behaviour, with patients setting their own behavioural goals along with the therapist and breaking them down into achievable subgoals. Patients were also encouraged to self-monitor and self-reinforce examples of positive social behaviour. In other words, in this therapy, the patients are in charge of their own therapy. Rehm's therapy emphasizes self-control: the individual has to work hard at overcoming the negative behaviour that is believed to be a factor in the cause of depression.

Evaluation of behavioural therapy

- *Improved self-control* – Improving self-control is a successful intervention for depression. In the study by Rehm and colleagues, this form of treatment led to a lower score on a depression inventory (questionnaire) after a 10-week trial.

- *Affordability* – This is a slightly more affordable treatment, because the patient is monitoring their own behaviour, rather than relying upon a therapist to do so.

- *Getting to the root of the problem* – It seems as though these programmes are successful because they force the patient to confront the problems in their lives. As depression makes people withdraw from society and company, these therapies simply encourage the patient to reverse this trend.

- *Social desirability bias* – Such studies measure improvement with self-report scales, which is a methodological problem in that the patient could simply be trying to please the therapist.

- *No scientific explanation* – Another potential problem is that we have no scientific explanation for why these therapies are successful. It could simply be that the therapy makes the patient think about their depression in a different way – as something they can fight and be their own agent of change.

Examiners' notes

In order to boost that all-important AO2 evaluation, you could try putting the terms 'effectiveness behavioural therapy depression' in your favourite search engine and see what you can find that you could use as critical evaluation.

Essential notes

These simple and effective treatments do work as long as the patient is prepared to work to change their life. The idea that having fun (or, at least, not sitting around doing nothing) can cause depression to lift is so simple. However, not all patients are so motivated, and alternative therapies need to be sought.

Psychological therapies: CBT

Cognitive-behavioural therapy (CBT) combines behavioural therapy with cognitive restructuring to create a full package of therapeutic treatment for depression. CBT is a successful and adaptable type of therapy that stresses the client's involvement in the process of changing their lives.

The cognitive elements

CBT addresses the fact that depression changes the way people think. When something goes wrong, people with depression tend to look to internal explanations (e.g. their own inability), rather than attributing the cause to external factors. For example, if a depressed person gets a bad mark in an essay, they might tell themselves that it is because they are stupid and that they will fail all their exams. Someone without depression might think this too, but also might consider the fact that the essay question was particularly difficult and that the whole class had problems too. CBT allows someone with depression to challenge their faulty hypotheses about events and to consider explanations other than the automatic self-deprecating one. For CBT to work, the negative thoughts have to be acknowledged by the client; then this gives the best chance for permanent relief from depression. CBT sets cognitive homework for the client that encourages them to address their mistaken perceptions.

The behavioural elements

The client and the therapist develop a programme to challenge the client's negative hypotheses through experimentation and role play. For example, when something bad happens, the client may be encouraged to keep a diary listing possible explanations for what has happened. Then they would be asked to rank them in terms of likelihood. The idea is that, in this way, the client sees that they are not always responsible for bad things.

Rational-emotive behavioural therapy

There are several different types of CBT, but one of the best known is Albert Ellis's rational-emotive behaviour therapy (REBT). This type of therapy confronts emotions, something that makes it especially successful for treating anger problems as well as depression. Ellis's model is called the ABC model (summarized in Fig. 5).

The ABC model

The bad event is called the activating event (e.g. getting a poor essay grade) and it leads to a set of negative beliefs (e.g. 'I must be stupid') and then to the consequences of those beliefs (e.g. 'I am going to fail the exam'). REBT challenges the client's beliefs by asking them to generate alternative causes for the bad grade (e.g. 'It was a tough essay', 'Everyone in the class struggled with the topic', 'I needed to do more research'). These alternatives lead to positive consequences where the client may still be

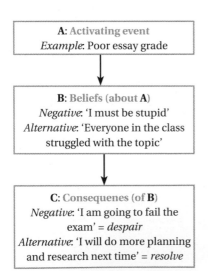

Fig. 5
Ellis' ABC model of therapy

disappointed with the grade, but has a plan of action to ensure it will not happen again (e.g. 'I will do more planning and research').

Evaluation of REBT

REBT challenges faulty logic by making the client confront their own beliefs, and this is a successful therapy for several reasons:

- The person is active in their own recovery.
- REBT teaches a set of skills that can be implemented not only when someone feels sad, angry and frustrated, but also to help them examine positive things and discover what makes them feel good. In other words, this is *individual* therapy; it does not assume that everyone is the same.
- Once the essential skills are taught, then the client can continue their lives without having to attend therapy sessions.

Aaron Beck's CBT

Beck's theory of depression underpins all 'talking cures', and so it is not surprising that he, too, developed a therapeutic programme for depression. It uses similar tools to REBT, with the therapy consisting of around 20 sessions. The client first draws up a list of activities that will make them feel more confident. They are then taught to acknowledge examples of negative thinking. These are talked through with the therapist with the aim of making the client recognize faulty cognition. Finally, the therapist encourages the client to try out their new thinking in real-life situations.

Evaluation of CBT

Good range of effectiveness
CBT is very effective (Butler *et al.* 2006) and is often given to depressed people at the same time as antidepressants. It is hoped that this package gives the moderately-to-severely depressed people the best hope of recovery. Those with mild depression are encouraged to use CBT alone.

Cost-effective
It is a cost-effective treatment and can even be implemented with a 'virtual' therapist; several computer packages for CBT are also available.

Client's motivation is essential
The major negative factor is that the client has to maintain their homework after contact with the therapist. This is considered an ongoing process. You cannot easily overcome the effects of many years of a depressed mind set; it takes perseverance and hard work.

Examiners' notes

Giving examples can be a useful way of elaborating a description, although it is more informative to include details of the psychological components of the therapy and only use examples when these are exhausted.

Essential notes

Of course, these strengths can be considered weaknesses if the client is not interested in feeling better. The client has to *want* to change their thinking; they have to want to recover and to put the work in to achieving change. If they do not, then they will not recover.

Essential notes

Another negative point is that it is difficult to measure the success of therapy effectively. Because there are no biological markers for depression, researchers are forced to rely on patient self-report. However, this is inevitable when dealing with mental health problems because diagnosis and recovery rely heavily on self-report.

Psychological therapies: psychodynamic

Psychodynamic theory is the therapy built upon the ideas of Freud and his followers. It uses the same principles to treat depression as it does other conditions, the most important being the therapist– client relationship. An important factor is that the client is open and trusts the therapist. As with other types of individual therapy, psychodynamic therapy realizes that the client brings a unique set of problems and will therefore require a unique treatment. Blatt (1992) has looked at trials comparing different types of treatment for depression and realized that what is most important is that the type of therapy fits the personality of the client.

Different psychotherapies for different types of people

It has been suggested that people who respond well to psychodynamic therapy are mostly people with higher social functioning, whereas CBT works more successfully with people with higher cognitive functioning (Blatt 1992). The reason for this is probably that the more intellectual a person is, the more likely they are to want to take charge and be a part of their own recovery. CBT enables this approach among such people. Psychodynamic therapy, on the other hand, attracts those who are better at relationship-building and conversation, which are both important skills within psychodynamic therapy. It also works better with ideational people (those who enjoy exploring new ideas) (Blatt 1990).

Bowlby's ideas and the treatment of depression

Bowlby believed that a susceptibility for developing depression was a consequence of an insecure attachment between child and caregiver (see p. 43). Therefore, one strategy in psychodynamic therapy is to provide the patient with a secure base. The idea is that the therapist leads the client through the stages of a healthy attachment and separation, with the client learning to understand their motivations and past more fully. This type of

Essential notes

YAVIS vs HOUND: Critics of talk-based therapeutic methods say they favour Young, Affluent, Verbal, Intelligent and Successful individuals (Schofield 1964) rather than people who are Homely, Old, Unattractive, Nonverbal and Dull. This limits their accessibility to all 'talking cures'.

Psychodynamic therapy is thought to be more effective with people with higher social (rather than cognitive) functioning therapy may best suit someone who wants a long-term exploration of their problems rather than a short-term fix (Blatt 1990).

Short-term psychodynamic psychotherapy (STPP)

There is a lot of literature on short-term psychodynamic psychotherapy (STPP) for depression. In this type of therapy, the analyst tries to uncover the unconscious mental processes that underpin a person's depression. One of the techniques used to do this is an exploration of the predisposing factors in that patient's life. The client has between seven and 40 sessions with the analyst. The aim is that the client–analyst relationship will encourage the client to come to terms with the bad things that have happened to them, allowing them to focus on the future with a clearer mind.

Evaluation of STPP and depression

STPP has been criticized as a treatment option for depression because of the way it views depression as the result of things that happened in childhood (e.g. Roth and Fonagy 1996). This seems to exclude many people whose depression is the result of other factors. However, when medication is being used alongside the therapy, there is more evidence for success, showing the benefit of using a combination of treatments.

Evaluation of psychodynamic therapy

Comparing CBT and STPP

There seems to be more success for STPP when the therapy is over a slightly longer period. Barkham *et al.* (1996) compared CBT and psychodynamic therapy over either eight or 16 weeks. Their results found that both packages were equally successful in the level of improvement they achieved at the end of the course of therapy. The one-year follow-up found that those who experienced the eight-week CBT package had maintained their improvement compared to those who had STPP. However, those who had the 16-week STPP had maintained their improvement (as had the CBT group). This leads to the tentative suggestion that the more severe the depression, the longer the course of therapeutic sessions should be.

One size does not fit all

It seems that this type of therapy is as successful as the other types, especially when the right fit between client problems and personality is identified. Psychodynamic therapy will not suit everyone, but it will suit some people.

Long-term benefit

It also has the potential to change the patient's behaviour in the long term, through a process of self-exploration alongside a therapist rather than the more client-driven CBT approach.

Value for money?

On the negative side, although it seems to work for some people, psychoanalysis is a costly process and it is difficult to show tangible evidence of its success.

Essential notes

This illustrates a common theme in the evaluation of treatments for depression: just as no one approach can explain the cause of depression, neither can one treatment method used in isolation effect a complete recovery from depression. This is because depression is an extremely heterogeneous (varied) condition.

Essential notes

Although psychodynamic therapy can alleviate depression, it is only as good as other forms of psychotherapy. This makes it a useful contribution to treatment options.

Clinical characteristics

What are phobic disorders?

Phobic disorders (phobias) are classed as anxiety disorders. Anxiety disorders are among the most reported mental health problems in the world, and they cover a broad range of different conditions, ranging from phobias to **obsessive-compulsive disorder (OCD)**. The chances of developing an anxiety disorder in the UK seem to be around 10 per cent, according to the NHS. It is important to realize that although everyone feels anxious sometimes, anxiety disorders reflect the kind of anxiety that interferes with day-to-day living. Phobias tend to reflect specific fears and anxieties (e.g. a fear of spiders), whereas generalized anxiety disorder is not so specific.

Fear and anxieties

Anxiety is a specific term referring to biological changes that occur when the person perceives themself to be in some kind of danger.

Fear is a physical and emotional reaction to a specific object. People who have phobias tend to be afraid of specific things, such as spiders (arachnophobia), heights (acrophobia) or clowns (coulrophobia). The fear will make people strive to avoid the thing they are afraid of. It is vital to distinguish a phobia from a general dislike: phobias reflect a fear that is recognized to be out of proportion to the actual damage the object or situation could cause.

Different kinds of phobia

Because phobias reflect specific fears, there are specific terms for various phobias. Both of the main diagnostic manuals, **DSM**-IV-TR and **ICD**-10, tend to reflect this by grouping types of phobia into three categories:
- specific phobia (fear of certain situations or things)
- social phobia (fear of social situations or performances)
- agoraphobia (fear of public spaces).

The latter can occur with or without panic disorders.

Specific phobia
Specific phobias are persistent and irrational fears of a particular object or situation (excluding social phobia and agoraphobia). Specific phobia is subdivided into three categories: fear of animals, blood/injury and situational (e.g. flying).

People will alter their daily routines to avoid the object or situation. Encountering the object/situation leads to an immediate fear response (e.g. heart racing, quickened breathing, dry mouth). It is estimated that 8 per cent of people are affected by specific phobia at any one time. More women than men suffer from a specific phobia; in fact, it is the most common mental health problem for women. An important diagnostic point is that people with specific phobia realize that their fear is irrational.

Clown phobia is quite common, but people phobic for clowns know that clowns are unlikely to hurt them, but this does not stop the fear.

Social phobia

Social phobia, or social anxiety disorder, is an excessive fear of social situations, such as being asked to make a presentation. The condition frequently begins in adolescence and continues into adulthood. It is difficult to establish a true prevalence figure, because people with this condition would avoid seeking help as part of their problem. However, prevalence in England has been rated 0.4 per cent, 0.6 per cent in Wales and 1.8 per cent in Scotland according to Meltzer *et al.* (2004). Women are more commonly affected than man by a ratio of 3:2 (Kessler *et al.* 2005).

The disorder frequently occurs alongside drug and alcohol problems (as people try to self-medicate) and also with depression. There is a crucial difference between social phobia and shyness. Many people are shy but are able to lead normal lives; someone with social phobia will go to extreme lengths to avoid social situations and will find it very difficult to live a normal life. Some social phobics have a specific fear of certain events, such as blushing or stammering when being asked to give a presentation, but others have a more general fear that they will do something embarrassing when in public.

Agoraphobia

The DSM defines **agoraphobia** as an anxiety of being in a public place where escape is difficult (e.g. stuck in the middle of a crowded bus) or where it would be difficult to seek help for treatment of a panic attack. The ICD sees it slightly differently, restricting the diagnosis to one of four situations: being in crowds, in a public place, travelling away from home and travelling alone. In both diagnostic manuals, the idea that the person will avoid social situations is stressed. The condition can occur alongside panic attacks. A lot of the anxiety about being in public is connected to the possibility that a panic attack will be experienced.

The UK estimates that between 4 and 5 per cent of the population are affected at any one time, with women twice as likely to be diagnosed with agoraphobia than men. Agoraphobia generally onsets in early adulthood.

Agoraphobia is not a specific phobia because it is not a fear (as sometimes believed) of being outside, but rather a fear of being unable to escape to a safe place when outside the home; it is the fear of being exposed and losing control.

Gender differences

As more women in general are reported as suffering from these conditions more than men, it could be that they are just more likely to seek help, whether for these anxieties or for depression. Men might simply 'suffer in silence'. Both genders might use drugs or alcohol to help them with their anxieties (although obviously these substances offer, at best, a short-term solution).

Issues in classification and diagnosis

There are many potential 'issues' in classifying somebody as having a mental disorder. These include ethical issues, gender issues, cultural differences in diagnosis and the problems of labelling somebody as 'mentally ill'. However, the two issues most commonly cited are reliability and validity.

- Validity refers to whether phobia actually exists or not. For example, is there enough evidence consistently to differentiate phobia from extreme fear?

- Reliability refers to the issue of making a diagnosis of phobia consistently; is a person living in the UK who is afraid of spiders as likely to be diagnosed with arachnophobia as someone in the USA (for example)?

Validity

Medicalizing normal life

Although everyone has things that they are afraid of or do not like, there is normally a rational explanation for this fear. However, a phobia is diagnosed on the basis that it is an *irrational* fear. This is quite a fine distinction for the clinician to make, and a phobia should only be diagnosed if it is serious enough to justify treatment. Fear is a healthy emotion; it helps you to survive. It does not need to be treated unless it massively interferes with life at home and work. For some people, something that is repeatedly put off (e.g. giving a presentation) becomes larger and larger. Dealing with it once can eradicate that fear in future.

Differences between DSM and ICD

The **ICD** offers a more focused set of criteria for agoraphobia than does the **DSM**, which might lead to underdiagnosis for clinicians who use this manual (or overdiagnosis for those who use the DSM) (see p. 6). This reflects the uncertainty that exists with regard to the precise nature of mental health problems; there is no diagnostic test for the presence of phobias as there is, for example, for diabetes.

The DSM also looks at the presence of panic attacks as important in agoraphobia. This is because panic disorder is a diagnosis in its own right, and the clinician has to be careful to diagnose the appropriate condition.

Both manuals look at phobias as being a long-term problem. A short-term fear, such as being anxious about giving a presentation to secure a promotion, is a reasonable anxiety to have. Leaving a job because of it and then failing to apply for others is a more serious indication that treatment is warranted.

Examiners' notes

There are two main ways of asking a question about 'issues of classification and diagnosis'. If there are 10 marks for a question on issues of classification and diagnosis, then it is AO2 only. However, it can also be a 24-mark question (25-mark prior to 2012), in which case it would be AO1 and AO2.

Reliability of diagnosis

Usually, patients with specific phobias seek treatment and are, therefore, easier to diagnose than people with agoraphobia and social phobia, for whom the picture is not so clear cut. There are a number of overlapping anxiety and emotional disorders, and the clinician has only what the patient reports as evidence for the diagnosis. Essentially, it is the patient who is responsible for outlining their behaviour in enough detail to allow an accurate diagnosis.

For all classes of phobia, there is the problem that these fears are exaggerations of normal behaviour. Everyone has some things or situations they would prefer to avoid and so the clinician has to make sure that they are not diagnosing a psychiatric illness when the person has a rational basis for their fears. This problem is amplified by the fact that there are no diagnostic tests for any of the phobic behaviours; ultimately, the clinician has to use their own judgement in deciding whether to treat or not.

Comorbidity with depression

A more serious problem is **comorbidity** (a person experiencing two or more mental health problems at the same time). Anxiety disorders including social phobia frequently present in association with depression, but psychiatry has problems in establishing whether the social withdrawal causes the depression or the depression causes the social withdrawal. Someone who withdraws from life because of depression and develops social phobia as a result, will not recover without consideration of the depression.

This means the clinician has to establish which disorder is the primary disorder for the most effective treatment.

Comorbidity with substance abuse

Another common comorbidity is substance abuse, especially for social phobia. This can be because people start to abuse alcohol to make any social situation easier. This may be a short term fix, but can become a long-term disaster. Randell *et al.* (2001) estimate that 20 per cent of those treated for alcohol-related disorders have some form of social phobia.

As the socially phobic avoid talking to other people, they are particularly difficult to treat with conventional therapeutic support. The primary treatment for alcoholism is a social support network, which only makes the situation worse for people who dread contact with others. However, treating one of the conditions seems to improve the other.

Biological explanations: genetics

Biological explanations of phobic disorders fall into two categories:

- The view that phobias arose as a result of a survival tactic from our evolutionary past. This would mean that there could be a genetic predisposition to develop phobias.
- The view that phobias are the result of abnormal brain processes.

Genetic explanations

One of the oldest of human behaviours is the 'fight or flight' mechanism. When something frightens us, or has the potential for harming us, the emotional areas of the brain release neurochemicals that give a sudden release of energy so that we can either stand and fight, or run away. It could be that people with phobias (specifically those of specific objects or situations) are experiencing the inappropriate triggering of the fight or flight mechanism. In short, phobias could be caused by an overzealous fear mechanism. Although this could be a neurochemical problem, it is also studied by looking at genetics. A family predisposition for phobias could be evidence for an evolutionary explanation.

Evidence from family history studies

Family history studies look for incidence of certain conditions within a family. A researcher interviews several generations of a family with a family member who has been diagnosed with a particular disorder and then compares the results to the incidence for the same condition among the general population. This gives an idea of how heritable the condition is, i.e. to see whether there is an indication of genetic transmission.

Many studies that have demonstrated a familial predisposition to phobia. For example, Noyes *et al.* (1986) found a higher incidence of agoraphobia in first-degree relatives (11.6 per cent). Lautch (1971) found that the fear of dentists runs in families. Kendler *et al.* (1992) gave evidence of many phobias shared among family members. However, the evidence is not clear cut.

Evaluation of family history studies

There are several problems with this type of research. One problem is that you might not be tracing evidence of genetic transmission but rather the incidence of social learning. If, as a child, you witness a parent with an irrational terror of spiders, it seems likely that you will also develop the same irrational fear.

A second problem is that, when taking a family history, you are relying on the interviewee to establish the extent of someone else's fears. There may be no established evidence for the incidence of phobic behaviours in the family other than a patient's memory, which seriously devalues this kind of study.

Examiners' notes

When choosing material for an answer in this area, you should prioritize the actual research that describes the genetic explanation and then draw upon any of the evaluation on these two pages for your critical commentary. In other words, there is a need to be *selective* in your choice of appropriate material.

Essential notes

First-degree relatives (parents, siblings and offspring) share about 50 per cent of their genetic material. As the relationship between family members gets more distant, this percentage decreases. Cousins share at most 25 per cent of their genetic material.

Twin studies

Twin studies offer more reliable evidence. Here, the incidence of phobic behaviour is measured in monozygotic (MZ) twins and is compared with that of dizygotic (DZ) twins. The studies look at **concordance rates**, i.e. the probability of both twins in a pair having the same psychiatric disorder.

Evidence from twin studies

There is some evidence that phobic behaviour has a genetic component. Torgersen (1983) examined the incidence of panic disorder and agoraphobia in 13 MZ twin pairs and found 31 per cent concordance. The 16 DZ twin pair comparison had no incidence of concordant phobias. However, this is a very small sample size.

However, Kendler *et al.* (1992) interviewed 722 female twins with a history of agoraphobia and found almost the opposite to Torgersen. The MZ twins had significantly lower concordance rates than did the DZ twins.

Kendler and colleagues have had better success investigating social phobia. They interviewed 2000 female twins and found a 24 per cent concordance in MZ twins compared to 15 per cent concordance for DZ twins.

Kendler *et al.* (1993) interviewed 2163 female twins and found that agoraphobia seemed to be more genetically determined than specific or social phobias. However, their research suggested that it was agoraphobia appearing comorbidly with major depression that was genetically determined rather than agoraphobia alone.

Evaluation of twin studies

- *Ambivalent evidence* – Twin studies have provided ambivalent evidence for phobias. This may be because some phobias are comorbid with major depressive disorder (see p. 32), and the two are becoming confused. It could be that only some phobias are genetically determined while others are caused by more social factors. There is also the possibility that the diagnostic manuals need to look more closely at the incidence of depression with agoraphobia; perhaps agoraphobia is a symptom of depression rather than a disorder in its own right.

- *Shared environment* – Twin studies such as these never provide perfect answers to the question. Twins share an environment and MZ twins are more likely to be treated alike than DZ twins. It is hard to factor out the effects of the environment without a biological examination of people's DNA to look for common genetic mutations.

- *Methodological problems* – The methodological problems with family history studies described opposite are also problems in twin studies.

- *Limited evidence* – Finally, Kendler's studies only look at women and phobias, and this ignores a huge proportion of the total population of those with phobic disorder.

(see p. 32)

Essential notes

MZ (identical) twins share the same genes, whereas DZ or non-identical (fraternal) twins have only 50 per cent of their genes in common.

Examiners' notes

Research evidence can also be used as AO2 evaluation, but you need to set this evidence in the context of a critical argument. For example, after citing 'Kendler *et al.* (1992) found a 24 per cent concordance for social phobia in MZ twins compared to 15 per cent concordance for DZ twins...' you might add '... which supports the claim that social phobia has a strong genetic influence'.

Essential notes

Genetic studies are limited by the methodological weaknesses. There is some evidence that there might be a genetic predisposition to phobias, but the importance of the environment cannot be factored out entirely. Researchers would need to look for specific gene mutations to have solid evidence for a genetic – and therefore evolutionary – explanation for phobias.

Biological explanations: biochemistry

Biochemical explanations focus on the contribution of chemical processes (such as **neurotransmitters** and **hormones**) in the onset of a mental disorder.

GABA

Biochemical explanations of phobias focus on the role of gamma aminobutyric acid (GABA) in the brain. GABA is a neurotransmitter that acts as the main inhibitory chemical in the nervous system. In other words, GABA is the neurotransmitter that enables you to reduce stress and anxiety and increase focus on a task. (Neurotransmitters are chemicals that enable neurons to talk to each other across the synapse – the gap between adjacent nerve cells). It seems logical, therefore, that a phobia would be caused by a reduction of GABA levels in the brain.

GABA responds to arousal, which includes anxiety. In a healthy person, when the time for the anxiety is passed, GABA is released to inhibit (stop) the activity of the neurons passing on the anxious signals. This means that anxiety levels drop – and so do the signs of high arousal (racing heart, dry mouth, sweaty palms, etc.). High arousal is modulated by the neurochemicals glutamate and noradrenaline.

Glutamate and noradrenaline

Glutamate is the neurochemical involved in high arousal. It is also important for things such as learning and is involved in neurodevelopment (the creation and maintenance of neural networks). The release of glutamate is a natural reaction to stress, but some studies have shown that chronic stress and illness can lead to too much glutamate being released in certain areas of the brain (Vyas *et al.* 2002). This can lead to permanent alterations of neural function in these areas. The areas affected are the hippocampus and amygdala – both areas involved in emotion. Noradrenaline is released as part of the body's response to stress. The action of both of these neurochemicals has to be inhibited with GABA.

A biochemical theory of phobia

It is hypothesized (e.g. Millan 2003) that the presence of an object of which someone is afraid (e.g. a spider) would lead to a release of neurochemicals, including glutamate and noradrenaline. In someone without phobia, the first response of fear would stop as soon as they realized they were in no danger or had run away. This would be caused by the release of GABA inhibiting the fear response. In someone with phobia, the fear remains.

Evaluation of the biochemical theory

This theory seems to be very plausible, but there are problems with it. For example, most of the evidence comes from animal models of panic and stress. It is considered unethical to submit a human to high levels of stress to see what happens in the brain, so the early development of a biochemical theory used animal research. Although we share similar

Examiners' notes

Questions often ask either for two (or more) biological explanations, or one biological and one psychological explanation. What that means is that you are usually only expected to offer a précis of the material on this page, although the action of the different neurotransmitters discussed here could count as two different explanations if you make this intention explicit e.g. by stating… 'The first explanation is…' It is acceptable to use abbreviations such as GABA for long names.

Examiners' notes

You might consider *why* animal research would not be as reliable as data derived from human studies, and then use your conclusions to elaborate the critical point being made (see p. 101 for more on 'elaboration').

neuroanatomy and neurochemicals to some animals, this evidence is obviously not as reliable as data from human sources.

The best support for this theory is that medications that mimic the action of GABA, called benzodiazepines, seem to reduce anxiety. Although this treatment is effective, it is not the same as saying phobia is caused by a lack of GABA, because it is the symptoms, not the cause of the problem that are being treated.

Neurological explanations

Biochemical explanations focus on the central nervous system – particularly changes in brain activity.

The amygdala

The amygdala mediates fear and stress responses. When this area is lesioned (deliberately damaged) in animal studies, animals show a reduction in innate fears (Kemble *et al.* 1990) and conditioned fears (Applegate *et al.* 1982). Applegate's study shows that when you pair an aversive stimulus with a neutral stimulus, neurons fire in the amygdala. Fredrikson and Furmark (2003) have shown that regional cerebral blood flow (rCBF) is reduced in the right amygdala when you show someone with a phobia the thing they are afraid of. These researchers also demonstrated that reduced right amygdala rCBF was the result of provoking anxiety in people with a fear of public speaking (Furmark *et al.* 2002).

The amygdala is known to contain GABA-releasing neurons, which supports a role for these brain structures in phobia.

Evaluation of the role of the amygdala

It seems as though the amygdala (especially the right amygdala) is responsible for the feelings of fear that someone with phobia feels when confronted with the object they are afraid of. However, this is not the same as saying that the amygdala is responsible for the phobia itself. Although most phobias lead to an excessive and irrational fear response, the fear normally appears as anticipation of seeing or being in the presence of the phobic item. The fear comes as a result of the phobia, but we cannot say with any certainty that it is the cause of the phobia.

However, the knowledge that the amygdala contains GABA offers the possibility of developing medication to treat phobias and the other anxiety disorders.

Essential notes

The role of the brain in the development of phobia is not entirely clear. However, research into the neurochemicals involved in stress and fear has helped the development of medication to treat these problems. This research does not just help those with phobia, but can also help treat post-traumatic stress disorder and obsessive-compulsive disorder.

Psychological explanations: behavioural

A behavioural explanation for phobia, which involves learning and conditioning, seems to be the most promising psychological explanation, because it offers a clear description of the development of phobias.

Learning theory

Learning theory proposes that we learn by association. If you experience a panic attack when in a crowded bus, you associate buses with panic attacks and avoid buses as a result. This is an example of **classical conditioning**. This theory is based on work by Pavlov (1927), who worked on salivary reflexes in dogs and is best illustrated by the Little Albert case study (Watson and Rayner 1920). This child was taught to associate a loud noise with his pet rat and so learned to fear the rat. Classical conditioning builds on an innate, unconditional reflex consisting of the unconditional stimulus (UCS) of a sudden loud noise which is automatically followed by the unconditional response (UCR) of startling. Pairing the loud noise with a previously neutral stimulus such as a rat on several occasions can bring about a new, conditional reflex such that the conditional stimulus (CS) of the rat brings about the new conditional response (CR) of startling.

Operant conditioning also plays a role in phobias, for example, avoiding buses and walking instead leads to a reduction in the anxiety, In this case the consequences of behaviour alter the frequency with which it occurs.

Another example of learning theory illustrates the development of phobias. Mineka and Zinbarg (2006) talk of a boy who saw his grandfather vomit while dying. The boy went on to develop a phobia for vomiting. This is called vicarious conditioning because it depends on the person witnessing something occurring to someone else. This type of conditioning means that witnessing someone else's fear is enough to induce fear. Phobias can be acquired through social learning.

Evaluation of learning theory

The first part of learning theory, that classical conditioning is the origin of phobia, works very well for the anxiety disorders like panic disorder and some instances of agoraphobia and social phobia. In these disorders, people can offer a memory of either a painful or shocking incident (for example in the case study by Mineka and Zinbarg above) that is the direct cause of their problems. The second part (that avoiding the feared object reduces anxiety) is more problematic because it cannot be tested with any accuracy. It hinges on someone's interpretation of an event, which is not the same as actually experiencing it. Therefore, Munjack (1984), who found that only 50 per cent of people with a driving phobia could recall an accident, also needed to ask people if they had witnessed a serious accident, or if a loved one had experienced an accident.

Mineka and Zinbarg (2006) have shown that previous experience has to be taken into account when assessing the likelihood of developing a phobia. They suggest that if two people are bitten by dogs, the chances of either one developing a phobia depends to an extent on their previous experiences with dogs. Someone with happy memories is more likely to continue their positive experiences with dogs regardless of the bite.

Learning theory was first popular in the 1970s and then fell out of favour, but studies such as those by Mineka and Zinbarg (2006) are showing it could still be relevant, and it can offer useful ideas for the treatment of phobias.

Preparedness theory

Evolutionary theory proposes that we are afraid of certain things because we have an innate biological memory that certain things can harm us. This theory stems from that of Seligman (1971), who proposed that we are instinctively prepared to avoid certain stimuli that will harm us.

Experiments have demonstrated this theory in humans. Öhman *et al.* (1975) paired pictures with electric shocks. The pictures were either things that might harm us, such as spiders and snakes, or things that cannot, such as flowers and houses. When shown the pictures later without the shocks, people showed fear responses for the spiders and snakes very quickly, but it took five times longer for the harmless stimuli. This can be interpreted to show that we are biologically predisposed to fear things that can harm us.

Evaluation of preparedness theory

- *Inadequate explanation of all phobias* – Preparedness theory explains potentially dangerous stimuli, such as fear of heights and the dark, but it is not so good at explaining fear of clowns (coulrophobia) or trees (dendrophobia) – things that very rarely harm people. Perhaps in these cases, learning theory offers the best explanation.

- *Ease of developing particular phobias* – Preparedness theory is good at explaining the ease with which fear for something can develop. Öhman *et al.* (1975) only had to pair a shock with a picture of spider or snake once for people to show a fear response the next time they saw the stimuli. For the harmless stimuli, it took five shocks. Mineka *et al.* (1984) was able to condition fear of snakes in young monkeys who had seen their parents react fearfully to a snake.

- *Fear or phobia?* – It is easy to learn fear. However, would the participants in the study by Öhman *et al.* (1975) go on to develop a phobia when they were no longer being given the shocks: were they developing a phobia or just afraid? Another factor is whether the participants of Öhman and colleagues' research were more concerned by the memory of the shock than the picture of a spider. Would these participants have gone on to develop a phobia? The problem is that Öhman and colleagues couldn't extend their study to find out because it would have been unethical. Psychologists cannot knowingly cause people to develop a phobia.

Essential notes

The recent success of cognitive-behavioural therapy (CBT) has led to people exploring older theories again. Learning theory has been shown to be resilient and is a useful starting point for developing new therapeutic strategies.

Essential notes

There is evidence that shows us that there is some evolutionary preparedness for certain stimuli, but this cannot explain every instance of phobia.

Psychological explanations: cognitive-behavioural

Cognitive psychology is the study of how mental processes operate. When we combine it with behavioural psychology (how learning affects behaviour), we have the basis of a therapy that can alter behaviour by challenging thought processes. This type of therapy is used a great deal for mental health problems.

Cognitive-behavioural theories combine the behavioural ideas outlined on pp. 64–5 with the cognitive ideas about how thought processing alters a situation. Cognitive-behavioural theories believe that the learning principles are not sufficient to explain every instance of a phobia.

Thought processes

Cognitive theorists ask people with phobias to describe their thought processes when they encounter a phobic object or situation. For example, if you are afraid of lifts because you once got stuck in a crowed lift and felt you could not breathe properly, you might associate lifts with suffocation. However, lifts mostly work; this fear is irrational because the thinking behind the fear is irrational. Aaron Beck (1963) believes this catastrophic thinking ('If I go in a lift, something terrible will happen') is a major factor in the development of phobias.

Beck *et al.* (1985) showed that people's phobic beliefs grow as the feared object gets closer to them. People were not afraid of the object as long as it was perceived to be at a safe distance. This shows that this is a genuine fear; however irrational, it is real to the person.

The fear of fear

Beck and colleagues also showed that people with phobias were preoccupied with their fear and symptoms of their anxiety. A series of studies (e.g. Williams *et al.* 1997) has shown that people with agoraphobia or social phobia are more concerned with the bodily sensations of rising anxiety than they are of the feared situation itself. As agoraphobia can occur with panic attacks, those patients are more afraid of the panic attack than they are of being outside their homes. People with social phobia worry more about what people think of them than they do of the social event itself. There is a tendency for social phobics to have high ratings of the need for perfectionism combined with low self-esteem (Bieling and Alden 1997). In other words, these people are extremely sensitive to criticism so that, eventually, avoiding criticism becomes pathological, meaning that a phobia may develop.

Evaluation of Beck's theory

As Beck's ideas have been successfully turned into therapeutic interventions, they can be said to be successful at explaining some phobias. There is a great deal of supportive evidence that demonstrates that certain people are more prone to developing an anxiety disorder such as phobia than are others (Ashbaugh *et al.* 2007). This helps counter the largest criticism of behavioural theory that not all people remember an initiating incident that led to their phobia.

Cognitive-behavioural theory can be said to be a theory that explains more instances of phobia, especially when combined with biological predispositions.

Diathesis-stress model explanation of phobias

The **diathesis-stress model** proposes that an individual's biological predisposition to phobias interacts with various stressful situations in the environment. This means that each person's propensity to develop a phobia varies from the next person. We each have a tolerance level for stress (our diathesis or vulnerability factor) that is probably inherited or the result of early experiences. When an individual suddenly experiences a stressful life situation (e.g. bereavement, unemployment) this vulnerability might become pathological and a phobia might develop.

Evidence for the diathesis-stress model
The diathesis-stress model sees phobias as the result of an unexpected addition of stress on top of the individual's background stress level. To support the theory, you would have to find people with phobias who had experienced major life events before the onset of the phobia:

- Kleiner and Marshall (1987) found that 84 per cent of 50 agoraphobics had experienced severe and prolonged relationship conflicts prior to the onset of the anxiety disorder.
- Scocco *et al.* (2007) found a similarly high number (92.7 per cent of 55 patients) had experienced a role transition prior to the development of panic disorder.

Evaluation of the diathesis-stress model
There is evidence to suggest the role of life events and stress in the development of some phobias, especially social phobia and agoraphobia. However, this cannot be said to be a reasonable explanation for the development of a specific phobia; it applies to the more social phobias.

Neither can the theory offer an explanation for why not everyone who experiences a significant life event goes on to develop phobias. There must be something else, perhaps a biological vulnerability (genetics or biochemical) that makes some people develop phobias while others do not.

Examiners' notes

Remember that research studies can be a useful form of AO2 evaluation, provided that an explicit statement is made about how the study specifically supports or challenges the theory or explanation in question.

Psychological explanations: psychodynamic

The psychodynamic explanations were primarily suggested by Sigmund Freud and further developed by his associates. Freud suggested that phobias were not the cause of the person's original anxiety. Instead, they projected the anxiety and fear they feel internally on to an external, unrelated object.

Psychodynamic theory

Psychodynamics believes that these internal anxieties and fears reflect unconscious sexual fears (also known as **id** impulses). These impulses are repressed and displaced on to some other object in order to protect the **ego**. According to Freud, this explains why phobias are so often irrational; they do not represent the real fears.

Little Hans

Little Hans was a 5-year-old boy who developed such a severe phobia of horses that he was unable to go out in public (horses were then the main transport in Vienna). Hans believed a horse might bite him. Freud believed this phobia was a displaced fear for Hans' real fears, which he believed was a castration anxiety. Freud spoke to Hans about his fears and dreams and concluded that, in Hans' case, his father was the source of his real fear.

Evaluation of the Little Hans case study

- *Methodology* – Freud only met Hans for one session in the presence of his father. It seems unlikely that the little boy could have explained anything about the real nature of his fears, repressed or otherwise. Freud's explanation is purely the result of his own interpretation, presumably filtered through his own childhood experiences and memories. Little Hans's father was an admirer of Freud's philosophy and so would agree with his interpretation and the resolution of Hans's phobia without question.

- *An incomplete explanation* – Additionally, while Freud's theory might explain the phobia of Little Hans, it does not offer an explanation for every instance of phobia experienced by so many people. Freud extrapolated his theory from this one case study. He really had no evidence beyond the very limited exploration of Hans's psyche. Children have childhood fears that frequently disappear without explanation.

It is always important to look at the standard of evidence when evaluating a study. Single case studies are often important, especially within clinical psychology. However, in this case, Freud based his theory on a short conversation with a small child mediated by the child's father. It is not hard to see that this evidence is not conclusive. Freud (and his associates) needed to collect many similar cases before they devised a reasonable theory.

Examiners' notes

There is always a danger, whenever discussing Freudian explanations, that you drift into a lengthy description of Freudian theory without actually touching on how this explains the development of phobias. Avoid this temptation and make sure that at all times you are addressing the question of explaining phobias rather than offering a general explanation of human behaviour.

Bowlby's attachment theory of phobias

John Bowlby's psychodynamic theory used the same principles as Freud, but without the reliance upon the idea of unconscious id impulses. Bowlby based his explanation upon his theory of attachment. Attachment theory details the importance of the relationship between a child and their primary caregiver. This relationship has to be secure for a normal emotional and social develop to occur.

In the case of agoraphobia, Bowlby believed the person with the phobia is afraid of losing the person to whom they are closest. Bowlby saw phobia as a more grown-up version of separation anxiety, the fear a child experiences when left by a parent that they might not return. Bowlby believed that the quality of attachment between parent and child could lay the groundwork for the development of a phobia later in life.

Evaluation of Bowlby's theory

- *An incomplete explanation* – Bowlby's theory does not readily explain all incidences of phobia. You can imagine that a parent who is overprotective and sees fear in all kinds of objects could impart that fear to a child. If a parent screams every time they see a spider, then a young child will believe that spiders are dangerous and to be avoided. You might also concede that a social phobia might develop in response to the fear of loss; it is better not to have relationships because they will end some day. However, phobias are more subtle than this. Social phobia is linked to a specific fear of doing something embarrassing in public. This is not readily linked to separation anxiety.

- *Inconsistent evidence* – In addition, other theorists have disagreed with Bowlby's interpretation. Parker (1971) believed agoraphobia resulted from parents who did not show affection, and so separation anxiety is unlikely to be a factor. Other studies have found no link at all between parental rearing styles and phobic disorders.

- *Links with early abuse* – There are also more controversial studies (such as Finkelhor and Browne, 1985) linking social phobias to sexual and physical abuse in childhood. These studies were correlational, however, and as correlation does not equal causation, such links need to be treated cautiously.

Essential notes

Psychodynamic theory is always hampered by a lack of evidence because it is essentially unscientific. A major source of evidence in this area comes from patient conversations during therapy and you cannot rely upon patients always to have perfect recall or not to tell you what they think you want to hear.

Examiners' notes

What really adds to the impact of an answer is when the student appreciates why something is good or bad about the theory in question. So, don't just state a criticism, ask yourself 'so what'? For example: 'There are also more controversial studies linking social phobias to sexual and physical abuse in childhood.' What are the implications of this insight? You might point out that this raises significant ethical issues as an explanation of phobias, as it heaps blame clearly on the parents or significant others in the person's childhood.

Essential notes

It seems that all of these explanations offer suggestions for how some people acquire their phobias. All of these ideas probably have some validity, and a combination of all of them may explain every incidence of phobia. We all have fears and anxieties, but only some go on to experience these fears at a pathological level.

Biological therapies: drug treatments

The medical model

Biological therapies are therapies that use the medical model to explain and treat psychiatric disorders. In the medical model, symptoms are seen as manifestations of pathological physiological processes, which are diagnosed and then treated with whatever methods are considered appropriate.

For phobias, the most commonly used biological therapy is drug therapy; this is given on the basis there is a chemical imbalance in the brain that can be corrected. Other conditions (such as OCD and depression) have more intensive biological therapies (such as **psychosurgery** or **electroconvulsive therapy**), but these are very rarely required for phobias. Here, we will deal with the current medications available for the treatment of phobias.

Drug treatments

Psychoactive drugs (drugs that affect the mind) either decrease or increase the levels of neurotransmitters in the brain. The relationships between psychiatric problems and neurotransmitters – and also the relationship between different chemicals – are not straightforward. Scientists are making progress towards understanding the way the brain works, but there is a lot still to do. We may not fully understand why medication for conditions such as phobia works, but if there is evidence that they help, they will obviously be used.

Anti-anxiety drugs

The oldest treatment for phobias is drugs that reduce the feeling anxiety produces in the body (e.g. racing heart, sweating). These drugs are the benzodiazepines (Valium, Librium) that were discovered in the 1950s. Benzodiazepines are GABA **agonists**; they enhance the amount of GABA in the brain. These drugs enforce relaxation; in other words, they get rid of the symptoms, but the underlying condition (the irrational fear of something) remains.

Evaluation of anti-anxiety drugs

The main problem with benzodiazepines is that it is easy to become dependent upon them. This dependence is mostly psychological; living without anxiety is seductive. The medication not only got rid of irrational fears, it got rid of all fear and anxiety responses. Patients never had to face up to their fears. Many people became dependent upon the drugs in the 1960s and 1970s after being encouraged to use the drugs for years. Now, it is acknowledged that these drugs are for acute use only. A short course is given alongside psychotherapy, which provides an effective treatment for anxiety disorders.

Antidepressants

Antidepressants affect the availability of serotonin and noradrenaline, the neurotransmitters implicated in depression. The first antidepressant drugs to be discovered were the monoamine oxidase inhibitors (MAOIs). These drugs block the action of monoamine oxidase, a chemical that breaks down noradrenaline and serotonin, and therefore increasing the presence of these neurotransmitters in the synapse. These drugs reduce panic symptoms effectively, but they can also lead to a dangerous rise in blood pressure when combined with certain foods. For this reason, they are infrequently used today.

SSRIs

The second generation of antidepressants are SSRIs (selective serotonin reuptake inhibitors, drugs which leave serotonin in the synapse for longer, boosting its effectiveness). Serotonin is not directly implicated in the development or maintenance of the phobia itself, but it is an important modulator of other chemicals that are implicated (noradrenaline and possibly GABA). The evidence that serotonin is involved in panic mostly stems from studies that report that antidepressants work, in that they are effective at reducing the anxiety associated with the phobic object or situation.

Evaluation of antidepressants

Antidepressants are effective at reducing social phobia and agoraphobia. However, how they do this is largely unknown. As the drugs are antidepressants, and depression is frequently comorbid with anxiety disorders, it could be that the improvement is as a result of depression remitting, with the improvement in the phobia being a secondary effect. If the SSRIs are treating the anxiety, then again we have the problem of treating the symptoms of phobia rather than the actual condition. This means that when the patient has finished a course of antidepressants, the phobia might return.

Evaluation of drug treatments

- *Treating the symptoms not the cause* – Although the medications can ease the symptoms of phobias and the other anxiety disorders, they do not treat the cause of the original fear. This means that the phobic behaviour may return when the drugs are no longer taken. In the past, this has meant that many patients remained on the medication for a long period of time.

- *Side effects* – Although this solution is initially cost-effective for organizations such as the NHS, a patient on these drugs long term is likely to experience other side effects with time.

- *A combined approach* – Ultimately, the best treatment for phobias is a combination of medication and psychotherapy (e.g. Vliet *et al.* 1994; Gould *et al.* 1997). The drugs reduce the anxiety while the therapy gets to the cause of the phobia. Together, it seems they can lead to long-term behavioural change.

Essential notes

The fact that we are uncertain of the exact action of these drugs indicates how much we still have to learn about the way the human brain works. There is almost certainly the potential to manufacture a more effective medication for anxiety disorders, but not until we better understand the interaction of neurotransmitters involved in anxiety and fear.

Psychological therapies: behavioural

Behavioural therapies are the oldest treatments for anxiety disorders, pre-dating any medication options. Behavioural theory states that phobias are learned behaviours, just as normal behaviour is acquired through learning. Behavioural therapy believes that abnormal behaviours, such as phobias, can be unlearned and replaced with normal behaviour.

Behavioural therapy is especially useful with phobias when the client is specifically afraid of a situation or object. It is less useful when the client's anxiety is less focused. It is fair to say that you have to really want to get rid of your phobia to undergo any behavioural therapy; the treatment requires exposure to the phobic object or situation.

Systematic desensitization

Systematic desensitization was devised by Joseph Wolpe (e.g. 1958). It is a direct attempt to counter-condition the client, replacing the fearful reaction to the phobic object or situation with a different emotion. It is called systematic because it has a number of distinct steps. There are two versions:

- *In vitro* desensitization works through imagination.
- *In vivo* desensitization works using the real phobic objects or situations.

The first step in either version is to teach the client relaxation techniques. Then the therapist and client work out a list of the things the client fears, starting with the thing that causes a minimum of anxiety.

The therapist asks the client to relax and then either imagine or experience the object or situation that causes the least anxiety. They concentrate on this object until the client can do so without experiencing anxiety. Then they move on to the next object on the list, and so on. This continues until the client has worked their way through all of their fears without anxiety. *In vivo* desensitization is most effective for specific phobias because they are more tangible than social phobia or agoraphobia.

Evaluation of systematic desensitization

The idea of systematic desensitization is that gradually the client learns to overcome the brain's desire to avoid the object. Behavioural psychologists would say that the evoking of the fear response is extinguished.

McGrath *et al.* (1990) found that this form of behavioural therapy helped 75 per cent of people with a specific phobia. Of course, the client has to be quite brave and motivated to undergo this type of therapy, and this means they have to be open to the experience of losing their phobia.

Examiners' notes

When describing (and evaluating) systematic desensitization in this context, you must tailor your answer specifically to the treatment of phobic disorders rather than write a general discussion of the nature of this form of treatment. To do this effectively, make sure that all your examples are relevant to phobic disorders, and that any research studies you cite are ones that have explored the use of systematic desensitization in the treatment of phobic disorders.

Flooding

Flooding is an even more extreme technique than *in vivo* desensitization, as it does not involve the relaxation techniques. The client is just exposed to the phobic object without reducing prior anxiety. It can be (and has been) done *in vivo*, but there are obvious ethical concerns here. If the client has claustrophobia (fear of enclosed spaces), they would be asked to sit alone in a small room and monitored until anxiety reduces. If the therapy is *in vitro*, the client imagines the situation. Flooding can also be done using virtual reality (Price *et al.* 2008) with some success.

Evaluation of flooding

It works because it is impossible to maintain a high state of anxiety for very long. Eventually, the neurochemicals maintaining the panic are exhausted, as is the client. The therapist obviously has to keep a careful check on the client to monitor their health, but if the client can endure this type of therapy, it is very effective. It would not take many sessions before the client learns that nothing more terrible than panic will happen to them. Flooding works, but *in vivo* flooding could potentially be dangerous and therefore should only be practised on very healthy clients. The client has to be open to the amount of anxiety they will feel during this process.

Essential notes

Behaviour techniques do work and, with the advent of virtual reality, they may become more popular. They will only work with the kind of client who really wants to eradicate their phobia. It is not 'pain free' therapy, but it is effective.

Modelling therapy

Modelling therapy is based upon social learning theory. It is a very simple technique that involves those with phobias observing others with their phobic object. So if someone has arachnophobia, then observing someone handle a spider should make the fear diminish. Then the client is asked to join in and hold the spider themselves.

Evaluation of modelling therapy

Modelling therapy has been shown to be very successful for specific phobias (e.g. Kelly *et al.* 2010). This study investigated whether children's fears of particular animals could be un learned using either modelling or through the provision of positive information about the feared animal. One hundred and seven children aged 6–8 years received negative information about a particular animal. Fear beliefs and behavioural avoidance of the feared animal were then measured. Children then received either positive information, modelling or a control task. Fear beliefs and behavioural avoidance were then measured again. Positive information and modelling both led to lower fear beliefs and behavioural avoidance than the control condition. With both methods, behavioural avoidance was significantly reduced, although positive information was more effective than modelling in reducing fear beliefs.

Modelling therapy is successful for exactly the same reasons as systematic desensitization; the client gradually comes to see that their fear is irrational. They learn that there is nothing to be anxious or fearful about, in the same way a child learns to overcome fear.

Essential notes

Social learning works because it mirrors how some people develop phobias in the first place. It is an effective way of getting rid of a specific phobia more gently than the other behavioural techniques.

Psychological therapies: psychodynamic

Psychodynamic therapy has been used in the treatment of phobias and the other anxiety disorders. As psychodynamic theory suggests that phobias are the consequences of repressed id conflicts, the therapist has to uncover the real reason for the irrational fear.

Methods of psychodynamic therapy

Psychodynamic therapy believes that as the true source of the id conflict is unconscious, the client will not know what they are most afraid of. Therefore the client has to use the established tools of psychodynamics, by talking to the client about their dreams and using word association. The idea is that this will lead the therapist to a deeper understanding of the client's psyche and so give access to the unconscious.

Evidence for the success of psychodynamic therapy

You would expect this type of therapy to have some success with treating phobias, as one of the core principles of psychodynamic theory is that anxiety and neuroses causes mental conflict. However, the evidence is mixed. Many of the studies that use psychodynamic therapy compare it to another therapy (CBT is most common), which is not a fair reflection on the success of the individual therapy. This is because therapy might work for lots of reasons, only one of which is type of therapy.

There have been no studies evaluating social phobia since the 1980s (Derubeis and Crits-Christoph 1998; Gibbons *et al.* 2008). There have been studies for agoraphobia (Hoffart and Martinsen 1990), but they compared traditional psychodynamic therapy with an integrated behavioural-psychodynamic therapy. The integrated therapy was found to be more successful.

Single case studies of phobia

Most of the evidence for the success of psychodynamic therapy in the treatment of phobia comes from single case studies. This includes the story of Little Hans and his phobia for horses. Freud eventually determined that Little Hans was suffering from an Oedipus complex (unconscious desires for the parent of the opposite sex, combined with a wish to get rid of the parent of the same sex), which may have arisen after the birth of his baby sister. Once this idea was explored by Freud, Hans' father and Hans, the phobia seemed to go away.

Evaluation of single case studies of phobia

Single case studies are interesting descriptions of the problems and treatment of one patient, but you should be wary when accepting them as evidence for the success of a therapy. Single case patients may recover for all kinds of reasons, and the therapy is only one of these. It is always better to confirm results with a series of patients before making conclusions.

Evaluation of psychodynamic therapy for phobias

Lack of evidence

Psychodynamic therapy is difficult to evaluate because there are few completed group studies in the research literature. There are single cases, but these do not have enough in common to combine them to see the bigger picture. It is simply not possible to evaluate psychodynamic therapy in the same way as we evaluate other forms of treatment for phobia, and this is a big problem.

Subjective nature of interpretations

A second, and perhaps more serious problem for the use of psychodynamic therapy in phobia, is that there is no evidence that phobias are caused by unconscious repressed id conflicts. If something is unconscious, it cannot be measured objectively. We are relying on the psychoanalyst to interpret what the client is telling them. It could be that other analysts will have a different opinion of the true cause of a phobia. If John Bowlby had treated Little Hans, it is likely he would have said the child's problems were caused by an insecure attachment. Both Bowlby and Freud are psychodynamic theorists, yet each has different interpretations of the situation. This subjectivity does not help the scientific standing of psychodynamic therapy.

Psychodynamic vs combined therapy

There is evidence that a combination of psychodynamic therapy and behavioural techniques is effective (Wolitzky and Eagle 1990; Hoffart and Martinsen 1990), but only limited evidence for psychodynamic therapy alone.

Examiners' notes

If you want to add a bit more clout to your evaluation, why not do a bit of research of your own. Ask yourself, 'what research can I find that supports (or perhaps challenges) the use of psychodynamic therapies in the treatment of phobias?' A little bit of Googling should do the trick!

Essential notes

Psychodynamic therapy might be a successful treatment for phobia, but the nature of the therapy makes it difficult to evaluate systematically.

Psychological therapies: CBT

Cognitive-behavioural therapy (CBT) is a combination of behavioural therapy and cognitive restructuring. As the concept of phobia includes an irrational fear, CBT theory would suggest that exploring the irrational nature of the perception of some object or a certain situation would make the client think differently.

CBT normally involves both therapy sessions and homework, i.e. tasks the client has to do between sessions, such as keeping a diary about incidences of phobic behaviour, or looking for photographs of the object/situation of which they are most afraid. Clients may also be taught to monitor their own health, by learning the signs of rising blood pressure (which might lead to fainting or a panic attack) so that they can establish when their fears are most active.

The idea of the homework is that the clients have to do work themselves; they are not reliant on the presence of the therapist to face their fears. This offers the best possibility that any behavioural change that occurs is likely to be lasting.

An example of a CBT session for a specific phobia

Panzarella and Garlipp (2009) describe a patient with a blood-injury phobia. This phobia was so bad that the client didn't leave the house if she had a cut finger because she thought she might get seriously ill and require hospitalization (and injections). It stopped her going on trips to distant places, just in case she might require hospitalization. She had decided to get help because she needed a diagnostic blood test and also because she was afraid she would damage her relationship if she continued with this behaviour.

The therapy
The therapy involved the client making a fear hierarchy: a list of things she was afraid of, with the most feared thing at the top. Then the therapist and client discussed the less feared aspect of the phobia until the client was able to do so without anxiety. She was encouraged to discuss any coping strategies she could think of to get her through the exposure sessions. She was asked to find a photograph of a painful situation as homework and to become desensitized to it. She made a recording of 'coping statements' ('I can get through this', etc.) to play before the blood test. In other words, the client directed the pace of the therapy to some extent, by being an active participant in the process of recovery. This particular patient went on to make a full recovery.

Essential notes

The therapist has to watch each stage of the process to deal with the way the client is evaluating their own success. People with anxiety disorders tend to evaluate themselves negatively. The therapist has to make sure the client gets the credit they deserve when they do things well, as it is difficult for the client to see improvement on their own.

Aaron Beck and CBT

The strategy outlined on p. 76 is a typical CBT session that shows the relationship between client and therapist. Beck (e.g. Beck *et al.* 1985) believed that the client has to be actively involved in the process, unlike psychodynamic therapy when the therapist guides the sessions. This is the strength of CBT, and it can be very effective – if the client wants to change their behaviour. It is a very individual therapy, reflecting that each patient has individual fears and thoughts about that fear. However, the techniques used are taken from an established collection of strategies and are therefore comparable between patients. This is a huge advantage because it allows studies into the effectiveness of CBT.

CBT with medication

Black (2006) did a **meta-analysis** of studies that used combined CBT and medication, and those that used therapy alone. He found there was no difference in results. This is good news in so far as patients can be treated successfully without a long course of antidepressants, as long as there is no underlying depression, and CBT is not known to have any unpleasant side effects.

Evaluation of CBT

Clear goals and measurable outcomes
Cognitive-behavioural therapy uses structured tasks with clear goals set by the client and therapist together. Because of this, we are able to evaluate the success of CBT very clearly. However, effectiveness depends to a large extent on the skill and experience of the therapist.

Success with different phobias
CBT is very successful at treating all kinds of phobias, but especially agoraphobia and social phobia (Barlow and Lehman 1996). The evidence is not as conclusive for specific phobia, where it seems the behavioural therapy alone is the most effective. When this review was carried out in 1996, CBT was not as popular as it is now. A more recent review of meta-analyses of CBT by Butler *et al.* (2006) suggests that CBT is very effective at providing long-term solutions to social phobia especially. Other anxiety disorders, such as panic disorder, also respond well to CBT. Barlow and Lehman's review did not look at specific phobias, but, as it seems as though behaviour therapy is very effective for this condition, it was perhaps not warranted.

Need for client's motivation
CBT is an effective treatment for phobia if the client wishes to do the hard work to change their behaviour. Without the willingness to work, the therapy will not be successful.

Examiners' notes

Questions in psychopathology require students to have studied therapies such as CBT in the particular context of the disorder they have studied. You may have met CBT before, but to answer a question about phobias, you must make it explicitly relevant to the treatment of phobias.

Essential notes

A meta-analysis is a research technique where the results of several similar studies can be combined to give a larger overall picture of the situation. They tend to offer strong evidence for the effectiveness of something and for this reason they are frequently used in medical fields.

Examiners' notes

You should always remember that criticisms should be backed up by appropriate argument or research evidence. Unsubstantiated assertions aren't worth much and receive very little credit.

Clinical characteristics

What is obsessive-compulsive disorder?

Obsessive-compulsive disorder (OCD) is an anxiety disorder. There are two elements:

- obsessions – i.e. persistent thoughts, ideas and impulses that enter and invade conscious experience
- compulsions – i.e. repeated acts that people feel they need to perform in order to rid themselves of anxiety, such as washing hands repeatedly to get rid of imagined contamination.

The differences between normal anxieties and OCD

Many people have obsessive thoughts at times or experience compulsions or superstitions (e.g. saluting lone magpies). However, these experiences are nothing like the way OCD makes you feel. OCD is extremely invasive, and the anxiety it provokes makes it almost impossible to function normally. For example, case studies show that someone with a contamination obsession will spend up to eight hours a day hand-washing, and that even this does not completely eradicate the fear of contamination.

Obsessions

Most obsessions fall into at least one the following six categories:

1. dirt and contamination
2. aggression
3. orderliness
4. illness
5. sex
6. religion.

For example, someone with an aggression obsession might worry that, without frequent rituals to keep the aggressive thoughts at bay, they might harm a family member.

Types of obsessions

Obsessions can take several forms, the most benign of which is doubt (about whether you have locked the front door, for example). **Rumination** is a term for thinking deeply about even the simplest things. Sometimes this can take the form of an internal debate, with the thinker presenting both sides of the argument. More sinister are obsessive thoughts, which interrupt normal cognitive processing to give an image or belief that cannot be shaken without going to the compulsion. These thoughts may appear as if they come from an outside agency. Occasionally, the person with OCD may try to resist the thoughts.

Obsessions can sometimes lead to phobias, whereby the person tries to avoid something they are obsessing about. So, for example, a fear of contamination may mean the person develops **agoraphobia** (a fear of crowed spaces) so as to avoid exposure to germs.

Compulsions

The purpose of the compulsion is to ward off some imagined horrible consequence. A failure to perform the compulsion results in extreme and invasive anxiety. Compulsions take several forms:

1. checking – e.g. checking and rechecking that you have unplugged the iron
2. seeking order – e.g. making sure that things are arranged in a particular way
3. cleaning – e.g. repeated hand-washing, clothes-washing or cleaning the house
4. counting rituals – e.g. counting things around the person, avoiding certain numbers, saying a phrase a certain number of times
5. touching – e.g. repeatedly touching, or avoiding touching certain items.

Giving in to compulsions

People with OCD may feel that giving in to the compulsion is giving in to the obsession; it does not make them feel good. The compulsion merely makes the obsession easier to handle. Some people who imagine loved ones with horrific wounds might start to worry that they will be the person to do the wounding. This can lead to them staying away from that loved one in order to alleviate the worry, or avoiding potential murder weapons, such as knives. Commonly, people know that their obsession is unfounded, but this does not make it go away.

Epidemiology

The mean age of onset for OCD ranges between 22 and 36, but it can begin in the late teens. Men tend to have an earlier age of onset than women, and the incidence of the disorder between the genders is approximately equal. It has a worldwide incidence of between 0.3 and 3.1 per cent of the population (Fontenelle *et al.* 2006); the wide range reflects the fact that OCD is very difficult to diagnose. It is still a comparatively poorly understood disorder, although there has been a recent increase in research papers, especially those focusing on risk factors for the onset of OCD.

Criteria for diagnosis

There are a number of criteria specified in diagnostic manuals for a diagnosis of OCD:

- Both the **ICD**-10 and **DSM**-IV-TR (see p. 6) stress that the patient has to acknowledge that the obsessions come from their own mind. This is because there seems to be an overlap with the symptoms of **psychosis** (e.g. schizophrenia).
- The diagnostic manuals also stress that the patient has to find either the obsession or compulsion excessive and intrusive, and that they try to resist them.
- The other feature that the patient must show is that neither obsession nor compulsion is pleasant.
- The diagnostic manuals say that either obsessions or compulsions have to be present on most days for a period of two weeks.

Examiners' notes

As with the list of obsessions, there is no need to include all the compulsions listed here. One or two might be used as a way of elaborating an answer. (See p. 101 for more about how to elaborate points in your answers.)

Examiners' notes

Questions on 'clinical characteristics' tend to be worth only 4 or 5 marks and are always descriptive (AO1). Your answers to such questions would be about 125 to 150 words in total (see Question 2(a) and the sample answers on p. 146).

Essential notes

When using either the DSM and ICD to assess a patient, it has to be very clear from the criteria that the patient is not suffering from a psychosis. Features of psychotic thinking would be that the need to do these compulsions is inflicted by an outside agency. Therefore, the criteria stress that the patient knows they are doing this to themselves and that they try to resist acting on the obsessions.

Issues in classification and diagnosis

Validity

In general terms, a measure is valid if it does the job it sets out to do in a way that is accurate, meaningful and relevant. In terms of identifying a disorder, diagnostic criteria are valid if they distinguish clearly between what can be considered 'well' and 'unwell'. Valid criteria also distinguish effectively between different conditions and minimize the possibility of misdiagnosis or overdiagnosis. In the context of OCD, this is not without its problems, so each of the points made about this below are evaluative.

Pathologizing normal behaviour

The fact that many of us check and recheck whether we have locked the door or may experience a sudden feeling of anxiety about whether we turned the gas off, shows that some elements of OCD are common to many people's experience. However, we are not all in need of treatment for these feelings. Recognizing this, the psychiatric profession seeks to make the diagnostic criteria for OCD specific enough to identify those people for whom OCD makes it impossible to live a normal life. At the same time, it is important not to overdiagnose the condition. An accurate diagnosis is very difficult to achieve, however, and it is inevitable that some people are either falsely diagnosed or misdiagnosed. As the diagnostic manuals were created with the specific aim of improving reliability and validity, this occasional failing is a problem. One potential solution is to subdivide different manifestations of OCD.

Subtypes of OCD

OCD is a heterogeneous disorder, i.e. there is a lot of variation between patients. As diagnostic criteria work better the more specific they are, some researchers have suggested dividing OCD into various subcategories (e.g. Ball *et al.* 1996). For example, about 60 per cent of patients present with more than one obsession, and a smaller number (48 per cent) present with more than one compulsion. There might be advantages in terms of more accurate diagnosis to breaking the disorder OCD down into smaller components.

Benefits of subdividing OCD

Before subdividing OCD, it would have to be demonstrated that there are additional benefits, other than improved reliability and validity. One justification for the subdivision would be if the subtypes responded differently to various forms of treatment. For example, Ball *et al.* (1996) reports that people with cleaning or checking rituals respond better to behavioural therapy than do those with other compulsions.

Validity: conclusions

So far, research in this area has been mixed. It is uncertain whether different types of obsessions and compulsions have different causes (Rasmussen and Eisen 1992). The patients all have features in common: the anxiety they experience that something terrible will happen to themselves

Examiners' notes

There are many potential 'issues' in classifying somebody as having a mental disorder. These include ethical issues, cultural differences in diagnosis and the problems of labelling somebody as 'mentally ill'. However, the two most commonly cited are reliability and validity. You could also try doing some of your own research on other potential 'issues' associated with OCD. For example, try putting 'cultural differences in diagnosis of OCD' into your favourite search engine, and then use this information to build a critical argument concerning the diagnosis of OCD.

or others if they do not go through their rituals. This means that, although there might be different subtypes of OCD, it might not make much clinical difference to reflect this formally in diagnostic manuals. More research needs to be carried out to find out if different treatments are more effective with certain subtypes.

Reliability of diagnosis

In a word, reliability means consistency. Diagnostic criteria are reliable if clinicians agree that an individual's symptoms indicate a particular condition (this is a kind of inter-observer reliability). The same clinician should also diagnose different individuals presenting with similar symptoms to each other as having the same disorder (this is a kind of intra-observer reliability). The following points evaluate reliability of OCD diagnosis.

The comparison between OCD and psychosis

There is a fine line between knowing that you are responsible for intrusive thoughts and believing someone else has put these ideas into your head. One of the criteria for OCD stresses that the patient has to know that they are causing these behaviours themselves. It is sometimes difficult to get at this information when the patient is embarrassed by these thoughts. However, the DSM also has criteria for those with 'poor insight'. This may cloud the distinction between OCD and a condition such as psychosis. The clinician making the diagnosis has to be very sure of the condition they are diagnosing because the treatments for the conditions are different.

Comorbidity

OCD is frequently **comorbid** with (i.e. occurs alongside) other disorders. For example, 62 per cent of all those diagnosed with OCD are also diagnosed with depression (Torres *et al.* 2006). In fact, the majority of people with OCD have another psychiatric disorder, such as other anxiety disorders, e.g. phobia, depression or substance abuse (Fontenelle and Hasler 2008). The reason is probably due to the fact that all these conditions have anxiety at their centre. This might indicate a biological cause for the problem, although the importance of family influences must not be ruled out.

Lack of inter-rater reliability

Stein *et al.* (1997) claims that diagnosis of OCD by lay interviewers specially trained to use an OCD assessment tool but who had no clinical experience overdiagnosed the disorder considerably. Stein and colleagues found that when the information obtained in these interviews was reappraised by clinical research personnel experienced in assessing OCD, the rate of diagnosis dropped considerably. This shows a lack of reliability in the diagnosis of OCD.

Essential notes

The main problem with the diagnostic category of OCD is that it is very broad. More effort is needed to discover whether OCD should be subdivided because of any potential benefits to treatment.

Examiners' notes

There are two main ways of asking a question about 'issues of classification and diagnosis'. If there are 10 marks for a question on issues of classification and diagnosis, then it is AO2 only. However, it can also be a 24-mark question (25-mark prior to 2012), in which case it would be AO1 and AO2. Part (b) of Question 2 on p. 147 is an example of a 10-mark version of a question about issues of classification and diagnosis.

Essential notes

The fact that OCD is comorbid with other conditions tells us that these disorders have something in common. However, this knowledge has not yet been used to provide better treatment for people diagnosed with OCD.

Biological explanations: genetics

As with other psychiatric disorders, it is believed that many people inherit a predisposition to develop anxiety disorders like OCD. Genetic explanations of OCD are perhaps not as established as other biological factors, but the search for the 'anxiety gene' is well under way. Information for a genetic component for OCD comes from three sources: family studies, twin studies and the use of newer technology to study genetic material. The hope is that the identification of specific genes involved in OCD might lead to better treatments.

Family studies

First-degree relatives share around 50 per cent of their genetic material. In family studies, the researchers look at the incidence of the disorder in families with a diagnosed **proband** (the starting point for a genetic investigation; the first person in the family diagnosed with the disorder). The incidence of OCD in proband families is then compared with similar families without a history of the disorder.

Research findings

There are very few studies that have looked at the family and OCD. The first is by Pauls *et al.* (1995). They found the incidence of OCD to be almost five times greater when a first degree relative also has OCD. A second study by Nestadt *et al.* (2000) found a similar risk of 11.7 per cent of families when a first-degree family member has been diagnosed with OCD, compared to a general risk of 2.7 per cent in the general population. Therefore, both studies have shown a genetic risk for OCD when a family member has the disorder. The Nestadt study was particularly well controlled. It showed that obsessions were more commonly shared than compulsions. They also found that those families where the proband was young at onset seemed to have a greater genetic risk than those with a later age of onset. This seems to suggest that there are at least two distinct forms of OCD.

Evaluation of family studies

The contribution of nature and nurture is unknown. The major problem with estimating heritability in studies like this is that it is hard to know how much the propensity to develop OCD is caused by learning from simple observation of family members. Although OCD is not an enviable condition, it is possible that younger families learn OCD-type behaviour purely as a function of spending a lot of time together. As these studies do not identify a gene, the evidence must therefore be treated with caution.

Examiners' notes

When choosing material for an answer in this area, you should prioritize the actual research that *describes* the genetic explanation and then draw upon any of the evaluation on these two pages for your critical commentary. In other words, there is a need to be selective in your choice of appropriate material.

Twin studies

Slightly more robust evidence comes from twin studies, especially studies using monozygotic (MZ) twins (i.e. identical twins), who share 100 per cent of their genotype. Unfortunately, there are few twin studies of the incidence of OCD. Some of the studies that exist look at one set of twins over a long period (which helps to separate the genetic from environmental effects) or use a very small sample (which can make conclusions unsafe).

A review of twin studies by Grootheest *et al.* (2005) estimates the heritability of OCD symptoms (rather than a diagnosis of OCD) to be between 27 and 47 per cent. This suggests a genetic influence for OCD, but the data are very limited.

Evaluation of twin studies

- *A lack of data* – The data are very limited, presumably because researchers cannot find enough twins to meet the necessary criteria. Instead, research has tended to focus on subclinical features of the condition, that is, when it is at a stage where it has begun to develop but symptoms are not yet apparent. Here, there is evidence for a familial factor, but there is no way of separating the genetic influence from the environmental.

- *A general genetic predisposition to anxiety* – The second important point is that perhaps the genetic predisposition involves anxiety disorders in general rather than OCD specifically. This is much more promising research in terms of potential for treatment, but again it is made difficult by the heterogeneous nature of OCD and the other anxiety disorders.

Other gene research

Advances in technology have enabled the investigation of candidate genes for OCD (i.e. those genes suspected of being involved in the development of the disorder). However, it is early days for this research, and no conclusive evidence has been discovered. Most of the work is looking at genes associated with the serotonin and dopamine systems. As of yet, no studies with a large population have been completed, although many candidate genes have been proposed (Pauls 2008).

Evaluation of gene research

- *Genetic factors* (above) *are not the answer* – It is possible that only some forms of OCD are heritable and have a genetic basis. Because we know so little about the disorder (compared to depression, for example), it is difficult to conclude anything from this work. However, we do know there is not a 100 per cent **concordance rate**; there must be influences other than genetics factors involved in OCD.

Essential notes

Monozygotic (i.e. identical) twins share the same genes, whereas dizygotic (DZ) or non-identical (fraternal) twins have only 50 per cent of their genes in common.

Examiners' notes

Research evidence can also be used as AO2 evaluation, but you need to set this evidence in the context of a critical argument. For example, after citing 'Grootheest *et al.* (2005) estimates the heritability of OCD symptoms (rather than a diagnosis of OCD) between 27 and 47 per cent…', you might add '…which supports the claim that OCD has a strong genetic influence'.

Essential notes

Separating the genetic influence from environmental factors is a problem with all observational studies of psychiatric disorders. It is typical for families to share behavioural characteristics purely on the basis of learning – children follow in their parents' footsteps. If the parents exhibit anxious behaviour, then it is extremely likely that the children will learn this response.

Examiners' notes

It is early days for advanced genetic studies of OCD. It seems that more work needs to be done on identifying subtypes of OCD in order to move forward in this area.

Biological explanations: biochemistry

Biochemical explanations of OCD focus on two aspects:

- neuroanatomical explanations – based on dysfunctions of the brain and nervous system
- neurochemical explanations – focusing on the action of neurochemicals such as serotonin and dopamine.

Neuroanatomical explanations

Impulse control

There is a cluster of disorders, some of them neurological and some psychiatric, that cause a problem with impulse control. This is the mechanism whereby you can stop yourself doing things – for example, putting off eating a bar of chocolate until you finish some task or stopping yourself doing or saying something you know to be inappropriate. With OCD, the urge to go through with the compulsion can be overwhelming. This indicates that OCD is something to do with the brain's reward system, which makes you feel good when you finish a planned task.

The orbitofrontal cortex

The orbitofrontal cortex is right at the front of the brain, immediately above the eyes. It is thought to play a role in the mediation of socially accepted behaviours (Friedlander and Desrocher 2006). Brain scans of people with an OCD diagnosis typically show an increased metabolism in the orbitofrontal cortex (Swedo *et al.* 1989). It is thought that this increase reflects the persistence of obsessional thoughts. This finding has been reported in adults, but not in children.

The caudate nuclei

Another area that seems to be involved in OCD is the caudate nucleus, part of the basal ganglia (see Fig. 4 on p. 49). Most imaging studies of the basal ganglia indicate that the caudate nucleus is altered in OCD, but the nature of that change is inconsistent (Friedlander and Desrocher 2006).

The caudate nucleus is connected to part of the dorsolateral prefrontal cortex (situated behind the orbitofrontal cortex). Adults with OCD show decreased volume in this area (Lucey *et al.* 1997), but children typically do not. This might be because children's brains are still in a process of functional development. This area is thought to be involved in signalling the completion of behaviours, by stopping certain thoughts and actions. Damage here would leave the patient stuck in a thought or action, unable to move onto the next task.

Evaluation of neuroanatomical studies

The jury is still out. These studies do not yet offer conclusive findings. This is partly because of small sample sizes and also because some studies combine children and adults – and, as you can see, there seem to be different brain changes in these two groups. Friedlander and Desrocher

(2006) suggest that most patients with OCD had other (comorbid) disorders, which might confuse understanding of the brain changes caused by OCD. It is fair to say that, as of yet, we are reasonably certain which areas of the brain are involved in OCD, but we are still in a process of gathering supportive evidence.

Neurochemical explanations

We are perhaps more certain of the neurochemicals involved in OCD. Many people believe OCD reflects a deficiency in the **neurotransmitter** serotonin, a hormone important in transmitting nerve impulses. The evidence for this is that OCD can be eased (but not cured) by antidepressants in some patients. Antidepressants are known to boost the levels of serotonin in the brain (e.g. Fineberg and Gale 2005).

Serotonin and dopamine

Anxiety disorders tend to respond to drugs that affect either the dopamine or serotonin systems. Serotonin is known to be a neuromodulator for other neurochemicals, including dopamine and GABA, such that it can dampen down or enhance their activity, so a problem with serotonin might lead to problems with other neurotransmitters.

Dopamine is the main neurochemical involved in the brain reward pathway. It is an important neurochemical in the caudate nuclei and the basal ganglia in general. It seems as though there is a decreased number of dopamine receptors in the basal ganglia of OCD patients.

Evaluation of neurochemical explanations

Research evidence – Supporting evidence for the involvement of dopamine comes from two sources:

- It has been observed that, for some people, atypical antipsychotics (the medicine given to some people with schizophrenia – see p. 23) causes a reduction in OCD symptoms (Westenberg *et al.* 2007).
- Long-term heroin addicts can develop OCD symptoms (Papageorgiou *et al.* 2003). Heroin addiction is known to disrupt the brain's dopamine levels, which may, in turn, lead to the symptoms typically observed in OCD patients.

Limitations of neurochemical explanations – Although this research is promising because it offers a chance at developing medications for OCD, there are problems:

- We can never be sure about cause and effect. Does OCD cause changes in neuroanatomy and neurochemistry, or is it the other way around? It is very difficult to answer such questions.
- Without certainty about the exact nature of the mechanisms involved, we are medicating relatively blindly. More needs to be understood about the way the brain works before effective treatments – or even cures – for OCD can be found.

Examiners' notes

What always adds authority to an answer is being able to add research evidence to support the claims you are making. Try putting 'research study serotonin OCD' into Google and see what you can find.

Essential notes

There are several promising leads in terms of the biology of OCD, but they need to be more fully developed before we understand this disorder. The problem of cause and effect is not easily solved, and we must bear this in mind as we look at other potential causes.

Psychological explanations: behavioural

Behavioural explanations of OCD focus around the learning theories of classical and operant conditioning. The leading proponent of the behavioural explanation of OCD is Mowrer (1960).

Mowrer's two-process theory of OCD

Mowrer's theory explains the development of OCD as a consequence of learning inappropriate or maladaptive fears. Mowrer highlighted two processes:

1. Neutral objects become associated with anxiety through the process of **classical conditioning**, whereby a previously neutral stimulus becomes associated with a traumatic event. For example, seeing a used syringe in a disgustingly unclean environment might become associated with the frightening thought of contamination.

2. The anxiety is reduced by engaging in a repetitive compulsion. This happens through **operant conditioning**, whereby an action which has rewarding or reinforcing consequences increases in frequency. In this case, **negative reinforcement** occurs because the reward is in the reduction of unpleasant feelings of anxiety. For example, hands are washed time and again to reduce the fear of contamination, perhaps with the knowledge that this action cannot really work; however, anxiety is reduced and so the behaviour is continued.

Evaluation of the behavioural model of OCD

Evidence for (some of) Mowrer's theory

- *Problems with part 1 of the theory* – Much of the evidence for Mowrer's theory has come from Rachman and Hodgson (1972). However, these theorists, as well as others, have concentrated on the second part of the theory at the cost of the first part. This is partly because the establishment of this classical conditioning has to be remembered by the patient; it is unlikely ever to be documented at the time. Someone with a contamination fear who is asked if there was an incident to justify their fear might be able to provide one, but it is very difficult experimentally to prove that the remembered event actually took place. It could just as easily be a constructed event designed to make the behaviour appear logical. There is no way to test this first part of the theory and as behaviourism is grounded in the idea of observation, the theory is compromised at the start.

There are rare papers that provide an association between an event and the start of an obsessive idea that leads to a compulsion. For example, Pitman (1993) described a case study of a woman who developed serious checking, hoarding and hand-washing compulsions after a sexual assault. There are also many papers tying combat situations that lead to post-traumatic stress disorder (PTSD) with various compulsions.

Examiners' notes

Pages 86–91 cover several psychological explanations of OCD. In exam questions that ask for 'explanations' or 'theories' in the plural, it is often more effective to cover just *two* explanations or theories. Trying to cover too many explanations can make your description and evaluation less detailed than it should be for the higher mark bands.

Examiners' notes

Mowrer's theory is based on the principles of classical and operant conditioning, but, when answering an exam question, you should not spend too long describing the principles of these two types of conditioning, other than to explain how these might be linked to the development of OCD.

However, these should be treated with caution because of the potential confound of PTSD. There are many, many other cases where a trauma or negative memory can be tied to the start of OCD.

It is nevertheless difficult to provide convincing experimental evidence for the first part of Mowrer's theory. Instead, the onset of OCD seems to be more gradual (Abramovich *et al.* 2007). If patients cannot recall a specific incident that triggered this pattern of behaviour, then the classical conditioning part of the theory cannot be supported.

- *Support for part 2 of the theory* – The second part of the theory however has received strong experimental support. Hodgson and Rachman (1972) showed that OCD patients demonstrate increased anxiety, shown in an increased pulse rate and a rating of discomfort. The pulse rate would then decrease as the patient was allowed to wash. This experiment has been supported many times, and it fits with patients' own comments that going through with their compulsions is the only thing that reduces their anxiety. As some aspects of this behavioural model have received little support, this theory cannot be accepted as a whole. However, Mowrer seems to have developed an explanation for why compulsions arise and continue.

- *Subjective evidence for part 2 of Mowrer's theory* – People confirm that going through with their compulsion avoids the negative consequences of their disturbing thoughts for themselves or the people around them. One patient states that they 'wash until it feels right' (Wahl *et al.* 2008). This study also gives the example of a patient who washes their hands until they bleed, continuing 'because they are uncertain they have washed enough'. As the theory predicts, people go through with their compulsion until their anxiety has decreased to an acceptable level to continue with normal behaviour. This strongly suggests that the behaviour has been conditioned within the patients; they have learned that their compulsion is the only thing to reduce their anxiety.

Effective behavioural therapy

There is evidence for the effectiveness of treatments based on behavioural theory (see pp. 96–7). Studies (e.g. Schwartz *et al.* 1996) have found that behavioural therapies not only reduce symptoms of OCD, but also bring about changes in biochemical activity. Marks (1981) found that behavioural therapy was very effective in treating compulsive cleaning and checking behaviour, but not so effective for obsessional thoughts.

Treatment etiology fallacy

The fact that a behavioural therapy successfully treats a particular disorder does not mean that the cause of the disorder can best be explained in behavioural terms. To make that assumption is to commit what is known as the 'treatment etiology fallacy' – the mistaken notion that the success of a treatment reveals the cause of the disorder so, although behavioural models form the basis of psychological treatments for OCD, they cannot be said to have accounted for the reasons why the disorder begins in the first place.

Essential notes

The evidence supporting a behavioural theory of OCD is a little mixed. The second part of the model, which explains the development of compulsions, has received a great deal of research support. This support has been developed into behavioural therapies for the treatment of OCD, which in turn have been quite successful. However, this theory has failed to develop an explanation for the development of obsessions.

Examiners' notes

Remember that in every question, the overall mark division has twice as many marks for AO2 evaluation than AO1 description. Remember this when constructing your response to any examination question.

Psychological explanations: cognitive

Obsessions (intrusive thoughts)

The cognitive model has grown out of the behavioural model's failure to explain how obsessions originate. Cognitive models start from the perspective that most people experience intrusive thoughts; these are exactly the same as the obsessive thoughts in people with OCD, but most people do not become obsessional about them.

Rachman and de Silva (1978) reported that 80 per cent of people admit to occasionally thinking things that made them uncomfortable. This raises the question of what is different about people with OCD? Is it what they think, or how they handle the thoughts when they have them?

OCD without the compulsions

There are people who report intrusive thoughts, but can force themselves to stop without a compulsion. These people sometimes have cognitive (thought and belief-based) rituals (e.g. touching wood, saluting magpies, distraction) rather than compulsions. They report that these rituals neutralize the intrusive thought; they are coping mechanisms (Salkovskis *et al.* 2003). They seem to differ from OCD patients in that they do not attach the same level of threat to the intrusive thoughts.

What makes OCD intrusive thoughts so uncomfortable?

The Obsessive Compulsive Cognitions Working Group (OCCWG 1997) looked at the reasons given by people with OCD for being afraid of their thoughts. They identified the following four thought processes:

1. People with OCD thought that the things they were thinking would really occur (including that they had special powers to cause the event to occur).
2. They thought they had to neutralize the thoughts – that they were the only person who could prevent these things occurring.
3. They overestimated general threats (i.e. they thought that catastrophic events were more common than they actually are).
4. They believed that total control of thoughts was possible and that failing to do so was dangerous in some way.

Thought–action fusion (TAF)

All of these above reasons show **thought–action fusion (TAF)**, the belief that thoughts can influence the world. People without OCD will respond to the discomfort that intrusive thoughts cause, but they do not experience TAF; they recognize that their thoughts are just thoughts.

The degree of TAF an individual experiences is related to the severity of their symptoms. When people believe that their thoughts cause events to occur, then trying to suppress the thoughts only makes them worse.

Salkoviskis and Kirk (1997) asked people with OCD to keep a diary of whenever they experienced intrusive thoughts. They were asked to suppress the thoughts on some days, but on other days to record them and then go on with their neutralizing action as they would normally. They found that, on the days people had been asked to suppress only, they recorded almost twice as many intrusive thoughts.

This experiment goes back to the research of Wegner *et al.* (1987), who found that telling people to think of something (in this case, a white bear) produced more thoughts of the bear after a period of being asked to suppress the thoughts.

Overvalued ideation
Another indication of the cognitive processes in OCD is those patients whose symptoms show **overvalued ideation**. Most people with OCD realize that there is no logical connection between their obsessions and compulsions (although they do the latter anyway). Those with overvalued ideation believe there is a link between the two; they have to go through with the neutralizing action so as to avoid the intrusive thought becoming reality. People with overvalued ideation generally have a poor chance of recovery and are difficult to treat (Kovak and Foa 1994). This type of behaviour is like a **delusion**, similar to those seen in schizophrenia and other psychoses.

Evaluation of cognitive theories

Research evidence
Dysfunctional beliefs do come first – Many of the predictions that are part of a cognitive-behavioural explanation of OCD are supported by research evidence. For example, a cognitive explanation would predict that dysfunctional beliefs about the world would precede the symptoms of OCD. This prediction was supported by Tolin *et al.* (2003), who found that the tendency to overestimate threat (a dysfunctional belief) significantly predicted the OCD symptoms of washing, checking and hoarding.

Strengthened dysfunctional beliefs increase OCD intensity – A cognitive-behavioural explanation would also predict that anything that strengthened a dysfunctional belief (e.g. confirmed a threat) should increase the associated obsessions and compulsions typical of OCD. This prediction was supported by a study by Abramowitz *et al.* (2005), who found that the development of OCD symptoms often followed some change in personal circumstances such as becoming parents for the first time, thus fostering an irrational preoccupation with dirt, danger and parental responsibility.

Successful therapies
The value of cognitive-behavioural explanations of OCD is enhanced because of the success of therapies based on this approach (see pp. 98–9). For example, Huppert and Franklin (2005) found that most of those who completed a course of cognitive-behavioural therapy (CBT) showed a significant improvement in their symptoms. Salkovskis (2007) found that CBT was superior to other forms of psychological therapy in reducing the symptoms of OCD, which emphasizes the important role played by cognition in the onset and maintenance of this disorder.

Essential notes

People who develop OCD believe their thoughts are more important or dangerous than other people who can experience intrusive thoughts and suppress them. It is likely that this difference is biological (whether because of genetics or neurochemical causes).

Examiners' notes

Remember that research studies can be a useful form of AO2 evaluation provided that an explicit statement is made about how the study specifically *supports* or *challenges* the theory or explanation in question, as is done here with the research evidence of Tolin *et al.* (2003) and Abramowitz *et al.* (2005).

Essential notes

Cognitive theories are the most successful theories to explain the onset and progression of OCD. It seems that the way we think is important in the development of obsessions and the continuation of compulsions. Experiments into cognitive theories can successfully identify those individuals who are both treatment-resistant and experience the most serious symptoms of OCD.

Table 3
Defence mechanisms important in OCD

Psychological explanations: psychodynamic

Psychodynamic theorists, such as Sigmund Freud, believe that children develop an anxiety disorder like OCD when they start to fear the content of their **id** drives and impulses. The id is part of Freud's model of the psyche that consists of basic drives and acts according to the pleasure principle (the drive to ignore pain and maximize pleasure). It is unconscious and, in itself, has no conscience or morality (Freud 1916), but children come to fear these impulses and so use defence mechanisms to reduce the anxiety caused by this fear. Defence mechanisms are tools used by the **ego**, the part of the personality responsible for decision-making and dealing with reality.

Psychodynamic explanation of OCD

Defence mechanism	Explanation	Example
Repression	The pushing-away of an unwanted idea or impulse	In an attempt to stop thinking a bad thought about harm coming to their family, the OCD person focuses on the socket-checking compulsion instead
Reaction formation	The conscious fixation on a desire that is opposite to an unacceptable unconscious (id) thought	'My family is going to die' (unacceptable unconscious thought). 'I don't want my family to die' (opposite, acceptable conscious thought). 'Nothing bad will happen to my family if I check the sockets'
Undoing	The performing of certain acts to cancel out an undesirable id impulse	'I've thought about my family dying again so I'll re-check the sockets to undo the thought'
Denial	The conscious refusal to perceive that painful thoughts exist	The socket-checking compulsion distracts from the obsessive thoughts and denies they exist
Rationalization	A substitution of a reasonable explanation for the true (undesirable) explanation for behaviour	'Socket-checking is a good way to protect my children from harm' (as opposed to 'I want my family to die')
Isolation	Disowning an undesirable impulse by blaming an outside influence; separating feelings from ideas and impulses	'If people could be trusted to install sockets properly, my family would be safe, and there would be no need for me to check the sockets'

According to the psychodynamic explanation, OCD is the conscious acting-out of the unconscious battle between id impulses and defence mechanisms that the ego employs to reduce the resulting anxiety. The id impulses are things such as the person imagining their family dying in a fire. The intense anxiety that this unacceptable thought produces would lead to repeatedly checking that there was no risk of fire in the house, e.g. by checking electric sockets. The defence mechanisms important in OCD are listed in Table 3.

Reaction formation and repression

There are many defence mechanisms, but some are more important in OCD than others. Some of the defence mechanisms, like repression and reaction formation, refer to the concept of denying ideas. In repression, the individual buries their unwanted idea, which will only lead to increased anxiety and greater risk of OCD developing. Reaction formation is when you convert an idea to its opposite; so, to rid oneself from an unwanted idea of harming people, you instead do things which indicate you care about them.

Undoing, isolation and denial

Undoing and isolation are, in some ways, quite similar because they all involve pushing away undesirable ideas. So, if the unwanted thought were a danger of infection, the undoing defence mechanism would result in hand-washing or house cleaning. Denial and isolation are when the ideas causing the anxiety are rejected.

Development of OCD

Freud believed that the seeds for OCD develop in the anal stage of development, the second of Freud's stages, when the child is between 1 and 2 years of age and is learning toilet training. Freud believed that, at this stage, the child has the potential for enormous rage and shame. How the parent handles the toilet training is crucial; if they are too harsh or try to toilet train too quickly, the child will feel shame and dirty, leading to conflict between the id and the ego. If this conflict is very strong, then development is arrested in this stage, causing the issues in adulthood that result in OCD. This would explain why someone with a contamination fear becomes so clean and tidy; they want to let go and be dirty (id), but they feel the shame and need for control to be clean (ego).

Evaluation of the psychodynamic theory of OCD

Limitations of the psychodynamic explanation

This theory is difficult to test experimentally. Few people can remember anything about their toilet training, and even if people did feel a degree of shame, why would this develop into such a specific behavioural problem? The theory seems best to fit ideas about cleanliness and contamination, and yet this is only one aspect of OCD behaviour. This theory is too specific and does not explain every incidence of OCD, whereas cognitive models (see pp. 88–9) explain the development of the disorder in more people.

Lack of therapeutic success

Most psychiatrists agree that psychodynamic theory is not particularly effective in the treatment of OCD. However, the symptoms of OCD may indicate a more significant underlying psychopathology; in this respect, the focus on personality reorganization that is the emphasis of psychodynamic therapy can produce a significant improvement in the individual's personal functioning (Gabbard 2005).

Essential notes

This theory is quite complicated. It seems to explain cleanliness compulsions and obsessions very well, but is perhaps not so convincing for the other types of obsession. However, describing OCD as a means to reduce anxiety seems logical.

Examiners' notes

What really adds to the impact of an answer is when the student appreciates *why* something is good or bad about the theory in question. So, don't just state a criticism, ask yourself 'so what'? For example: 'As with all psychodynamic theories, this theory is difficult to test experimentally.' What are the implications of this insight? You might point out that this raises significant problems of scientific validation and makes the psychodynamic explanation difficult to falsify, which limits its value as a scientific explanation.

Biological therapies: drug treatments

Biological therapies are the most common methods of treating OCD. Although there is research into the potential of genetics treatments for certain types of OCD, those treatments are too early in development to be used yet. These two pages will, therefore, focus on drug therapy for OCD.

Drug therapy for OCD

Although there is no specific drug treatment for OCD, clinicians will frequently prescribe medication given for other psychiatric conditions. These drugs are designed to redress a problem with the normal neurotransmitter levels. Most psychiatric disorders are thought to involve either the dopamine or serotonin systems, so medications that target these systems are typically used to control the symptoms of OCD. There are three types of medication suitable for use in OCD, the first two are considered primarily as antidepressants. The third class is antipsychotics, typically given for psychoses such as schizophrenia; this medication is reserved for the most severe cases of OCD.

Tricyclics

Although tricyclics are primarily considered to be antidepressants, they are also used in anxiety disorders, including OCD. One tricyclic, clomipramine, has been used since the late 1960s with relative success (Jenike *et al.* 1989). Clomipramine works by inhibiting reuptake (drawing a neurotransmitter back from the **synaptic cleft** into the neuron) of serotonin. In fact, it was the success of this particular drug that was responsible for the implication of serotonin in OCD.

SSRIs

SSRIs are the second generation of tricyclics. (SSRI stands for selective serotonin reuptake inhibitors – drugs that leave serotonin in the synapse for longer, boosting its effectiveness.) Generally, SSRIs have a more specific effect on the brain and, as a result, have fewer side effects. This is why they are the medication of choice for OCD and the other anxiety disorders. SSRIs start to work between two and four weeks after starting the treatment. Most trials have found that they are not quite as successful as the tricyclics, but they do successfully reduce symptoms without the same level of side effects.

Antipsychotics

The observation of the connection between the brain reward system and OCD led to the inclusion of dopamine **antagonists** (antipsychotics) as a therapy for those OCD patients resistant to SSRI therapy. Evidence from disorders similar to OCD, such as Tourette's syndrome (an inherited neurological disorder chararacterized by physical and vocal tics), had shown that antipsychotics could be useful in addition to SSRIs. Patients resistant to SSRI therapy tend to show more severe symptoms, and so the use of this medication seems justified. Clinical trials suggested that the atypical antipsychotics (e.g. haloperidol) were effective as long as the patients were also taking SSRIs (e.g. Fineberg *et al.* 2006).

Evaluation of drug treatments

Tricyclics

Most studies of clomipramine show the drug is a more effective treatment than a placebo. Success in drug trials is usually classed as a 25 per cent reduction in symptoms. On this basis, tricyclics were proved to be very successful. However, there are some problems. Tricyclics have unpleasant side effects, especially at the start of treatment. As well as nausea, dizziness and dry mouth, the medication can increase feelings of jitteriness, which the patient might interpret as anxiety. So initially, the symptoms may increase. Many people do not tolerate tricyclics well, and today it is generally considered that SSRIs have reduced side effects and are preferred for this reason.

SSRIs

As with tricyclics, there is a risk that the medication will initially make anxiety symptoms seem worse. SSRIs can also cause sexual problems, such as impotency. There is also an increased risk of suicide in people aged below 18 years of age (Nutt 2005), which has led to these drugs being removed from the list of acceptable treatments for children in the UK. Although the medication does make a difference for some patients, it has been estimated that 40 to 60 per cent of patients do not respond completely to SSRIs alone.

Antipsychotics

Antipsychotics are effective for some of the patients resistant to SSRI treatment alone. This is probably because the severity of the symptoms requires this stronger medicine. However, it has to be recognized that this is a lot of medication, and both sorts of drugs have side effects, such as weight gain, which lead some patients to discontinue the treatment.

General issues with drug treatment

Drug treatment can be successful for 50 to 70 per cent of patients, although the side effects may outweigh the benefits for some people. As with all psychiatric medication, this treatment for OCD will only minimize the symptoms; the reasons for the patient's obsessive-compulsive behaviour will remain. This means the patient has to stay on the medication long-term or seek another way of treating OCD.

Examiners' notes

It is essential that your description (and evaluation) is specifically and *explicitly* aimed at the treatment of OCD rather than drug treatments only. It is easy to get carried away with a discussion of the antidepressant effects of these drugs without actually covering their use with OCD sufferers. Make sure you don't make this mistake.

Essential notes

The fact that antidepressants have some success in the treatment of OCD shows the close relationship between depression and anxiety disorders.

Biological therapies: neurological treatments

A more dramatic treatment for OCD involves direct treatment to the brain. There are three therapies currently used for OCD:

- psychosurgery (reserved for very severe patients)
- deep brain stimulation (DBS)
- transcranial magnetic stimulation (TMS) – a new, experimental treatment that is not so invasive as surgery.

Psychosurgery

Psychosurgery is defined as any operation performed on the brain with the aim of alleviating the symptoms of mental illness. It is sometimes used in the small percentage of patients with OCD who are not helped by SSRIs or a combination of SSRIs and antipsychotics, and is regarded as a last resort. Psychosurgery is not a cure for OCD, but it does make the symptoms easier to deal with.

The operation

The operation most commonly used in OCD is similar to the operation used in depression. It is called a bilateral cingulotomy and it targets the cingulate cortex, an area involved in mediating the brain's emotional centre (the **limbic system**) and prefrontal cortex (the areas that deal with impulse, reward and motivation). The neurosurgeon burns out a tiny portion of this area bilaterally. If the surgery is successful, the symptoms of OCD improve, and depression and anxiety are lifted.

Evaluation of psychosurgery

- *Success in treatment-resistant OCD sufferers* – Psychosurgery has been found to be successful, with Cosgrove (2000) reporting that around 30 per cent of treatment-resistant OCD sufferers are helped. However, this improvement is often hard won, with several patients having more than one surgery.

- *Undesirable side effects* – An important issue is that of side effects. Post-surgery patients report problems sustaining attention and other mild cognitive deficits. More serious are those patients who have gone on to develop epilepsy and, although this number is relatively small, these side effects have to be taken into account before agreeing to the operation.

- *Ethical issues* – The use of psychosurgery has always been controversial. A particular ethical issue is whether or not people suffering from the kind of mental torment that severe OCD must involve are in a position to give informed consent for the surgery.

Deep brain stimulation and transcranial magnetic stimulation

More promising are the newer techniques of deep brain stimulation (DBS) and transcranial magnetic stimulation (TMS).

Deep brain stimulation (DBS)

DBS is a technique whereby tiny electrodes are planted in part of the basal ganglia called the subthalamic nucleus (see Fig. 6); when switched on, the electrodes act to stimulate the brain tissue. Although this is very early days for this procedure, and the number of patients who have undergone this type of surgery is very small, the operation led to a 97 per cent reduction in symptoms in one patient (Fontaine *et al.* 2004).

Transcranial magnetic stimulation (TMS)

TMS is a less invasive technique than DBS. It involves placing magnets onto the surface of the skull in specific locations to stimulate brain cells. It has been mostly used in the treatment of depression, but is increasingly being attempted with other psychiatric conditions. The advantage of TMS is that the patient remains awake while short bursts of magnetic pulses are delivered; the procedure is totally painless. It is not clear exactly how TMS works, but animal models have shown an enhanced release of serotonin after treatment.

Evaluation of DBS and TMS

DBS is expensive but seems to be very successful. TMS, on the other hand, is comparatively cheap and relatively simple. Remember, however, that DBS is brain surgery and should not be considered lightly, as the mechanisms being operated upon are not yet fully understood. However, it seems to work and is a promising area for further investigation.

These newer techniques are included here because they show that the study of treatments for OCD is continually evolving. Both techniques can still be considered experimental, but offer some hope for those patients whose OCD is so severe there are no other options.

Research support

There are very few studies using OCD patients, and the results so far are mixed. However, TMS has to be considered because it is a relatively simple treatment with few side effects. For example, Greenberg *et al.* (1997) studied 12 OCD patients with moderately severe OCD symptoms. They administered single sessions of TMS to the dorsolateral prefrontal cortex or to a control site in a different part of the cortex. This was followed by a significant reduction in compulsive urges that lasted at least eight hours in those patients who received TMS in the dorsolateral prefrontal cortex. The same reduction was not found in those patients who received stimulation in the control site. This study suggests that a single session of TMS might reduce compulsive urges by changing neuronal activity well beyond the initial period of stimulation.

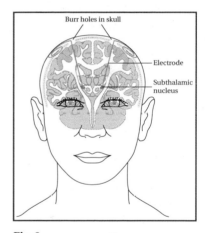

Fig. 6
The technique of deep brain stimulation

Psychological therapies: behavioural

Behaviour therapy (BT) concentrates on modifying observable behaviour. It is not concerned with the underlying cognitive processes. This means that BT is unlikely to offer any real treatment for the obsessions part of the condition because these are disrupted cognitions. However, BT might be useful in the treatment of the more overt symptoms of the disorder, the compulsions. It mainly treats these using the exposure techniques of modelling and ERP (exposure and response prevention).

Modelling

Two of the earliest behavioural techniques used in the treatment of OCD are modelling and systematic desensitization. In both of these techniques, Pavlovian (classical conditioning) techniques are used to reduce anxiety in the patients.

Modelling is based on social learning theory (SLT) Bandura *et al.* 1969). This states that we learn some of our behaviour by watching others (models). We internalize modelled behaviour, but whether we reproduce it or not depends on what the consequences of the behaviour were for the model. In this type of treatment, the therapist simply models the behaviour the patient regards as dangerous. So, for a patient with a contamination fear, the therapist will hold the dirty cloth without signs of fear or anxiety. The client will at first feel anxious but after some time will become calmer and will also be asked to handle the cloth. It is hoped that the therapist's behaviour will have shown the client that the consequences of handling the cloth are not to be feared. The technical term for the disappearance of the fear is **extinction**.

Systematic desensitization is essentially the same process as modelling, but delivered at a slower pace, with the client being trained in relaxation techniques and then exposed in stages to the object of their fear in much the same way that phobias are treated. At each stage, the client works on mastering their fear before going on to the next (see p. 72). This type of therapy does work for anxiety disorders, but is thought to be more useful when the client has a specific fear.

Examiners' notes

When describing modelling as a technique, you should try to focus on how this has been used in the treatment of OCD rather than in the treatment of some other disorder (such as a phobia).

Evaluation of modelling

- *Limited range of application* – This type of therapy may not be easily applied to all types of OCD. Where the obsessions are associated with the fear of contamination, the patient may have a list of specific things that trigger their anxiety (e.g. a dirty cloth, a used syringe and messy kitchen). In this case, you can see how modelling might relieve their anxiety when the therapist shows them there is nothing to fear. However, what do you do when the fear is not as tangible? For example, what if someone avoids the number three because they think harm may come to loved ones? It is difficult to see how the therapist could successfully demonstrate that there is nothing to worry about here.

Exposure and response prevention (ERP)

ERP is a method designed to stop people carrying out their compulsions. Again, it uses Pavlovian conditioning techniques to convince the client that they have nothing to be worried about if they do not go through with a compulsion. If a patient feels the need to wash their hands after touching a door handle because of a contamination fear, the therapist will simply ask them not to. The client has to refrain from their compulsion for a set period, e.g. between therapy sessions. As you can imagine, this can be extremely difficult for them at first. However, with the addition of relaxation techniques and support from family, the fear caused by the intrusive thought will gradually fade away.

Evaluation of ERP

- *Neurological support* – ERP has been shown to be successful, even to the point where the effects of the training can be seen to reduce overactive areas of the brain (Saxena *et al.* 2008). This improvement can happen after a relatively short series of therapy sessions (Saxena and colleagues used a four-week intensive session). It has even been shown that computer-mediated ERP training can be successful (Baer *et al.* 1988).

- *Associated reduction of obsessional thinking* – ERP seems to work by breaking the ritual of the compulsions. There is evidence that shows that once the ritualized behaviour stops, the obsessional thinking reduces too, (Rachman *et al.* 1970). ERP works for between 55 and 85 per cent of people prepared to try it.

- *ERP + medication* – There are many people with OCD who are either resistant to trying ERP or who try and fail in the first few days. There is some evidence that adding in medication might help a proportion of these people.

Overall evaluation of behavioural therapy

- *The commitment of the client* – BT techniques seem to be very effective, but really only when the client wants to recover. Although ERP is successful, this type of therapy requires the client be prepared for discomfort (at least initially) and hard work. This type of therapy is not for everyone.

- *The importance of cognitions* – The larger problem lies, perhaps, in treating the ideas that cause the association between an intrusive thought and a compulsion; to do this, attention needs to be paid to cognitive processes. For this reason, the fusion of cognitive therapy and behavioural therapy seems to make more sense for a more rounded therapy for OCD.

Examiners' notes

Writing the full term 'exposure and response prevention' is time-consuming, so the usual (and accepted) way to deal with this in an exam is to state the full term the first time and then use ERP after that.

Essential notes

The success of ERP leads to the suggestion that the OCD behaviour is self-perpetuating; people become less anxious during and immediately after their ritualized compulsive behaviour, but this gradually wears off. This increased anxiety makes the possibility of intrusive thought more likely, and so the cycle continues. Break the cycle, and the client improves.

Examiners' notes

Look at the 'Strong answer' to question 2(c) on p. 149 for an excellent description and evaluation of ERP given in around 250 words in response to a question worth 10 marks.

Examiners' notes

Stating that behavioural therapy is 'not for everyone' can be elaborated if you think of the implications of this statement. A major problem with using behavioural therapy for OCD is resistance to the therapy process. The therapy can be hard work, requiring persistence and a high level of motivation on the part of the patient. The major implication of this problem is that, unlike drug therapies used to treat OCD, therapeutic success is highly correlated with the patient's level of motivation.

Psychological therapies: CBT

Behaviour therapy is effective, but therapists realized that it could be improved after seeing the success of Aaron Beck's cognitive-behavioural therapy (CBT) for depression (see p. 40). CBT attempts to connect the best features of cognitive psychology with the therapeutic ideas of behavioural psychology. So, instead of the emphasis only being on observable behaviour (as behavioural therapy advocates), CBT focuses on the thinking processes that contribute to the initial development of the disorder.

The principles of CBT

(see p. 40)

CBT aims to challenge – and hence alter – the irrational thinking that underlies OCD. It does this in therapy sessions, but also by giving clients homework to do between sessions. A typical homework assignment for OCD would be to keep a diary of the incidence of intrusive thoughts and emotions. CBT aims to rid the client of their anxieties as well as teaching them strategies to avoid compulsions. It helps clients to uncover information about the cycle of intrusive thoughts and compulsions so that they can understand what is happening to them. In this way, it offers a more rounded treatment than behavioural or cognitive therapy alone.

Neutralizing intrusive thoughts

Therapists such as Paul Salkovskis expanded these ideas to OCD. Salkovskis (e.g. 1996) realized the people with OCD blamed themselves for the intrusive thoughts, believing that, as they had had the thought, they were responsible for putting it right. Their compulsion could, therefore, be seen as a neutralizing action – either thinking or behaving in a positive way to make up for the negative thought (e.g. saying a prayer a fixed number of times in order to neutralize an intrusive thought about harming a family member). Eventually, the neutralizing act is repeated so often that it becomes compulsive (e.g. constantly saying the prayer). At the same time, the neutralizing action becomes not quite enough to dispel the negative thought, which gradually becomes obsessive, leading to the person having to repeat the action more and more frequently. This is the beginning of OCD. This idea fits in with what people with OCD feel about their compulsions – that if they do not go through with them, either the thought will come true or someone close to them will be hurt in some way.

CBT and OCD

Clark (1988) believed that the best way to treat OCD was to correct the client's faulty thinking (in the example above, the idea of harming a loved one). If that idea is corrected, then the client will have no reason to go through with their compulsion. Salkovskis took this one step further and focused the therapy on the explanation for people's obsessive-compulsive actions.

Examiners' notes

The exam makes very precise demands about therapies being specifically directed towards the treatment of OCD. Therefore, while it is fine to outline the principles of CBT, these should be directed explicitly towards the treatment of OCD.

Essential notes

Whereas behavioural therapy focused on the compulsion, cognitive therapy focused on the obsession. This means that *together* they make a more rounded and better-defined treatment for OCD.

Habituation training

One simple CBT technique is habituation training, whereby the therapist encourages their clients to think their obsessive thoughts repeatedly. By being forced to confront the things that most frighten them, clients should experience a reduction in the level of fear they feel. In other words, they are encouraged to become more familiar with the concept. At first, the client may only do this within the therapy session, but homework may be set asking the client to confront their fears outside the therapy session. The client is asked to imagine their thoughts and keep picturing them for as long as they can without having to do their neutralizing action. The client repeats this until they no longer feel the need for the compulsion. Essentially, they become used to (habituated to) the thought that once scared them.

Evaluation of CBT

Limitations of CBT as a treatment for OCD

- *The client's honesty and motivation* – The biggest problem with this method is that it relies on the patient doing the task and reporting back their progress honestly. Client participation is essential because if people show the corrected behaviour only in the therapy sessions, they will soon remit when asked to cope without therapy. In fact, remission rates (people coming back for more therapy) are quite high for CBT, reported at 40 per cent by Salkovskis and Kirk (1996). Therefore, CBT does not offer an easy solution, but it does offer a potential way of treating OCD for those patients who really want to get better and are prepared to work hard towards their own recovery.

CBT in addition to drug treatments

- *The supportive effect of medication* – CBT has been shown to be more effective when the client is also taking medication (SSRIs or in more serious cases, SSRIs *and* antipsychotics) (Kampman *et al.* 2002). Kampman and colleagues examined the effectiveness of combining CBT with SSRIs in cases where OCD patients had been unresponsive to SSRI treatment on its own. Fourteen patients who had shown only 8 per cent reduction in OCD symptoms on SSRI drugs alone, experienced a much greater reduction in symptoms (41 per cent) when drugs were combined with 12 sessions of CBT.

Answering A2 examination questions

AO1, AO2 and AO3

The A2 examination assesses three 'assessment objectives' known as AO1, AO2 and AO3:

- **AO1** assesses your ability to recall and show your understanding of scientific knowledge – e.g. describing a theory or study.
- **AO2** assesses your ability to analyse and evaluate scientific knowledge – e.g. evaluating a theory in terms of research support.
- **AO3** is concerned with 'How Science Works' – e.g. methodological criticisms of research studies.

Be prepared

A2 questions will often occur as questions in parts and these different parts can also occur with different mark allocations. For example, question (a) on a particular topic could be worth:

- 4, 5 or 9 marks (for exams up to 2011), or
- 4 or 8 marks (for exams from 2012 onwards).

This means that not only should you be aware of all the topics on which you may be questioned, but you should also have practised examination type answers for these to fit the varying mark allocations. For example, if you have covered the Unit 4 topic of schizophrenia and included the dopamine hypothesis as one of your biological explanations of schizophrenia, then you should be able to produce a 'shorter version' outline of the theory to answer a shorter 4- or 5-mark question, as well as being able to produce a 'longer version' outline of the explanation for an 8- or 9-mark question.

Use your time wisely

Examinations are held under time constraints, and so you must use your time wisely. Students often waste far too much time doing things that are not required, e.g. stating '*In this essay I am going to…*' or providing irrelevant information. This means that they don't have sufficient time to do the things they *should* be doing, and so lose many of the marks available.

Read for understanding

When reading a question, ensure that you fully understand its requirements. Far too often, students focus in on a certain word or phrase that identifies the particular topic being examined and base their answer solely on that. After expending much time and effort, they then realize that they are not answering the question as it should be answered or discover they cannot answer the question as well as they first imagined. Therefore, make sure you have read the entire question and fully understand its requirements *before* starting to answer it.

Make a plan

When you have fully understood the question and have decided that you are able to answer it, then it's also a good idea to prepare a small plan of points to be made, possibly in bullet point form numbered in a logical order. This not only gives you a plan to follow, but also protects against forgetting some of these points mid-answer. It also helps you to engage with the material, which again is a useful strategy towards producing higher-quality answers.

Effective evaluation

Students can often become confused, especially under exam conditions, as to what to include in an answer requiring evaluation. A good way to combat this problem is to include the 'recipe' method as a regular part of your revision. Thus, when planning the evaluative content for an answer, list all the different elements that could comprise evaluation. This will vary slightly from question to question depending on the wording, but generally you should have:

- examples of research that both supports and weakens points being made
- practical applications
- methodological points (especially in questions specifically about research studies)
- implications
- theoretical support.

You may not actually use all of this material, but you should produce answers with good breadth of evaluation, as well as reducing the chances of having insufficient material or of using non-creditworthy material.

Elaboration in AO2 evaluation

AO2 assesses your ability to analyse and evaluate scientific knowledge relevant to a specific topic area. When allocating marks for AO2 questions, examiners look for appropriateness and *elaboration*. One way of elaborating effectively is to use the 'three-point rule'. This involves *identifying* the critical point, *justifying* it, and then *explaining* why this is good (or bad) for the theory or explanation being evaluated.

Using the right terminology

As well as having a good understanding of psychological concepts and topics, you also need to be able to communicate your understanding to others. A useful and simple means of achieving this is by using psychological terminology wherever relevant in exam answers. Try to develop a good working knowledge of psychological terminology throughout your studies – and practise using it – in order to become proficient in this skill. However, be careful not to use jargon for its own sake, as this can lead to the danger of writing incomprehensible answers that appear muddled.

Example questions and answers with examiner comments

On the following pages you will find sample questions followed by sample average and strong answers, and also tinted boxes containing the comments and advice of examiners. Answers refer to content within the revision section of this book and additional content, providing you with opportunity to consolidate and extend your revision and research.

Examiners' notes

It is worth placing obvious 'tags' on your evaluation. For example, instead of just describing a supporting research study, you should preface any such description with a phrase such as 'This claim is supported by research by... which showed that...'

Examiners' notes

Below is an example of the 'three point rule' for elaboration (AO2) if your criticism is that a study lacks ecological validity:

'This study lacks validity (*identification*), because research by X failed to replicate the findings of Y (*justification*), which therefore means that the findings of Y's research cannot be generalized beyond the specific situation of that experiment (*explanation*)'.

Examiners' notes

Unlike the topics in Unit 3, there is no *requirement* for Issues, Debates and Approaches (IDA) material in your answers. However, that doesn't mean that any such material would fail to earn marks, as it would still be credited under AO2/AO3. If you do include any IDA material (e.g. gender or cultural bias, reductionism, real-world applications), don't just tag it on to the end of an answer, but make sure it is effective by elaborating the points.

Example Paper AQA Unit 4 Psychopathology: Schizophrenia

Question 1

*Outline and evaluate **one or more** psychological explanations of schizophrenia.* [**9 + 16 marks** (2009 onwards)]
[**8 + 16 marks** (2012 onwards)]

There are a number of important requirements in this question, so it pays to read it carefully.
- It requires both AO1 description ('outline') and AO2 evaluation ('evaluate'). The marks in brackets indicate the number of marks available for each aspect, so for this question, about one-third of your answer should be AO1, and two-thirds should be AO2.
- The offer of 'one or more' should be considered carefully. Writing about more than one explanation offers the opportunity for increased breadth; restricting yourself to just one offers greater depth. It really is your call: either approach is acceptable, and neither one is more highly valued than the other.

- The question asks for *psychological* explanations (e.g. cognitive, psychodynamic), so any inclusion of biological explanations would have to be made explicitly relevant as part of an AO2 critical point.
- Although the question does not specifically *require* research evidence, it is always a good idea to back up any assertions with solid evidence. You could then also gain AO2 credit for methodological evaluation of this evidence. Using research evidence also makes your answer appear more authoritative and better informed, and so is more likely to push your answer into the higher mark bands.

Average answer

The first psychological explanation is the cognitive approach. This argues that people with schizophrenia have problems filtering out inappropriate information in their world and so are more likely to experience delusions or hallucinations. People with schizophrenia may also fail to activate schemas. Schemas are ways of understanding situations and knowing what to expect and what we might ignore. For example, if we go to a restaurant, we know what to expect and so would not be surprised by someone suddenly appearing and asking us what we would like to eat. This explanation is criticized however, because there is no really convincing evidence to support this claim. The explanation is also criticized because it is reductionist and ignores the important role played by other influences, for example genetic influences or environmental influences, both of which have been shown to influence schizophrenia. For example, the dopamine hypothesis explains schizophrenia in terms of excess dopamine activity in the brain. Cognitive explanations do not take this into consideration, which is why it is reductionist.

A second psychological explanation is the expressed emotion explanation. This claims that when schizophrenics live in an environment where there is high expressed emotion, e.g. high levels of ☛

The description of this explanation is both accurate and appropriate, but it lacks development. We are given an irrelevant exposition of how schemas might operate in a restaurant, but not how they may (or, rather, may not) operate in the mind of a schizophrenic. Evaluation is fairly superficial: an appropriate point is identified (that such an explanation is reductionist), but it is not explained why this cognitive explanation is considered reductionist, apart from making the fairly basic point that it doesn't take into consideration other explanations of schizophrenia.

criticism or concern, they are more likely to relapse than schizophrenics who live in an environment characterized by low levels of expressed emotion. The expressed emotion explanation is supported by cross-cultural studies, which show that in countries where schizophrenia is not stigmatized, levels of expressed emotion are lower and relapse rates are also lower. The expressed emotion explanation is criticized, however, because many schizophrenics live apart from their families and have little to do with them, so they would not be exposed to high levels of expressed emotion from other family members. Despite this, they still do not recover, which challenges the claim that their schizophrenia is maintained by being constantly exposed to high levels of expressed emotion in their family environment.

A third explanation is the psychodynamic explanation of schizophrenia. This sees schizophrenia being caused by a disturbed family environment, known as the schizophrenogenic family. Bateson came up with the idea of the double-bind hypothesis, where family members, particularly parents, give conflicting messages about what is acceptable behaviour. This explanation is criticized because studies in this area did not use control groups and also the families were studied retrospectively, so it is possible that it was not the 'sick' family that caused the person's schizophrenia, but it was living with a schizophrenic that caused the family members to act in that 'sick' way.

Sociocultural explanations of schizophrenia stress the contributory role of the culture in which a schizophrenic lives. There are a number of contributing factors. The first of these is the socio-economic status of the individual. Schizophrenia is more likely to be found among lower socio-economic groups. It is possible, however, that this doesn't cause the schizophrenia, but that people drift into these groups when they are rejected by the rest of society (the social drift hypothesis). A second factor is that schizophrenia is found more among immigrant populations living in the UK than among non-immigrants. However, this may be due to a cultural bias when diagnosing schizophrenia, or the fact that the behaviour or beliefs of some immigrant groups may appear strange or even frightening to the doctors doing the diagnosis, who are then more likely to diagnose a mental disorder because of this strangeness. Alternatively, it could be the case that ☞

This is a decent outline of the expressed emotion explanation, although it might have earned more credit if it had explained why high levels of EE are associated with the maintenance of schizophrenia. The second two-thirds of this paragraph are good, particularly the last part, although more might have been done with this material to increase its impact.

As elsewhere in this essay, we are introduced to the central claim of the explanation (that schizophrenia is something to do with disturbed family functioning), but it is not explained how schizophrenia develops as a result of this exposure. The two critical points are appropriate, but insufficiently elaborated to earn more than basic marks.

Again, this is accurate and appropriate, but again there is insufficient detail to lift the answer into the higher mark bands. The student has probably been too ambitious in trying to cover so many different explanations, and this has compromised the amount of detail they have been able to provide.

members of immigrant populations find it more stressful living in another country, and this causes some of the symptoms (e.g. paranoia) that are associated with schizophrenia.

Average answer: overall comment

Lack of detail has been the problem throughout this essay: there is good material, but not enough is done with it. By choosing four distinct types of explanation, this student has tried to do much too much and has ended up with a superficial gloss-over of all four rather than a more detailed discussion of just one (or two) of these. There is also the problem of not paying enough attention to the specific requirements of the question, which asks for research evidence, of which there is very little. This is not disastrous, as the answer would still earn marks consistent with a C grade, but there is the potential for a much higher mark (and therefore a much higher grade) if the coverage had been less ambitious.

Strong answer

The cognitive explanation of schizophrenia believes that the disturbed thinking processes found in schizophrenia are the cause rather than the consequence of schizophrenia. One part of this explanation is that the experience of schizophrenia arises from a failure in the attention systems, which work to filter out stimuli in the world that are not worth processing. If there is a failure in this system, then the world becomes unpredictable, and the person is inundated by external stimuli, which they are unable to interpret appropriately, leading to delusions and hallucinations. The relevance of attentional failure in schizophrenia has been demonstrated in experiments where participants are required to pay attention to one stimulus while ignoring another. For example, in the Stroop test, people who are schizophrenic find it very difficult to ignore the written word when trying to identify the colour the word is written in (Barch *et al.* 1999). Research has also suggested that cognitive problems such as attentional failure may have a genetic origin. Faraone *et al.* (1995) found that relatives of schizophrenic patients tended to show similar (although milder) cognitive impairments, such as attention failure, to those shown by their schizophrenic relatives.

Frith (1993) explains schizophrenia as a failure to understand the context of a particular situation. For example, situations that most people would interpret as being completely normal (e.g. being looked at in the street) might be interpreted with feelings of paranoia by a person with schizophrenia. Frith claims that this inability to understand the motivation or actions of ☞

This is a very competent opening paragraph. Rather than just stating that there may be an attention problem in schizophrenia, this student explains *why* a failure of the attentional system might be implicated in schizophrenia. This explanation is both accurate and detailed. Research evidence is offered as evaluation, and this, too, is both appropriate and accurate, as well as being suitably elaborated. A good start.

Including a second aspect of the cognitive explanation adds breadth to this answer. The description is suitably detailed and so has sufficient depth for the higher mark bands. The latter half of this paragraph provides research evidence as well as appropriately elaborated AO2 material; this again places this answer solidly in the higher mark bands.

others is caused by underactivity in the frontal lobes of the brain. Liddle *et al.* (1992) provide some evidence for this explanation, showing differences in cerebral blood flow in the brains of schizophrenics compared to non-schizophrenics when they are interpreting ambiguous situations. The problem with this explanation is that although there is some evidence that the frontal lobes of schizophrenics are less active than in non-schizophrenics, it is difficult to judge whether this is a cause or consequence of schizophrenia – that is, whether the lack of contextual understanding causes the other symptoms of schizophrenia, or is just one of them.

Hemsley (1993) suggests that the main cognitive problem in schizophrenia is that there is a breakdown in how the person deals with the relationship between information that is already stored in memory (schemas) and new information coming in from the environment. Hemsley claims that schizophrenics fail to use these schemas properly, and as a result, each situation is treated as being completely novel, which would be very confusing. Hemsley also argues that the breakdown between internal schemas and external stimuli means that schizophrenics sometimes cannot tell the source of internal thoughts. This means they are interpreted as being voices that arise from someone else and so are experienced as auditory hallucinations.

Hemsley has attempted to provide a neurological basis for his theory, in particular highlighting the role of the hippocampus and related brain structures (such as the amygdala). However, there is little clear evidence to support this. For example, a study in Finland by Tanskanen *et al.* (2005) compared hippocampus and amygdala volume in schizophrenics and a control group of normal individuals. They found no significant volume or shape differences in the hippocampus or amygdala between the schizophrenics and controls. This failure to provide neurological evidence for the cognitive explanation challenges the claim that these cognitive problems are a cause of schizophrenic symptoms rather than a consequence.

Cognitive explanations, such as those proposed by Frith and Hemsley, might be seen as reductionist in much the same way that biological psychological explanations are reductionist. They argue that the complex experience and behaviours that are described as schizophrenia can be reduced to faulty neuropsychological processes such as those that normally operate in the frontal lobes ☞

This paragraph is entirely descriptive and so picks up solid AO1 credit for its accurate and detailed exposition of the role of the failure to activate schemas in schizophrenics.

This paragraph, the second of two linked to Hemsley's theory, is a very well-elaborated discussion of the failure to provide neurological support for this explanation and is high-quality AO2.

Biological explanations of schizophrenia are often described as being reductionist, but in this case, the student has made a very good case for cognitive explanations also displaying a reductionist bias. This is well explained and fully deserves credit.

of the brain, or a failure of the attentional system. However, because of the many different characteristics of the disorder, cognitive explanations may not be able to explain the origins of all its symptoms, although they do provide a believable explanation for hallucinations and delusions.

Strong answer: overall comment

Overall, this is a very well-constructed and accurate discussion of cognitive explanations of schizophrenia. There is plenty of research evidence, which contributes to the overall impression that this is an *informed* response to the question. There is an appropriate balance between AO1 and AO2, and this answer would, therefore, easily fall into the Grade A standard.

Question 2

Part (a)

Outline clinical characteristics of schizophrenia. [**5 marks** (2009 onwards)] [**4 marks** (2012 onwards)]

- The term 'clinical characteristics' does not have one specific meaning, so could be a brief outline of the different forms of schizophrenia and their characteristics, although it is most likely to mean the 'symptoms' of schizophrenia.

- As this question is only worth a few marks, you would not be expected to cover *all* the possible symptoms of schizophrenia. A good strategy would be to illustrate the concept of positive symptoms with a couple of examples and then the same with negative symptoms. For 5 marks, about 150 words would probably suffice; for 4 marks (2012 exams onwards), 125 words or so would be enough.

Average answer

There are two main types of clinical characteristics in schizophrenia. These are the positive and negative symptoms. Positive clinical characteristics are symptoms like hearing voices or seeing hallucinations. A person who sees things that aren't there, or hears things that aren't there, is experiencing hallucinations. Another important positive symptom is experiencing delusions, like a delusion of grandeur, e.g. a person imagining that they are famous. Negative symptoms include things like not being able to experience pleasure or responding to questions using a meaningless phrase.

There is nothing really wrong with this answer – the material used is appropriate and accurate, but it simply lacks detail. In order to push this from a Grade C standard answer to a Grade A standard answer, it simply needs detail. Contrast this answer to the strong answer below – they are similar in content, but the strong answer is better developed (not just *longer*).

Strong answer

The symptoms of schizophrenia are divided into positive symptoms, where the person shows behaviours that a normal person would not have, and negative ☛

symptoms, which are an absence of behaviours that a normal person should have.

A person diagnosed with schizophrenia is likely to experience delusions and hallucinations. The most common hallucinations are auditory hallucinations, where the person with schizophrenia may hear voices, even though there is nobody actually there. Delusions involve the individual losing control of their thoughts. For example, they may have paranoid delusions, where they believe that they are being followed or spied upon by others. Negative symptoms can result in the individual appearing apathetic and without emotion (flatness of affect). They may also show anhedonia, an inability to respond to pleasurable experiences. In order to be diagnosed with schizophrenia, the individual must be experiencing at least two of the more important positive symptoms (delusions and hallucinations) for over a month.

In this answer, the 'clinical characteristics' are interpreted in terms of the positive and negative symptoms, along with the necessary requirements for diagnosis of schizophrenia. This is a good general response to the question and is sufficiently detailed to receive the maximum marks available.

Part (b)

*Explain issues associated with the classification **and/or** diagnosis of schizophrenia.* **[10 marks]**

- Questions that use the term 'explain' can be hard to decipher, as sometimes 'explain' can imply both AO1 and AO2, whereas sometimes (as here), it is AO2 only. It is exam board advice simply to ignore the injunction and answer the question, and this is one occasion where that advice is helpful.
- Remember to cover at least two issues. Covering *one* issue would count as 'partial performance' and would lose you marks, although covering too many may make your answer too superficial.

- Identifying the issues would be considered the product of analysis (and therefore AO2), and further elaboration of those issues would push the mark up into the higher mark bands.
- Reliability and validity are the usual issues in this context, although there are others, such as labelling and stigmatizing, overlap with other disorders and so on.
- Note that this question is about schizophrenia and should be restricted to this disorder.

Average answer

There are several issues that could affect the diagnosis and classification of schizophrenia. The first of these is reliability. Reliability means that if a classification system is used by different people, then they should produce the same outcome. If they do produce the same outcome (i.e. a diagnosis of schizophrenia), then they have inter-rater reliability. Early versions of the DSM were less reliable than later versions such as DSM-IV, and are therefore considered to be of more use to psychiatrists. ☞

The second issue is validity, whether classifying someone as schizophrenic means that the symptoms that they experience are the same and that they respond to treatment in the same way. If different patients respond to treatment in the same way (e.g. through drug treatments), then diagnosis has predictive validity. However, evidence suggests this is not the case, as drug treatments are not successful with all patients, and some people never recover from schizophrenia, whereas others recover more or less completely.

A third issue is the ethics of diagnosis. Some psychologists believe that by diagnosing someone with schizophrenia, they will be stigmatizing them, which will change their life for the worse because of the way other people will react towards them. However, others disagree, claiming that by diagnosing someone with schizophrenia, it makes their condition less frightening for them.

This is a good, if undeveloped, answer. As so often with 'average' answers, topics are raised, but not really elaborated. Reliability, validity and ethics are all appropriate issues in the diagnosis and classification of schizophrenia, but this is an AO2 question, so more analysis and evaluation are needed to push the answer up into the higher mark bands. One way of achieving this is to add research evidence to support the claims being made. As it is, this answer would be of about Grade C standard.

Strong answer

Reliability in the diagnosis of schizophrenia is very important. This has been difficult to achieve in the past, particularly when psychiatrists in different countries have used different classification systems. For example, in Europe, ICD-10 is used, whereas in the USA, DSM-IV is used. These classification systems have a different emphasis on the symptoms that are necessary for a diagnosis of schizophrenia. DSM requires symptoms to be present for at least six months for schizophrenia to be diagnosed, whereas ICD requires only one month. Because of this, it is possible that a person can be diagnosed with schizophrenia in one country but not in another, making the diagnosis of the disorder less reliable. This was demonstrated in a study by Copeland *et al.* (1971), who gave a description of a patient to US and UK psychiatrists. Sixty-nine percent of the US psychiatrists diagnosed schizophrenia, whereas only 2 per cent of the UK psychiatrists diagnosed schizophrenia.

A second issue involved in the diagnosis of schizophrenia is whether the condition actually does exist and whether it is distinct from other forms of mental disorder. A validity problem is that there is considerable overlap with conditions such as bipolar disorder. People with bipolar disorder also ☛

experience delusions and hallucinations; therefore diagnosing a person with schizophrenia may lead to a faulty diagnosis, because schizophrenia shares these important symptoms with bipolar disorder. A valid diagnosis, therefore, relies upon the psychiatrist's experience rather than simply the use of a classification system. One way around this problem is to diagnose on the basis of the severity of symptoms experienced by the individual, rather than just whether they are present.

There are two clear issues covered in this answer: reliability and validity. It is well focused throughout, and the 'explanation' of the two issues is sound and appropriate to the requirements of the question, showing good understanding of how these issues impact upon the diagnosis of schizophrenia. There is a good deal of appropriate elaboration, which would push this answer into the top mark band, and it clearly demonstrates a Grade A standard answer.

Part (c)

*Outline and evaluate **one** biological therapy used in the treatment of schizophrenia.* [**4 marks + 6 marks**]

- This question indicates the number of marks available for AO1 (4) and for AO2 (6). As is always the case, this should dictate how much you write for each in response.
- Note also that the therapy *must* be biological and you should only write about *one*.

- The most likely therapy would be drug therapy. This might be restricted to conventional antipsychotics or may also include a brief outline (most probably their mode of action) of atypical antipsychotics.
- Evaluation might include a consideration of the drugs' effectiveness, ethical issues in the use of drug treatments and so on.

Average answer

A common biological therapy used in the treatment of schizophrenia is antipsychotic drugs. These work by blocking the action of dopamine. Schizophrenia is thought to be caused by too much dopamine activity in the brain, which leads to the positive symptoms such as delusions and hallucinations. Antipsychotic drugs block the receptors that receive dopamine, so that the symptoms are reduced.

Drug treatments of schizophrenia are widely used because they are effective in reducing the positive symptoms. However, they are not effective in the treatment of negative symptoms, where psychological treatments are more likely to be used. Drug treatments are also more likely to have side effects. For example, drugs can become addictive if taken continuously. Drug treatments also tend to have side effects, which are often disturbing enough to stop the patient taking the drug. Drug treatments may not offer a complete cure – they may only have a positive effect on the symptoms of schizophrenia so long as the patient is taking the drugs. As soon as they stop taking the drug, the symptoms (and thus the schizophrenia) reappears. Finally, there ☞

Although this part of the question is only worth 4 marks, it still requires some elaboration to gain the full 4 marks. The student could, for example, have distinguished between the action of conventional and atypical antipsychotics. As it is, this response would probably only gain 2 of the 4 marks available.

A number of critical claims are made in this answer (e.g. that drug treatments are effective in reducing positive symptoms but not negative symptoms). While this is more or less true, the point would be made more effectively (and earn more marks) if evidence had been used to support it. The other critical points tend to be more general rather than specific to the treatment of schizophrenia. Some of these points are true (e.g. that there are side effects), whereas others are not (e.g. that they are addictive). However, none are focused specifically on schizophrenia, which they need to be to earn marks. The concept of a 'chemical straitjacket' is never explained, although consideration of the motivational effects of drug treatment is a good point. Overall, this answer fails to address the explicit requirements of the question, although it would be easy enough to take this material and mould it into a Grade A answer.

are ethical issues in the use of drugs for the treatment of schizophrenia. The use of antipsychotics has been likened to a chemical straitjacket, and they also take away the personal responsibility of the schizophrenic for their own recovery.

Strong answer

Drug treatments for schizophrenia use antipsychotic drugs. These drugs are used to reduce the action of dopamine in the brain, which is thought to be the cause of the positive symptoms of schizophrenia. The main form of antipsychotic are the conventional antipsychotics, which act as dopamine antagonists, binding to dopamine receptors, reducing the effects of dopamine, and so reducing the positive symptoms of schizophrenia. By reducing dopamine activity, antipsychotic drugs can reduce the hallucinations and delusions that are typical of schizophrenia. The atypical antipsychotics work by temporarily blocking the dopamine receptors, thus allowing relatively normal levels of dopamine transmission. Atypical antipsychotics are also thought to block serotonin receptors in the brain as well.

The effectiveness of drug treatments for schizophrenia has been demonstrated in a number of studies, although most of these studies have a follow-up period of just a few months. As schizophrenia is a life-long condition, this does not tell us much about their long-term effectiveness. Rzewuska (2002) found that symptoms tend to return if patients stop taking the drug. In addition, it is generally estimated that about 25 per cent of patients do not respond to conventional antipsychotics, and these drugs appear to be ineffective in the treatment of the negative symptoms of schizophrenia. It is claimed that atypical antipsychotics are more effective at treating the negative symptoms of schizophrenia, although a meta-analysis that compared atypical with conventional antipsychotics (Leucht *et al.* 1999) found little evidence to support this. In addition, the most effective atypical antipsychotic, clozapine, can cause suppression of the immune system, which can be fatal.

This is accurate, appropriate and sufficiently detailed to be worth the full 4 AO1 marks available. Contrast this to the material provided in the average answer – it is essentially the same material, but the extra elaboration is the difference between a relatively weak answer and a very strong one.

This is well written and offers a concise and entirely appropriate evaluation of both conventional and atypical antipsychotics. Although it is not necessary to cover both, they have been woven together effectively in this answer. The elaboration of these points is clear, and there is, likewise, a clear logic in the way the points are developed. This would be worth maximum marks and is clearly equivalent to a Grade A standard answer for the 6 AO2 marks available.

Question 3

*Discuss the use of **two or more** psychological therapies as treatments of schizophrenia.* **[9 + 16 marks** (2009 onwards)] **[8 + 16 marks** (2012 onwards)]

- The use of the word 'discuss' in a question should not cause you concern. It is just another way of asking you to cover AO1 and AO2 in your answer.
- In this question you are asked to cover at least two *psychological* therapies (*not biological* therapies). Be careful about spreading yourself too thinly: covering more than two could lead to a response that is too superficial in both its coverage and in the elaboration of any evaluative points.

- An essential requirement of this question is that discussion is limited to therapies as they are used in the treatment of schizophrenia rather than general discussions of, for example, CBT or psychoanalysis.

Average answer

Cognitive-behavioural therapy is used to change the way people think about things. This has several stages. People are asked to keep a diary about what they think and the way that they feel. The therapist then helps them to see the connection between thinking negatively and feeling bad. The therapist will also challenge some of the beliefs that the schizophrenic has, for example that the 'voices' that they are hearing come from God. The patient is then taught to think more positively about things so that their symptoms are reduced.

There is a lot of research that supports CBT. One study followed an American woman over a period of four years. She was a graduate and came from a middle-class Christian family. Before receiving CBT she had been in hospital 12 times in seven years and was on daily medication for her schizophrenia. She then received CBT for a period of three years. After receiving CBT, her symptoms were reduced and she showed a significant improvement in her behaviour. Also she did not have to go back into hospital after receiving CBT.

It is believed that many schizophrenics have particular problems with their social skills, and this contributes to their social drift into loneliness and alienation. By teaching schizophrenics interpersonal skills, it is believed that they will be better able to deal with their lives, and therefore the illness will not have such a negative effect on them. Social skills training involves helping schizophrenics to deal with social interactions and stressful situations, as well as helping them become more self-aware and to manage their symptoms more effectively. ☞

There are a number of things wrong with the treatment of CBT in these opening two paragraphs. First, it is far too superficial and lacks the detail typical of a higher-grade answer. Second, much of the description of CBT is general rather than being tied specifically to the treatment of schizophrenia. Third, the lengthy description of a single case study is unnecessary and fails to make an explicit evaluative point other than hinting at the fact that this case demonstrates that CBT can be effective as a treatment of schizophrenia.

A problem with this sort of therapy is that the improvements appear to be short-lived, and the patients revert to their old ways when the intervention has finished. However, as a form of therapy it has been shown to be valuable when used together with antipsychotic medication. Studies have shown that people are less likely to be hospitalized because of their schizophrenia if they receive the 'double' treatment of social skills training and antipsychotic medication.

A third type of psychological therapy is family intervention therapy. This involves dealing with the family of a schizophrenic because the environment in which a schizophrenic lives can often make their symptoms worse. Therapists can visit the family and teach them how to recognize the symptoms and how to deal with their schizophrenic family member. Another important aspect of this type of therapy is expressed emotion. The family of a schizophrenic can often make things worse by trying too hard to help them or even by being hostile towards them. This is known as high expressed emotion, and this has been shown to increase the likelihood of a schizophrenic having a relapse. The family can be taught not to act in such a way, so that the schizophrenic is less likely to relapse.

Studies have shown that family intervention therapy is an effective way of reducing the likelihood of a schizophrenic requiring hospital treatment. In particular, studies have shown that, by reducing the amount of expressed emotion that is experienced within a family, the relapse rates of schizophrenics are also reduced. Critics of this type of therapy argue that it does not really help the schizophrenic that much, but just helps their family deal with them. Therefore, it might be seen more as a therapy for the family than a therapy for the individual schizophrenic.

The treatment of social skills training is more focused on schizophrenia, and so would be worth more marks than the treatment of CBT in the preceding paragraphs. However, it is still less detailed (albeit accurate and appropriate) and certainly requires a great deal more AO2, remembering that twice as many marks are available for AO2 as AO1. What is there is fine, but just lacks elaboration. For example, giving the specific details of the study alluded to would add much needed extra detail, as would a study to back up the assertion made at the beginning of the second paragraph.

The description of family intervention therapy is accurate and reasonably well-detailed. However, once again the AO2 is sadly underdeveloped. Considering the mark split in this question, this student has made the fundamental error of providing no more AO2 material than AO1 material.

Average answer: overall comment

To push this answer nearer towards the Grade A band, more detail is needed to flesh out the AO1, and *a great deal more* needs to be made of the AO2 points included. This answer would just about be enough for around a Grade C. The student has perhaps been overambitious in trying to cover *three* therapies – this has resulted in a lower mark than they could have earned. If the student had just gone for two therapies (as in the strong answer that follows), they could have provided more detail and that would have helped push this up to a much higher grade.

Strong answer

The first form of psychological therapy involves family interventions. These interventions involve family members of people who have been diagnosed with schizophrenia run in conjunction with other treatments (such as drug treatments). Family interventions have an educational component, with family members being given information about the disorder and how they might manage living with a schizophrenic, e.g. by improving communication styles or reducing expressed emotion within the family. These sessions do not need to have the patient present.

The reduction of expressed emotion within the family is an important part of this type of therapy. A high level of expressed emotion within the family may lead to hostility toward the family member with schizophrenia, or trying to help them too much. Family intervention therapy helps to reduce the level of expressed emotion within a family and as a result this reduces the likelihood of the recovering schizophrenic relapsing. If the schizophrenic stays in close contact with their family, it is necessary to repeat this form of intervention every few years. It can then contribute to a successful treatment for schizophrenia.

A meta-analysis of family intervention studies (Pharaoh et al. 2003) found that this type of therapy was effective in significantly reducing the rate of hospital admissions and the relapse rates for people with schizophrenia. An additional advantage of this type of therapy is that it improves compliance rates for taking medication, and as a consequence offers greater scope for overall improvement in an individual's condition.

Despite the apparent success of this form of therapy, however, the conclusions drawn from studies such as the Pharaoh et al. study may be more inconclusive than they appear. For example, the studies in this meta-analysis varied in how long they followed the individuals under study. Patients who have schizophrenia relapse at different rates. Therefore, the longer the study period, the more valid the study is as a test of the effectiveness of family intervention. There is also some disagreement in how 'relapse' is defined within a study. For example, some studies defined relapse in terms of time between hospital stays, whereas others defined it in terms of worsening symptoms. In some countries, patients would not be readmitted simply because their symptoms ☞

These first two paragraphs constitute the AO1 content for the first therapy (family intervention therapy). The therapy is clearly identified in the first sentence, which helps the examiner to see where one starts and the next begins. The student gives a clear and accurately detailed explanation of what is involved and why it should help the schizophrenic. This is a good opening.

The third and fourth paragraphs are all AO2. The effectiveness of family intervention therapy (i.e. does it work?) is clearly addressed in the third paragraph, and this is then followed by an intelligent discussion of the problems of reading too much into these findings. The student is aware of some of the problems inherent in meta-analyses (e.g. having different ways of measuring outcomes) and has dealt with these in a way that makes them explicitly relevant to studies of the treatment of schizophrenia. The first half of this essay is clearly a high Grade A standard.

have worsened – instead, their medication would be adjusted. This could make calculation of comparable relapse rates very difficult, making it harder to judge the effectiveness of the therapy.

The second therapy is cognitive-behavioural therapy (CBT). CBT is used in the treatment of schizophrenia because cognitive disorganization is an important part of the disorder. Benjamin (1989) suggested that the voices experienced by schizophrenics during their auditory hallucinations were directly responsible for their schizophrenic behaviour. He believed it should be possible to get rid of the abnormal beliefs (and behaviours) by using CBT to introduce normal thought processes. For example, a patient who experiences paranoid delusions (e.g. that they are being followed) would be asked to provide the evidence that this is really the case. By using a process known as belief modification, the therapist demonstrates to the individual the connection between their thought patterns and how they feel, and how this contributes to their illness. In CBT, the therapist challenges the patient's interpretation of events (e.g. the delusions they experience) and helps them to think about things is a less pathological way.

The effectiveness of changing thought processes as a treatment for schizophrenia was demonstrated in a study by Chadwick and Birchwood (1994). They found that simply by asking patients what they thought about the voices they reported, the amount of time that they spent hallucinating dropped significantly. Turkington *et al.* (2000) found that CBT was effective in the treatment of both positive and negative symptoms, which makes it particularly effective when used in conjunction with drug treatments that mainly address the positive symptoms of schizophrenia. CBT has also been shown to be particularly effective when used during a patient's first episode of schizophrenia. When used in this way, CBT shortens the length of the first schizophrenic episode, with patients continuing to be less negatively affected by their symptoms than those who have not had CBT. Despite this, relapse rates 18 months later are no better than for patients who have not had CBT (Lewis *et al.* 2002).

A limitation of CBT as a treatment for schizophrenia is that it is not a cure for schizophrenia, but rather it offers a way of decreasing the distress involved with ☞

Again, the student clearly identifies the second therapy. They have chosen to discuss just two therapies rather than 'more than two', which is probably a good idea as it gives greater opportunity for detailed discussion (a requirement for higher marks). An impressive feature of this paragraph (which is all AO1) is that the student explicitly addresses the relevance of CBT in the treatment of schizophrenia, rather than making the obvious mistake of just describing how CBT (in general) works.

Lots of good evaluation is presented in these final two paragraphs. The effectiveness of CBT in the treatment of schizophrenia begins this section, which is all AO2. Intelligent comment is made about the particular strengths (and limitations) of CBT in this context, and these points are appropriately elaborated. For example, the student offers the point that CBT may not *appear* to be as effective as some therapies in reducing the symptoms of schizophrenia, but it has the considerable advantage of reducing the distress associated with these symptoms. This is all good stuff: accurate, appropriate and well elaborated.

the symptoms. For example, Jones *et al.* (2000) found that, although CBT was not particularly effective in changing delusional beliefs, it did significantly reduce the distress that was associated with these beliefs. This has led some critics to conclude that CBT is less of a cure for schizophrenia and more of a way of normalizing symptoms.

Strong answer: overall comment

Overall, the entire answer is extremely well structured. The balance of AO1 and AO2 is well thought out, and this would certainly be marked at the top end of the marking scale – a clear Grade A.

Example Paper AQA Unit 4 Psychopathology: Depression

Question 1

Outline and evaluate **one or more** *biological explanations of depression.*
[9 + 16 marks (2009 onwards)] **[8 + 16 marks** (2012 onwards)]

There are a number of important requirements in this question, so it pays to read it carefully.

- It requires both AO1 description ('outline') and AO2 evaluation ('evaluate'). The marks in brackets indicate the number of marks available for each aspect, so for this question, about one-third of your answer should be AO1, and two-thirds should be AO2.
- The offer of 'one or more' should be considered carefully. Writing about more than one explanation offers the opportunity for increased breadth; restricting yourself to just one offers greater depth. It really is your call: either approach is acceptable, and neither one is more highly valued than the other.

- The question asks for *biological* explanations (e.g. genetic, biochemical), so any inclusion of psychological explanations would have to be made explicitly relevant as part of an AO2 critical point.
- Although the question does not specifically *require* research evidence, it is always a good idea to back up any assertions with solid evidence. You could then also gain AO2 credit for methodological evaluation of this evidence. Using research evidence also makes your answer appear more authoritative and better informed, and so is more likely to push your answer into the higher mark bands.

Average answer

The first biological explanation for depression is genetics, because depression seems to run in families. This tells us that there are probably genes involved. One method used to investigate the contribution of genetics is the twin study. Researchers use two different types of twin, identical and fraternal twins. Identical twins are genetically identical, so if one twin has depression, then the chances of the other twin having depression would be high if genetics is the most important cause. A twin study was carried out by McGuffin *et al.* (1996). They found that there was a 1 in 2 chance of an identical twin becoming depressed if the other twin was depressed. With fraternal twins, who share only half of their genes, there was a 1 in 4 chance of the other twin becoming depressed. A problem with twin studies is that if depression was due totally to genetics, then there should be a 100 per cent similarity between the twins. This is not the case, so this suggests that other factors (e.g. the environment) must be also responsible. The similarity between twins in terms of depression may be caused by the fact that twins share a very similar environment, so that might be the reason. ☞

This first section is appropriate in its choice of content and is generally accurate. There are some minor inaccuracies – for example, in the McGuffin *et al.* study, figure should be 1 in 5 for identical twins rather than 1 in 4, but this is not a significant error. The AO2 evaluative component towards the end of this paragraph is limited and lacks development, so, although appropriate, it fails to develop the arguments in an effective way.

Another way of investigating the role of genetics in depression is with an adoption study. These studies investigate depressed people who have been adopted at an early age. They compare these people with their biological parents to see if they were also depressed. If the biological parents are depressed and the adoptive parents are not depressed, then this indicates that there is a genetic influence at work. This was supported by research by Wender *et al.* (1986), who found that biological relatives of depressed individuals were eight times more likely also to be suffering from depression than were adoptive relatives. This shows that genetic factors are very important, and this cannot be explained by similar environments, because the depressed individual and their biological parents have not shared the same environments. It is possible that people do not inherit depression, but they just inherit a vulnerability for depression. This is known as the diathesis-stress model.

A second explanation concerns the influence of neurotransmitters. These transmit impulses across the synapse from one nerve cell to another. An example of a neurotransmitter is serotonin. Serotonin is necessary to make people feel good, and so if an individual does not have enough serotonin, they may feel depressed. Psychologists discovered this when treating depression with drugs that increased serotonin activity in the brain. People became less depressed after taking these drugs, which meant that they must have had a deficiency in their levels of serotonin. These drugs are known as SSRIs. The most common type of SSRI is Prozac. Prozac works by stopping the reuptake of serotonin into the presynaptic nerve cell. However, a problem for serotonin deficiency explanation of depression is that SSRIs only work for half of the people suffering from depression. Another problem is that antidepressants such as Prozac take several weeks to start working, even though their chemical effect must be immediate. A final problem for this explanation is the problem of cause and effect. The fact that depressed people have low levels of serotonin may be the cause of their depression, but it may also be a consequence of their depression.

As with the previous paragraph, the descriptive material is appropriate and accurate, but the evaluation lacks development. This is a worrying trend in this essay given that two-thirds of the marks available are for AO2. The student makes a valid point concerning the diathesis-stress model, but needs to develop this. They are implying that the diathesis is inherited and that environmental stressors trigger depression, but this needs to be made explicit. What would really boost the marks is some evidence that this is the case.

As is now becoming a pattern in this answer, about two-thirds of the material is AO1 and one-third AO2, when it should really be the other way around. We are given a fairly superficial explanation of the mechanism of SSRIs, with no real research evidence to back up the claims being made. Giving research evidence adds authority to an answer and turns assertion into informed psychology.

Average answer: overall comment

This is a reasonable answer, generally accurate and with no significant irrelevant information. However, there is a lack of research evidence and an overemphasis on AO1 at the expense of AO2. This means that, although it would receive a decent mark for AO1, it would be let down by a relatively low mark for AO2.

Strong answer

A number of studies have shown an increased risk for depression among first-degree relatives of individuals with major depressive disorder (clinical depression), with the chances of developing the disorder seemingly dependent on the closeness of the genetic relationship. Family studies have compared individuals of known genetic similarity to see if those who share more of their genes with an individual with depression also have a greater risk of developing the disorder themselves. For example, supporting this claim, Gershon (1990) analysed the results of ten family studies and found that the rates of depression in first-degree relatives (e.g. children of a depressed parent) was as high as 30 per cent, considerably higher than rates in the general population. However, this increased risk of developing depression when a close family member already has a diagnosis of the disorder might not be entirely due to genetics. It may instead be the result of a shared environment, with children acquiring their depressed mood and associated behaviours as a result of observing their parents.

Twin studies have also provided evidence for the link between genetics and depression. Monozygotic twins have identical genetic material, whereas dizygotic twins share only 50 per cent of their genetic material. If we assume that twins share roughly the same environment, then any greater similarity between MZ twins compared to DZ twins in terms of depression can be explained in terms of their greater genetic similarity. Evidence that supports this comes from McGuffin et al. (1996), who found a concordance rate of 46 per cent for MZ twins and 20 per cent for DZ twins, suggesting that depression has a substantial genetic component. However, this also demonstrates that genetics cannot be the only explanation, as otherwise the concordance rate for MZ twins would be 100 per cent. This might be explained by the diathesis-stress model, which suggests that individuals may inherit a vulnerability for depression (a diathesis), which only leads to depression when the individual is exposed to significant life stressors. A problem with the use of twin studies is that twins share their environment and so tend to be subject to the same influences. This has meant that researchers are turning to adoption studies as a better test of the genetic explanation, because such studies can use individuals who are genetically related but exposed ☞

This is a good opening for two main reasons:
- The AO1 material is clear and detailed, with a good rationale given for the use of family studies in the study of depression.
- The detailed AO2 claims are backed up by research, and overall, the AO2 content makes up about 60 per cent of the paragraph, which is more in keeping with the overall mark split for the question.

Again, this gives an impressively detailed description of the rationale behind the use of twin studies, and the remaining content has been carefully crafted so that it is virtually all AO2 evaluation. For example, the McGuffin et al. study might just have been described, but here it is stated explicitly that it *supports* the genetic explanation, thus turning it into AO2. Problems with twin studies are clearly identified and used to introduce the main advantages of adoption studies in the next paragraph.

to different environments as a result of being adopted. This enables researchers to study the influence of genetics without the confounding influence of environment.

The largest adoption study in this area was by carried out by Wender et al. (1986). They interviewed people who had been adopted and found that they were eight times more likely to develop depression if their biological parents were depressed. However, more recent studies have suggested that having an adoptive parent with depression was also a significant risk factor for developing depression. Tully et al. (2008) found that adopted children who had an adoptive parent with depression were significantly more likely to develop depression themselves than were children in an adoptive family with no evidence of depression. These two studies suggest that both genetics and rearing environment are influential in the development of depression.

The influence of genetics is also demonstrated in a study by Kendler et al. (2006). They studied over 15 000 twins using the Swedish Twin Registry and estimated from the data that the heritability of major depressive disorder is 38 per cent, with a higher risk for women than men. There are many explanations for why women should be more at risk of depression than are men. One explanation is that any gene for depression may be located on the X chromosome. Women have two X chromosomes, while men only have one, which might explain why women are generally twice as likely to be diagnosed with depression than men. However, psychological explanations (e.g. male reluctance to report illness) are more generally accepted as an explanation for this gender difference.

Trying to establish which genes are involved in depression has been a challenge for researchers. Some studies have found a defect in the 5-HTT gene responsible for the transmission of serotonin in people suffering from depression. Serotonin is linked to depression, with low levels of serotonin beings associated with low mood and the experience of depression. However, critics argue that genes such as 5-HTT do not directly cause depression but instead change the way the person responds to environmental stressors, which for some people makes depression more likely. This is further evidence for the ☞

There is lots of good material here in these two paragraphs about adoption, and they clearly display the key criteria of accuracy and detail. The discussion on why gender differences might exist is clearly informed and critical, and would earn AO2 credit. As with previous paragraphs, there is an appropriate balance between AO1 and AO2, and so the student is earning good marks on both skill divisions, unlike the previous answer where that student mainly picked up AO1 marks and lost out on the more lucrative AO2 marks.

An impressive closing paragraph. It doesn't matter that a specific study is not identified, as the student offers an overview of research in this area and makes a suitably intelligent critical point to close.

diathesis-stress model, as it demonstrates that some people are more likely to develop depression because of an inherited vulnerability, in this case an abnormality in the 5-HTT gene.

Strong answer: overall comment

Detailed, accurate and well structured. This student knows the material and uses psychological evidence sensibly to flesh out their AO2 content. Note that they have gone for the 'one' rather than the 'or more' option in the question, as they have been confident that they had sufficient depth and breadth to offer. They could have opted to include other biological explanations, but that might have diluted the overall depth of discussion that we see here. This is clearly a Grade A answer.

Question 2

Part (a)

Outline clinical characteristics of depression. [**5 marks** (2009 onwards)] [**4 marks** (2012 onwards)]

- The term 'clinical characteristics' does not have one specific meaning, so could be a brief outline of the different types of depression and their characteristics, although it is most likely to mean the 'symptoms' of depression. Remember that 'outline' requires descriptive (AO1) content only, so there is no need for any evaluation in this part of the question.

- As this question is only worth a few marks, you would not be expected to cover *all* the possible symptoms of depression or all the possible variants of the disorder. For 5 marks, about 150 words would probably suffice; for 4 marks (2012 onwards), 125 words or so would be enough.

Average answer

Depression is a mood disorder that involves feeling sad and not being very interested in things that are going on around us. It can be mild, moderate or severe, and at its worst can even make the person contemplate suicide. It is believed that about 17 per cent of the population will experience depression at some time in their life. In Japan, it is considered a sign of weakness, so not many people report the symptoms of depression. The main symptoms are feelings of sadness (a depressed mood), loss of interest or pleasure and a lack of energy, plus other symptoms as well, such as feelings of death or suicide and a change in appetite or sleeping patterns.

While all this is accurate, the answer would have been better if this student had concentrated more on detailing the symptoms chosen and had included the qualifying statements (e.g. symptoms must have been experienced for at least two weeks), rather than including statistics or cultural differences that do not constitute 'clinical characteristics' of the disorder.

Strong answer

Although there are different forms of depression, there are four general groups of symptoms that apply to all. These are: the affective symptoms, e.g. a depressed mood or feelings of sadness; cognitive symptoms, e.g. inability to concentrate or lowered self-esteem; behavioural symptoms, e.g. social withdrawal and restlessness; and finally physical symptoms, e.g. change in sleep patterns or appetite. For a diagnosis of major depressive disorder, the individual must experience either a low depressed mood or a loss of interest and pleasure in normal activities plus four other symptoms. These must cause significant distress or impairment of general functioning and must not be caused by illness, by the use of drugs or alcohol or by an event such as bereavement. The symptoms should also have been experienced for at least two weeks.

There are many ways of answering this first part of the question. This student has included the core diagnostic criteria and qualified this with accurate and detailed description of other relevant characteristics of depression. This is a concise yet detailed and effective answer that is worth full marks.

Part (b)

*Explain **two or more** issues associated with the classification **and/or** diagnosis of depression.* [**10 marks**]

- Questions that use the term 'explain' can be hard to decipher, as sometimes 'explain' can imply both AO1 and AO2, whereas sometimes (as here), it is AO2 only. Working out when a question is AO2 and when it is AO1 *and* AO2 can be tricky, but here it is simple mathematics. Part (a) is all AO1, and the skill division for part (c) is made clear with 4 marks for AO1 and 6 for AO2. So, as there are only 9 marks for AO1 *in total* (8 marks in exams from 2012 onwards), that means part (b) MUST be all AO2.

- Remember to cover at least two issues.
- Identifying the issues (remember to cover at least two) would be considered the product of analysis (and therefore AO2), and further elaboration of those issues would push the mark up into the higher mark bands.
- Reliability and validity are the usual issues although there are others such as difficulty in establishing the cause of symptoms, differential diagnoses and so on.
- Note that this question is about depression and should be restricted to this disorder.

Average answer

Depression is difficult to diagnose because the difference between normal low mood and depression can be quite small. For example, the doctor has to decide whether the patient's mood is low enough for it to be considered depression. Another problem concerns the person making the diagnosis. Most people who suffer from depression go to see their GP rather than a psychiatrist, but, because the GP is not skilled in using diagnostic criteria for mental disorders, people are often misdiagnosed and depression may be diagnosed when not there or missed when it is. GPs may also base ☞

their diagnosis on their previous knowledge of the patient, so this is not entirely objective. This means that diagnosis of depression may not be reliable.

Validity is another issue in the diagnosis of depression. There may be quite a lot of overlap between the symptoms of different disorders. For example, it is difficult to distinguish between mild depression and anxiety disorder because many of the symptoms are the same. This has important implications for treatment. Some people believe that it is wrong to label depression as an illness as having a low mood is just a normal reaction to some of the problems of life. By labelling someone as 'depressed', this could be potentially stigmatizing, and may lead them to stop trying to change the part of their life that is causing them problems.

This is a reasonable answer to the question, touching on three issues: reliability of diagnosis, validity of diagnosis, and the problem of labelling and stigmatization. Unfortunately, none of these is explored in any great depth, nor backed up with research evidence. However, they *are* appropriate points, and discussion is accurate and reasonably well informed, so this would earn decent marks, although development and research evidence would have pushed the mark up considerably.

Strong answer

The reliability of diagnosis is determined by whether the same diagnostic criteria are likely to produce the same diagnosis on two separate occasions and whether or not two independent doctors give the same diagnosis when presented with the same symptoms. One of the main issues around the diagnosis of depression is that reliability is not always as high as it should be. For example, in a study using DSM-IV, Keller *et al.* (1995) found that the reliability of diagnosis over a six-month period was poor for major depression. They suggested that one of the reasons for this is that a diagnosis of depression requires a minimum of five out of nine symptoms. If an individual is just at the threshold for depression, a disagreement about one item can result in either a diagnosis of depression or not. In the UK, diagnosis is frequently left to a GP, who might get the diagnosis wrong. Mitchell *et al.* (2009) claim that depression is misdiagnosed more frequently than it is missed in general practice, and this is probably due to the ambiguous criteria of classification systems such as DSM.

For a valid diagnosis to be made, the doctor must distinguish between depression and other disorders and also between the different forms of depression. However, when McCullough *et al.* (2003) compared nearly 700 patients with different types of depression, they found considerable overlap of symptoms and responses to treatment, which made it difficult to ☞

This is a very effective opening. The student has concentrated on reliability and this is clearly explained at the beginning of the answer. The student has then carefully illustrated the issues associated with lack of inter-rater and test-retest reliability *and* provided research evidence to support these assertions.

The student follows the same routine in this paragraph, outlining the appropriate issues of validity and then illustrating these with research. This is suitably evaluative and properly elaborated. There has to a trade-off between depth and breadth in response to a question like this, and, with just 10 marks available, the balance between the two is appropriate. This answer would most probably earn close to if not full marks.

Example Paper: Depression

diagnose distinctive types of depression accurately. For a doctor to make a valid diagnosis of depression, they must first rule out other possibilities. The doctor has to make sure that the physical symptoms are not caused by injury or physical illness. For example, some of the symptoms of anaemia resemble the physical symptoms of depression.

Part (c)

*Outline and evaluate **one** psychological therapy used in the treatment of depression.* **[4 marks + 6 marks]**

- This question indicates the number of marks available for AO1 (4) and for AO2 (6). As is always the case, this should dictate how much you write for each in response.
- The therapy *must* be psychological – any material relating to biological treatments would not receive credit *unless* it is used as part of a critical evaluation of the psychological treatment.

- You should only write about one therapy. This could be CBT in general, for example, but within that one 'type' of therapy, it would be fine to cover different types of CBT associated with different therapists (e.g. Beck, Ellis).

Average answer

Beck (1976) developed a CBT treatment that was specifically for depression. The person first draws up a list of things that will make them feel more confident. They are then taught to recognize when they are thinking negatively. They discuss these negative thoughts with the therapist, who helps them to change these thoughts so that they think more positively about their life and so become less depressed.

CBT is very effective at treating depression. It is relatively quick and inexpensive, and can even be used online or over the telephone. It is better for people who only have mild depression. A problem is that there is a lot of homework for the client to do, and many people may not be sufficiently motivated to do it. A good point about this type of therapy is that there are no side effects. Drug therapies, for example, can have lots of side effects, which may prevent patients from continuing with their medication. Research has also shown that patients are less likely to relapse with CBT.

This is a classically 'average' answer, with lots of assertions without the evidence to support them.

- The AO1 material in the first paragraph is accurate and appropriate, but simply lacks detail. Each of these points could have been fleshed out just a little to gain maximum AO1 marks.
- The second paragraph is all AO2, but again lacks elaboration. There are perhaps too many points attempted and not enough depth to any of them. A better approach would have been to take two critical points and flesh each of them out to make them more *effective*.

Overall, this student's answer to Question 2 is competent yet not always effective. There is a general lack of detail, with not enough supporting research evidence. Accuracy isn't a problem, but the lack of detail and elaboration would restrict this to around Grade C level.

123

Strong answer

Beck (1976) developed a CBT treatment that was specifically for depression. The therapy involves four phases. First, the person draws up a schedule of activities that will make them feel more active and more confident. Second, they are taught to recognize their automatic and negative thoughts, and they discuss these negative thoughts with the therapist, who helps them to test their reality. Third, the therapist helps them to understand the illogical thought processes that lead to these negative thoughts. Finally, the therapist helps individuals to change their maladaptive attitudes and to engage in pleasurable activities.

CBT is very effective at treating depression. A study by Brent *et al.* (1997) found that CBT was more effective and quicker than other forms of psychological treatment in adolescents diagnosed with major depression. CBT has been found to be particularly effective when given to depressed people at the same time as antidepressants (Butler *et al.* 2006). An advantage of CBT over antidepressants is that clients who receive CBT are less likely to relapse (Hollon *et al.* 1992), something that tends to restrict the overall effectiveness of drug treatments. A difficulty of assessing the effectiveness of a therapy such as CBT is that a control group is essential in order to judge the impact of the treatment condition. Control groups tend not to be appropriate because this would mean depriving depressed individuals of much needed treatment, and so would be considered unethical.

This answer is very similar to the previous 'average' answer, but demonstrates how material can be elaborated using supporting research evidence to make more of an impact and to pick up high marks. Unlike the previous answer, which has six distinct AO2 points yet none elaborated, this answer has just three points and lots of elaboration, so would get a much better mark.

Overall, this student's answer to Question 2 is competent and effective throughout, with all three parts answered accurately and in sufficient detail. The student has paid careful attention to the mark divisions for each question part and has provided the appropriate amount of material for each. The three answers combined would easily be worth a Grade A.

Question 3

'Depression is an illness that cannot be overcome by simply pulling oneself together. The good news though is that it can be treated.'

Outline and evaluate **two or more** *therapies used in the treatment of depression.* [**9 + 16 marks** (2009 onwards)] [**8 + 16 marks** (2012 onwards)]

- In this question you are asked to cover at least two therapies. Be careful about spreading yourself too thinly here: covering more than two could lead to a response that is too superficial both in its coverage and in the elaboration of any evaluative points.
- An essential requirement of this question is that discussion is limited to therapies as they are used *in the treatment of depression* rather than discussions of, for example, CBT or behavioural treatments of mental disorders generally.

- Note that the *type* of therapy is not dictated by the question. Thus, you could use two biological, two psychological, or one of each.
- Finally, don't worry about the use of a quotation in the question. Sometimes these are used to give you a few hints as to how you might answer the question, but at other times (as here), they are used merely to orientate you towards the main issue that the question is exploring.

Average answer

The first type of therapy I am going to cover is the use of antidepressant drugs. There are different types, but the most commonly used are the SSRIs, such as Prozac. SSRIs are selective serotonin reuptake inhibitors. This means they are selective, working only on serotonin, and they inhibit the reuptake of serotonin, and so reduce the symptoms of depression. The trouble with SSRIs is that they don't work with everyone, and with some people they may increase the likelihood of suicide. There was a case in the US where Joseph Wesbecker, who was on Prozac, shot 20 people and then killed himself. Another type of antidepressant drug that is no longer used is the MAOI type of drug. This drug was originally developed to treat TB, but doctors found that it lifted the mood of patients who took it, and so it was tried out on people with depression. MAOIs work by slowing down the production of monoamines within the brain and as a result they reduce the symptoms of depression. The trouble with MAOIs is that when they were taken with certain types of food they could kill the person, so they were gradually phased out. A problem with all drug treatments, including antidepressants, is that they have side effects, and people can become dependent on them rather than trying to sort their lives out. Psychological therapies such as CBT are more effective because they teach people essential skills for dealing with stressful events in their life rather than providing a chemical crutch.

The second therapy I am going to cover is ECT. This is where a patient is first given an anaesthetic, and then an electric current is passed through their brain to produce a seizure. It is not the shock that is thought to reduce the symptoms of depression, but the brain seizure that follows it. The use of this form of treatment has been popularized in films such as *One Flew Over the Cuckoo's Nest*, starring Jack Nicholson as Randle McMurphy, a man who receives ECT to control him while in a mental institution. As a result of films like this, ECT has received a very bad press, being seen as a barbaric form of treatment. There are also problems with ECT, particularly because of the side effects associated with the treatment, such as memory loss. ECT is very effective, particularly when used with people who have severe depression. It is used with patients where there is a high risk of suicide and where other treatments have failed. Research has found it has a 70 per cent ☛

There is some irrelevant information here that would not earn marks (e.g. the story of Joseph Wesbecker) and the fact that the MAOI drugs were originally developed for the treatment of TB. Unfortunately, it is the gory case studies like the Wesbecker case that are often the most memorable, yet they don't really contribute much, if anything, to the answer. There is also some inaccuracy: MAOIs do not work by slowing down the production of monoamines but by breaking down the enzyme that destroys them – therefore an opposite effect. There are a few evaluative points, which are appropriate yet lack evaluation. For example, we are told that there are side effects, but these are not identified, nor is any evidence offered.

Again there is some irrelevant information, this time about Jack Nicholson's role in *One Flew Over the Cuckoo's Nest*. There is also some inaccuracy, as evidence does suggest a significant difference between real and sham ECT. However, the AO2 material is better for this second form of therapy, so gains more marks. Even so, this answer would have benefited from some research to back up the assertions (e.g. about success rates and any side effects).

success rate when used with such patients. It also offers hope to people where there was none before. This makes it a very worthwhile type of treatment for depression, because it saves lives. However, a problem with ECT is that we don't really know why it works. Some critics have likened it to kicking a television set that doesn't work. There is also the problem that some research has shown that giving sham ECT (i.e. no shock is actually given although the patient thinks it is) can be just as effective as actual ECT. This suggests that the real value of ECT as a treatment for depression may lie in the extra attention given to the patient rather than the actual treatment itself.

Average answer: overall comment

There is lots of good material in this answer, and it would not take much to turn it into a Grade A answer.

The simple rules are to leave out anything irrelevant, flesh out what is relevant and provide psychological research evidence whenever possible. As it stands, this is somewhere around Grade C/D level.

Strong answer

The main form of treatment prescribed for depression is the use of antidepressant medication. Early forms of antidepressant medication (the MAOIs) worked by inhibiting the action of an enzyme that breaks down noradrenaline and serotonin, making more of these neurotransmitters available in the nervous system, which in turn decreases the symptoms of depression. The second class of antidepressants, the tricyclics, block the reuptake of noradrenaline and serotonin, again making more of these neurotransmitters available to excite neighbouring cells. The third class of drugs is the SSRIs, which inhibit only the reuptake of serotonin from the synapse. It usually takes about six weeks with SSRIs until their effects are noticeable. This is thought to be due to the fact that the nerve cells take time to adapt to the drugs. The more modern version of these drugs, the SNRIs, prevent the reuptake of both serotonin and noradrenaline.

Antidepressants have been found to be effective in relieving the symptoms of depression in about 70 per cent of patients compared to just 33 per cent for placebos. However, Kirsch et al. (2008), in a review of clinical trials of SSRIs, found that there was only a significant difference between the drug and a placebo in the most severe cases of depression. However, ☞

This is both concise and well informed. The main types of antidepressant are clearly identified and their mechanisms of action accurately explained. All of this is accurate and sufficiently detailed, and follows a logical sequence. So far so good!

they suggest that for moderately depressed individuals, even the placebo offered some hope for them, so had a beneficial effect that masked any superiority of the drug condition. This was not the case for the most severely depressed individuals, who had effectively given up hope, thus accounting for the greater difference between drug and placebo conditions. The use of a placebo condition raises significant ethical problems in these studies because the duty of care suggests that, if an effective treatment exists, it should not be withheld and a placebo substituted in its place. The use of SSRIs is also questioned for children and adolescents. Double-blind studies (e.g. Geller *et al.* 1992) have failed to show a significant superiority of SSRIs over placebos. Critics of SSRIs as a treatment for depression have also highlighted the greater risk of suicide among adolescents. For example, a review of studies (Barbui *et al.* 2008) found that SSRIs increased the risk of suicide among adolescents but reduced it among older adults.

For patients suffering from severe depression or patients who have not responded to drug treatment or psychotherapy, ECT is an option. It is particularly useful when there is a risk of suicide because it offers quicker relief from depressive symptoms than antidepressants. The procedure for ECT involves giving a short acting general anaesthetic to prevent the patient injuring themselves during the seizure that follows the administration of the shock. The standard procedure involves placing an electrode on one side of the head (unilateral ECT) and sending a current of between 70 and 130 volts through the brain. This produces convulsions for a brief period after which the patient comes round. There are usually six sessions given once a week over six weeks.

The effectiveness of ECT for patients who have not responded to other forms of treatment is quite high. Richards and Lyness (2006) estimated that about two-thirds of patients with severe depression improved significantly after treatment with ECT. However, Sackeim *et al.* (2001) found that a significant proportion of these relapsed within a year of receiving a course of ECT. Before the advent of unilateral ECT, the risk of side effects following ECT was high. These side effects included memory loss, headaches and, for some people, an increase in anxiety and fearfulness. Rose *et al.* (2003) found that about one-third of patients who had received ECT subsequently complained of persistent memory ☛

This paragraph is entirely evaluative and covers four distinct critical points (effectiveness, comparisons with placebo, ethical issues and appropriateness as a form of treatment). By limiting the number of points, the student takes the opportunity to elaborate each of the points made, thus increasing the impact of each point. The material is thoughtful and well-informed, and puts the answer well on course for a Grade A.

ECT is covered equally efficiently, with the role of ECT (for severe and treatment-resistant depression) and the method of delivery described accurately and in detail. The mode of action is not covered, but as there is no agreement on this, it is quite understandable.

As with the treatment of antidepressants covered earlier, the AO2 material does not try to cram too much in at the expense of elaboration. There is also a commendable amount of research evidence, clearly setting this apart from the 'average answer', which made claims without supporting them. Finally, the balance between AO1 and AO2 is appropriate, and the student is clearly mindful of the mark division for these two skills.

loss. Sackeim *et al.* (2001) found that unilateral ECT was just as effective as bilateral ECT but the risk of cognitive problems was less. In an equivalent to the drugs versus placebo studies, ECT has been compared to 'sham ECT', where the patient is anaesthetized but does not receive ECT. Studies (e.g. Gregory *et al.* 1985) have shown a significant difference in favour of 'real' ECT, thus supporting its effectiveness for treatment-resistant depression.

Strong answer: overall comment

This student earns good marks right from the first paragraph, showing a sound understanding of the two therapies chosen for this answer and an equally sound understanding of the requirements of the marking guidelines. This is clearly a Grade A standard answer.

Example Paper AQA Unit 4 Psychopathology: Phobic disorders

Question 1

*Outline and evaluate **two or more** therapies used in the treatment of phobic disorders.*
[**9 + 16 mark**s (2009 onwards)] [**8 + 16 marks** (2012 onwards)]

There are a number of important things to note here.
- For students taking this exam in 2011, questions include both types of anxiety disorder – phobias and OCD – and give you the choice which to answer. You will have probably covered only one of these, so that is the one to write about. Don't get distracted by the inclusion of the other in the question, and whatever you do, don't attempt to cover both phobias and OCD in your answer. From 2012 onwards there will be separate questions on phobias and OCD.
- The question requires both AO1 description ('outline') and AO2 evaluation ('evaluate'). The marks in brackets indicate the number of marks available for each aspect, so for this question, about one-third of your answer should be AO1, and two-thirds should be AO2.

- You are asked to cover at least two therapies relating to phobias. It is entirely up to you whether you write about two therapies or more than two. Bear in mind, though, that trying to include too many would make your answer more superficial.
- To answer the question as it is phrased, you must limit your discussion to therapies *as they are used in the treatment of phobias*, rather than discussing (for example) CBT or drug treatments of mental disorders generally.
- Note that the *type* of therapy is not dictated by this question. Thus, you could use two biological, two psychological or one of each.

Average answer

The first type of therapy is behavioural therapy. This type of therapy includes treatments like systematic desensitization, flooding and modelling. In systematic desensitization, the patient has to work through a hierarchy of situations. For example, if they have a spider phobia, they may begin by being exposed to a cartoon spider, then a stuffed spider then finally a real spider. It works because exposure to the feared object is gradual. Flooding doesn't have the gradual exposure to the feared object – the person has to face up to the feared situation all in one go. In modelling, the person with a phobia sees someone else modelling the desired behaviour. For example, the therapist may allow a spider to walk over their face so the person with the phobia can see that there is nothing to fear, and then they feel more confident about imitating that behaviour.

There is a great deal of research evidence that this sort of treatment can be very effective in the treatment of phobias. In flooding, there are some dangers because the person who has a phobia of something (such as a spider) may become very distressed if they suddenly get put in a room full of spiders. The good points about this sort of therapy is that it is quick and there are no side ☛

This is a reasonably accurate description of systematic desensitization, although there are some important omissions. For example, there is no mention of the relaxation training that is such an important aspect of systematic desensitization, nor its absence in flooding. The evaluation is better, but there is not enough of it (remember it should be twice as extensive as the descriptive content), and it is not developed enough.

effects, so people may prefer it to, for example, drug treatments, which do have side effects. These sorts of treatments appear to be more effective when they are used in the treatment of specific phobias rather than social phobias or agoraphobia.

The second type of therapy uses drugs to reduce the anxiety felt by phobics whenever they come across the thing they fear. These drugs include anti-anxiety drugs such as BZs and antidepressants such as the SSRI drugs. BZs work by enhancing the action of a neurotransmitter in the brain (GABA) and making the person feel more relaxed in the presence of the feared object. Antidepressants have a similar effect, making people less anxious when they are in a situation that would usually cause them to be fearful. Drugs are not really the best solution for someone with a phobia because they can become addictive, so they are only prescribed in the short term.

There are strengths of the drug treatment of phobias. For example, they help people deal with the fear they experience so they can live a more normal life. They are readily available from GPs and also relatively cheap. However, there are also a number of problems with the use of drugs as a treatment for phobias. They don't work for all people – therefore, other forms of treatment would be necessary for them. They can produce side effects, particularly if they are used for a long time, and can become addictive if taken for long periods. This raises ethical concerns about the use of drugs. The biggest problem with the use of drugs is that they only treat the symptoms of the problem (i.e. the fear) and do nothing about the problem itself.

The descriptive content is reasonably detailed and accurate, although the relevance of these drugs could be made more explicitly relevant to the treatment of phobias. There are quite a few appropriate points of evaluation made, but these lack elaboration. Research might have been used to add justification for each of the points, as detail is necessary for higher marks. The mention of the addictive nature of drugs is rather sweeping and is made twice, so is ignored the second time around.

Average answer: overall comment

This is a reasonable answer, but with a dearth of research evidence and a lack of elaboration, it would be restricted to around a Grade C.

Strong answer

The most commonly used biological therapy for phobias is drug therapy. This therapy assumes that there is a chemical imbalance in the brain that can be corrected by drugs, which either increase or decrease the levels of specific neurotransmitters in the brain. For example, benzodiazepines (BZs) bring about relaxation for the phobic by enhancing the amount of GABA in the brain. Although BZs have been shown to be effective ☞

This is an accurate and appropriate description of the action of BZs in the treatment of phobias. There is lots of detail and appropriate elaboration in the three evaluative points made in the second half of the paragraph.

(e.g. for people suffering from stage fright), they do not get rid of the underlying condition, but only treat the symptoms. An additional problem is that BZs have been shown to be addictive, with people becoming psychologically dependent on the drug to deal with their fear. As a result, BZs are prescribed only for short periods of time. If the underlying condition (i.e. the cause of the fear) has not been addressed, BZs would therefore have limited appropriateness for the treatment of phobias.

Antidepressants such as the SSRIs prolong the action of serotonin in the synapse. Serotonin is not directly involved in the treatment of phobias, but increases the effect of other chemicals (such as GABA) that are. Antidepressants are effective at reducing the panic that can accompany social phobia and agoraphobia, although the mechanism by which they do this is not known. However, even though they are effective at reducing the anxiety associated with phobias, they are still only treating the symptoms rather than the actual condition. This means that as soon as the person stops a course of antidepressants, the phobic reaction can return. Antidepressants are therefore more effective when combined with a course of psychotherapy (e.g. Gould *et al.* 1997). However, other studies have not found the same advantage of combined treatment – for example, Haug *et al.* (2003) found that combined drug and behavioural treatment actually led to an increase in anxiety following the termination of treatment.

The behavioural explanation of phobias claims that phobias are learned behaviours; therefore, in behavioural therapy, phobias can be unlearned and replaced with more adaptive behaviours. Systematic desensitization is used to replace the fearful reaction with a more positive emotion. The patient is first taught relaxation techniques. Then the therapist and patient work out a hierarchy of fearful situations, starting with a situation that causes the minimum of anxiety, then working towards a situation involving the feared object in its most fear-evoking state. The therapy can either be carried out 'in vivo' (which involves actual contact with the feared object) or 'in vitro' (which involves imagining contact with the feared object). This type of behavioural treatment has been found to be very effective in the treatment of specific phobias. McGrath *et al.* (1990) found that systematic desensitization helped 75% of people with a specific phobia, and Ost *et al.* (1991) also found that for people suffering from arachnophobia, ☛

This is an impressive description of the specific action of SSRIs in the treatment of phobias. Evaluation is reinforced by appropriate research evidence, and the material selected for this evaluation shows an excellent understanding of the area.

This is an appropriate description of systematic desensitization, which contains an accurate description of all the main parts of this therapy as it is used specifically in the treatment of phobias. Evaluation concentrates on the effectiveness of systematic desensitization and makes good use of research evidence, which is *made* evaluative by the use of phrases and terms such as 'has been found to be very effective' and 'however'.

working through the entire hierarchy in one session produced a significant improvement in symptoms that was still evident at a four-year follow-up. However, Menzies and Clarke found that in vivo techniques are usually more effective than in vitro techniques when used as a treatment for specific phobias.

Flooding is a more extreme version of systematic desensitization, where the patient is exposed to the feared object without moving through a hierarchy or any attempt to reduce anxiety. Although this can be done in vivo, that raises ethical concerns, e.g. the possibility of raised blood pressure or even heart attacks. As a result, the technique is more usually carried out in vitro, where the patient is required to imagine contact with the feared object. When used in vivo, research (e.g. Svensson *et al.*) has found significant and long-lasting improvements in a range of phobias, including claustrophobia and fear of flying. However, Bryan *et al.* (2003) found that, when used on its own, in vitro treatment of phobias is not as effective as in vivo treatment, but its effectiveness can be increased when used in conjunction with other forms of treatment, such as CBT. Behavioural treatments such as systematic desensitization are particularly appropriate in the treatment of phobias because they are relatively quick (compared to psychodynamic treatments, which may take many months) and, unlike drug therapies, there are no side effects or dependency problems.

Again, a very effective outline and evaluation of flooding. It introduces (as extra detail) the distinction between *in vivo* and *in vitro* treatments, which gives the opportunity to evaluate the treatments in terms of the difference between their effectiveness.

Strong answer: overall comment

Well-detailed, accurate and making excellent use of research evidence throughout, so thoroughly deserving of a Grade A.

Question 2

Part (a)

Outline clinical characteristics of phobic disorders. [**5 marks** (2009 onwards)] [**4 marks** (2012 onwards)]

- The term 'clinical characteristics' does not have one specific meaning, so could be a brief outline of the nature of phobias (e.g. specific and social phobias) and/or the 'symptoms' of phobias.
- Remember that 'outline' requires descriptive (AO1) content only, so there is no need for any evaluation in this part of the question.

- As this question is only worth a few marks, you would not be expected to cover *all* the possible symptoms or characteristics of phobias. For 5 marks, about 150 words would probably suffice; for 4 marks (2012 exams onwards), 125 words or so would be enough.

Average answer

Phobic disorders are anxiety disorders. About 1 in 10 people have an anxiety disorder. Phobias are a fear of something, such as arachnophobia, which is a fear of spiders, or acrophobia, which is a fear of heights. A phobia is a fear that is out of proportion to the actual danger posed by the object. For example, fear of clowns is quite a common phobia, even though people who suffer from this type of phobia know that clowns can't hurt them. For something to be classified as a phobia, the fear that a person feels when they are in that situation is excessive.

Although this material is accurate enough, it doesn't quite go into enough detail. It might, for example, have included more content relating to the actual diagnosis of a phobia (e.g. a marked or persistent fear for more than six months and an avoidance of the feared object or situation).

Strong answer

A phobia is an excessive and unreasonable fear of certain things or situations, even though the individual recognizes that the fear they feel is unreasonable. DSM and ICD list three different categories of phobia. Specific phobias are irrational fears of a specific object or situation. When the person encounters the feared object, they show an immediate fear response and so go to great lengths to avoid it. A social phobia is an excessive and persistent fear of a particular social situation, such as public speaking. The fear experienced in a social phobia is actually fear of the possibility of embarrassment or humiliation in front of other people rather than the situation itself. Agoraphobia involves being anxious about being in situations from which escape might not be possible. It may be diagnosed with or without panic disorder.

This is a very competent précis of a lot of information. It explains what phobias are, summarizes the different types of phobia and outlines their characteristics. This is both concise and informative.

Part (b)

*Explain **two or more** issues associated with the classification **and/or** diagnosis of phobic disorders.* [**10 marks**]

- Questions that use the term 'explain' can be hard to decipher, as sometimes 'explain' can imply both AO1 and AO2, whereas sometimes (as here), it is AO2 only. Working out when a question is AO2 and when it is AO1 *and* AO2 can be tricky, but here it is simple mathematics. Part (a) is all AO1, and the skill division for part (c) is made clear with 4 marks for AO1 and 6 for AO2. So, as there are only 9 marks for AO1 in total (*8 marks in exams from 2012 onwards*), that means part (b) MUST be all AO2.

- Identifying the issues would be considered the product of analysis (and therefore AO2), and further elaboration of those issues would push the mark up into the higher mark bands.
- Reliability and validity are the usual issues, although there are others such as cultural differences in diagnosis and co-morbidity of phobias with other disorders and so on.
- Remember to cover at least two issues. Answers that cover only one issue (e.g. reliability) would not attract full marks.

Average answer

The two main issues associated with the diagnosis of a mental disorder are validity and reliability. The first of these is all about deciding what is a real mental disorder (and therefore should be treated) and what is just normal behaviour. For example, the clinician has to decide whether a person's behaviour is serious enough to classify as depression or is just the sort of low mood that everyone experiences from time to time. In phobias, for example, some people may show fear of social spaces like shopping malls not because they have agoraphobia, but just because they don't like all the noise and bustle, and so find that a bit frightening. A diagnosis of phobia in that situation would then be invalid because it would be a fairly normal reaction rather than a characteristic of a mental disorder.

The second issue is reliability. Kendler *et al.* (1999) found that the diagnosis of phobias assessed at personal interview lacked reliability. Another problem is that of comorbidity, because often two disorders occur at the same time. For example, many people with a phobia are also depressed as a result of this. Treating the depression rather than the phobia would not be effective because the phobia (the primary disorder) would still be present. By treating the phobia, on the other hand, this would result in a reduction of depression symptoms as well.

This student has chosen reliability and validity as the two issues most affecting the diagnosis and classification of phobias. The explanation is reasonably detailed, but does lack development. For example, we are told that diagnosis using personal interviews lacks reliability, but not told why this is (e.g. through memory distortion or social desirability bias). In the paragraph on validity, just one point is made, so this part of the answer lacks breadth.

Strong answer

A problem for the diagnosis of phobic disorder is that the classification systems may not always produce a valid diagnosis. For example, when diagnosing someone as suffering from a specific phobia, the fear experienced should be considered 'excessive and unreasonable'. However, there is a fine line between what is considered normal fear towards something like a snake or heights (this may be perfectly reasonable and helps us to survive) and fear that might be considered excessive and unreasonable. Therefore there is a possibility that we 'medicalize' what is effectively normal behaviour, which then requires 'treatment'. However, to be diagnosed with a phobic disorder, the fear must be recognized as unreasonable by the individual and also interfere significantly with their everyday functioning, thus justifying attempts to treat and so alter their ☞

behaviour. A major problem when determining the existence of a phobia is that there are no diagnostic tests for phobic behaviours, and so the decision to treat or not to treat a particular type of behaviour comes down to the personal decision of the doctor.

A problem for the diagnosis of phobias is that the doctor has to rely on the patient's description of their behaviour in order for them to make an accurate diagnosis. The doctor must then distinguish the diagnosis of a phobia from other possible disorders. For example, specific phobias share some characteristics with OCD, as a person with OCD may fear objects such as knives. The doctor needs to look for evidence of underlying obsessional thoughts in order to dismiss this possibility. Social phobias can also share some characteristics with schizophrenia, although schizophrenics do not recognize that their fears are irrational, whereas people with phobic disorders do. Because phobias can co-exist with other disorders (such as depression), the doctor has to establish what is the primary disorder in order to treat that, as deciding the wrong disorder as the main one would result in ineffective treatment.

The first paragraph also concentrates on just the one point, but this time with lots of different facets to add detail. We are left with a good understanding of the problem of determining what is and what may not be a phobic reaction. The second paragraph also presents a suitably elaborated discussion of the issue of comorbidity. There is an appropriately evaluative tone throughout (remember that this is all AO2), so could receive full marks for this part of the question.

Part (c)

*Outline and evaluate **one** psychological therapy used in the treatment of phobic disorders.* [**4 marks + 6 marks**]

- This question requires *both* AO1 description *and* AO2 evaluation, but not in equal amounts, as the number of marks available shows (4 marks for AO1 and 6 marks for AO2). For a total of 10 marks, you should be aiming for about 250 words, but this should be split into about 100 words of AO1 and 150 words of AO2.

- Note also that the question requires only one psychological therapy, although variations of this therapy (e.g. different types of behavioural therapies) could count as just one therapy. Any material relating to biological treatments would not receive credit *unless* it is used as part of a critical evaluation of the psychological treatment.

Average answer

One psychological therapy for the treatment of phobias is cognitive-behavioural therapy. This involves changing the way a patient thinks about those things that cause them fear and so develop more effective ways of dealing with them. For example, Beck's cognitive therapy provides a series of tasks that will help the patient cope with difficult situations without experiencing fear. ☞

There is research evidence that shows that CBT can be effective for a range of different phobias, although it is more effective for social phobias than it is for specific phobias. There is also evidence that CBT works most effectively when combined with some other form of treatment, such as behavioural therapy or drug therapy. One of the main things that stops CBT being that effective for some people is the skill of the therapist. Some therapists apply CBT less competently than do others; therefore, it is this rather than the therapy itself that prevents the patient getting better. Drug treatments have also been used effectively in the treatment of phobias, and Fyer *et al.* (1987) found that about 90% of people with phobias got better after taking BZs.

- AO1: The descriptive part of this answer is accurate enough, but only mentions the specific treatment of phobias tangentially. It needs to be made far more explicit; otherwise, this could be a description of CBT in any disorder.
- AO2: The evaluative material is explicitly directed toward phobias, so is better. However, the last sentence on drug treatments is not made relevant and would, therefore, receive minimal credit.

Average answer: overall comment

This answer does show evidence of appropriate knowledge and understanding, and the student makes some decent evaluative points. However, the lack of development and elaboration does limit the overall effectiveness of the answer, and so it would be worth a Grade C only.

Strong answer

Cognitive-behavioural therapy (CBT) helps the patient to identify the negative thoughts that maintain their phobia, and then to replace these with more positive and rational ways of thinking about the object or situation (cognitive restructuring). The behavioural part of CBT gives patients the opportunity to test their irrational thoughts against reality (e.g. someone with a fear of flying may be given statistics about flying being the safest form of travel). They may also be given adaptive cognitive strategies to rehearse whenever they are in the feared situation, e.g. when they are in an open space or have to perform in public.

There are several advantages to using CBT in the treatment of phobias. It is particularly effective in the treatment of social phobias. Barlow and Lehman (1996) found it was more effective than behavioural therapies for social phobias, but less effective for specific phobias. Mansell and Morris did, however, find that CBT could be used effectively in the treatment of some specific phobias, such as fear of the dentist, and another study by Thorpe and Salkovskis (1997) reported significant improvements in spider phobics after just one session of CBT. The effectiveness of CBT has been enhanced when it is combined with graded exposure (systematic ☞

- AO1: Compared to the average answer, this is a much better description of CBT, made explicitly relevant to the treatment of phobias. It adds detail and maximizes the AO1 marks available.
- AO2: Again, this student makes excellent use of research studies to build their evaluation, and constructs a debate within the answer that addresses the 'logical error' that represents a publication bias.

desensitization). However, Cooper *et al.* (2010) claim that because more research focuses on CBT, more studies are published, creating the logical error that CBT is superior to other forms of therapy. They claim that in reality it is not, and that other forms of psychological therapy are equally effective in the treatment of phobias, but have smaller bodies of research.

Strong answer: overall comment

This is well informed, accurate and detailed, with an excellent attention to the need for research evidence. This is well worth a Grade A.

Question 3

Part (a)

Outline **one** *psychological explanation and* **one** *biological explanation for phobic disorders.*
[**9 marks** (2009 onwards)] [**8 marks** (2012 onwards)]

- This part of the question is entirely AO1 description ('Outline…').
- It also requires *two* different explanations (one psychological and one biological). This requires careful planning as an 8/9-mark answer should attract about 200 words in total, which would mean about 100 words for each explanation.

- Questions like this are relatively common, so it is worth practising putting together a concise yet suitably detailed précis of *two* psychological and *two* biological explanations of phobic disorders, so that you are prepared for any combination of requirements.

Average answer

The psychodynamic explanation of phobias claims that a phobia is an expression of an underlying anxiety that may have nothing to do with the feared object or situation. Freud studied a child called Little Hans in a case study. Little Hans had a phobia of horses, but Freud believed that really this was just an unconscious fear of his father. A problem with case studies like Little Hans is that they can't be generalized to other people, and Freud has also been criticized for being biased in his interpretation of the study so that it supports his theory.

The genetic explanation of phobias claims that the fear people have towards things such as snakes, spiders and heights has evolved because our ancestors thought these would have been dangerous, and so natural selection means that a fear of dangerous things would be passed through the genes. These then trigger fight or flight responses that are found when people come into contact with their feared object or situation.

This is a little short on detail and insight. Most of the description concerns the Little Hans case study rather than the explanation itself; also, the material evaluating this case study would not receive credit in this part of the question because the answer should be description only. The genetic explanation is brief but appropriate, and could very easily have been fleshed out to add extra detail for higher marks.

Strong answer

The psychodynamic explanation of phobias is that phobics have displaced an unconscious source of anxiety onto a neutral object or situation. This explanation requires the operation of two defence mechanisms: repression and displacement. The original source of the fear (usually a sexual or Oedipal anxiety) is repressed into the unconscious mind and then, because it continues to have an effect, may be displaced onto the phobic object or situation. This is why the fear appears irrational to the individual, because there is no conscious explanation for it. Another aspect of the psychodynamic explanation comes from Bowlby (1973), who claimed that school phobia and agoraphobia were a consequence of separation anxiety, a fear of losing someone to whom the person has become attached. This would explain why people with these phobias try to stay home to make sure they are not abandoned by the parent.

The genetic explanation is based on the belief that fear and anxiety that are associated with phobias are evolutionary adaptations that help us survive. Most phobias are towards objects that would have been dangerous for our ancestors, such as snakes (poisonous), closed spaces (person would be trapped) and the dark (dangerous because of predators). The adaptation would then become more widespread because individuals who responded to these dangerous objects and situations with the response of fight or flight (avoidance) would be more likely to survive and pass on these characteristics to their descendants. These characteristics would then become more common in the gene pool.

This is a much stronger description of the psychodynamic explanation. Extra detail comes from inclusion of defence mechanisms as well as detail on Bowlby's views on agoraphobia. Detail is vital to push the marks up. The genetic explanation is also far more competent, and the link between adaptive forces and the widespread existence of specific phobias in modern humans is made more explicit.

Part (b)

Evaluate the explanations for phobic disorders that you outlined in part (a). [**16 marks**]

- This part of the question is entirely AO2 ('Evaluate...').
- If part (a) should be answered in about 200 words, this second part should produce about 400 words. This is important because an examiner has separate mark allocations for each skill.
- You can include any combination of good points and bad points relating to each explanation.

- Research evidence is a useful way of building an evaluative response, but you must make it explicit by the use of phrases such as 'This is supported by...' or '...thus challenging the claim that...'. Higher marks are available for material that is elaborated, so bear that in mind when building your response.

Average answer

A problem for the psychodynamic explanation is that there is no evidence to support it. It is difficult to test scientifically, which makes it less acceptable as an explanation. Another problem is that it cannot offer an explanation for every example of phobias experienced. Freud read too much into the Little Hans study. It is also unparsimonious, in that Freud's explanation is very complicated compared to simpler explanations of phobias such as the behavioural explanation. For example, Watson and Raynor explained how phobias could be developed through the process of classical conditioning, which is a much more parsimonious explanation.

The genetic explanation is supported by family studies that show that phobias tend to run in families. For example, Fyer *et al.* found that when individuals with specific phobias were studied, they discovered that about 30% of their first-degree relatives also had a phobia. This supports the claim that there is a genetic basis to phobias. Support also comes from twin studies. For example, Kendler *et al.* found that there was a much higher concordance rate for phobias in MZ twins than there was for DZ twins. There are problems with family and twin studies, which limits the usefulness of these findings. For example, first-degree relatives, and particularly identical twins, share very similar environments – therefore, it is just as likely that they have learned their phobic behaviours from close family members. It is also possible that what is inherited is not the phobia itself but a tendency to develop anxiety toward most things, not just phobic situations. Because the genetic explanation is based on the claim that phobias are fears that evolved from our ancestors, this is impossible to test, because this is something that would have happened millions of years ago.

The choice of the psychodynamic explanation was perhaps not the wisest one for this student, as they have very little to include by way of evaluation. Although the lack of parsimony is appropriate, we are not really told what makes this explanation unparsimonious. Evaluation of the genetic explanation is much better, although the claim that evolutionary based explanations cannot be tested is false.

Average answer: overall comment

Questions in this area nearly always ask for two explanations; therefore, you need to make sure that you have sufficient material for a balanced outline and evaluation of both. This is not the case here, as the psychodynamic explanation is relatively poor. However, this answer may just creep towards a Grade C standard.

Strong answer

The psychodynamic explanation is difficult to test empirically and is based entirely on case studies such as the case study of Little Hans. Case studies such as this are open to subjective interpretation, and, in Freud's case, most of his information about Little Hans was gathered second-hand rather than from direct interviews with the child. However, this explanation does have some cross-cultural evidence to support it. For example, Whiting (1966) found that phobias are more common in cultures that are characterized by strict parenting and the use of punishment, supporting the claim that the anxiety associated with phobias can be traced back to unconscious anxiety toward the parents. The psychodynamic explanation also claims that simply treating the symptom of a phobia will result in symptom substitution, because the unconscious anxiety is still there. However, there is little evidence for this, as after treatment of phobias, there is no evidence of symptom substitution. The evidence for Bowlby's attachment claims is inconclusive. Bowlby did find patterns of anxious attachment in families of people with school phobia and agoraphobia, supporting the link between the two. However, many other studies have found no relationship at all between parental rearing styles (and attachment types) and the development of phobias.

Evidence for the genetic explanation comes from two main sources. Family studies compare the incidence of phobias in relatives of diagnosed cases of phobic disorder compared to relatives of controls who do not have the disorder. Fyer *et al.* (1990) studied first-degree relatives of people with specific phobias and found that 31% had also been diagnosed with phobia, although only 2% were diagnosed with the same form of phobia. Fyer *et al.* (1993) also found that 16% of first-degree relatives of people with a social phobia also had a social phobia, compared to just 5% of relatives of a control group. This suggests that people may inherit a vulnerability to anxiety, possibly due to an oversensitivity of the sympathetic nervous system. This would explain why first-degree relatives may develop a different form of phobia. There are some methodological problems with family studies because most of the data is acquired through family interviews, and these are prone to memory distortions and a social desirability bias. Twin studies compare the difference in concordance rates between MZ and DZ twins. For example, ☞

The inclusion of Bowlby's attachment-based explanation gives more scope for evaluation, which is one of the reasons why this is a much stronger answer. Every claim is justified with argument or research evidence, making the evaluation very effective. There is an impressive attention to detail in the evaluation of the genetic explanation, although exact percentages are not necessary for high marks. Again, lots of appropriate research evidence is included, which makes the evaluation more authoritative and adds that all-important elaboration.

There is lots of accurate and very relevant information in this discussion of the genetic explanation. As with the psychodynamic explanation earlier, it is focused on phobias throughout, and there is plenty of descriptive detail to earn high AO1 marks. The AO2 commentary is also very effective, with the student drawing appropriate conclusions from the material that they have included (e.g. 'This would explain why first-degree relatives may develop a different form of phobia'). There is an appropriate balance of AO1 and AO2, and the whole paragraph shows an excellent critical understanding of the role (and limitations) of a genetic explanation of phobias.

Torgersen (1983) found 13% concordance in MZ twins for agoraphobia and zero concordance for DZ twins. However, Kendler et al. (1992) found that MZ twins had lower concordance rates than DZ twins for specific phobias, which challenges the claim that these phobias have a genetic basis.

Strong answer: overall comment

This is a well-informed coverage of both the two explanations chosen. There is appropriate division of content into the one-third AO1 to two-thirds to AO2, and it is all accurate and detailed. This is a strong, Grade A answer.

Example Paper AQA Unit 4 Psychopathology: Obsessive-compulsive disorder

Question 1

*Outline and evaluate **two or more** therapies used in the treatment of obsessive-compulsive disorder.*
[9 + 16 marks (2009 onwards)] **[8 + 16 marks** (2012 onwards)]

There are a number of important things to note here.

- For students taking this exam in 2011, questions include both types of anxiety disorder – phobias and OCD – and give you the choice which to answer. You will have probably covered only one of these, so that is the one to write about. Don't get distracted by the inclusion of the other in the question, and whatever you do, don't attempt to cover *both* OCD *and* phobias in your answer. From 2012 onwards there will be separate questions on phobias and OCD.

- The question requires both AO1 description ('outline') and AO2 evaluation ('evaluate'). The marks in brackets indicate the number of marks available for each aspect, so for this question, about one-third of your answer should be AO1, and two-thirds should be AO2.

- You are asked to cover at least two therapies relating to OCD. It is entirely up to you whether you write about two therapies or more than two. Bear in mind, though, that trying to include too many would make your answer more superficial.

- To answer the question as it is phrased, you must limit your discussion to therapies *as they are used in the treatment of OCD*, rather than discussing (for example) CBT or drug treatments of mental disorders generally.

- Note that the *type* of therapy is not dictated by this question. Thus, you could use two biological, two psychological or one of each.

Average answer

The first therapy for OCD I am going to write about is drug treatments, which are usually prescribed by a GP or mental health specialist. Drugs are used to treat the physical symptoms of a disorder. Prozac, which is a SSRI, works by preventing the reuptake of serotonin into the neuron. This then reduces the symptoms of OCD. The problem with drug treatments is that they only address the symptoms rather than the underlying cause of the disorder. There are also side effects with many drugs, and Prozac is thought to cause suicide in some people. Another problem with the use of drug treatments for a disorder is that they are only a form of emotion focused coping, so that they only deal with the emotions associated with OCD rather than the actual problem, which requires problem focused coping methods such as CBT. Some people criticize drug treatments as using a chemical straitjacket. Therefore they are not considered an appropriate form of treatment for psychological disorders such as OCD.

A second type of therapy is also a biological treatment, psychosurgery. Psychosurgery is only really used as a last resort when all other types of treatment have ☛

Although the material in this paragraph is accurate, some of these points are more general than specific to OCD. For example, we are told that there are side effects with most drugs, but not told what these might be in the treatment of OCD. There are too many superficial points made here, some descriptive and some evaluative, and not enough elaboration or justification using research evidence to substantiate the assertions being made.

failed. A probe is used to destroy part of the brain that is thought to produce the symptoms of OCD. The probe is inserted into the appropriate part of the brain and then its tip is heated until that part of the brain is burned out and destroyed. A problem with this method, as with all forms of psychosurgery, is that it is irreversible and so might be considered to be unethical. The use of psychosurgery is very carefully controlled under the Mental Health Act. Psychosurgery has been found to be effective in reducing the symptoms of OCD, but it doesn't work for everyone. One study found that only about 1 in 3 patients showed a significant improvement after receiving psychosurgery. There is also a problem that people suffering from OCD may not be able to give their informed consent because their thinking abilities are disturbed.

This is better, as there is some detail about the procedure, although we aren't really told how this type of psychosurgery works. The student might have described the particular circuit that is being targeted and why. The descriptive content lacks detail, but the evaluative content is suitably elaborated.

Another form of treatment used for OCD is behavioural therapy. One type is called ERP, which tries to stop people with OCD carrying out their compulsive behaviours. In this treatment, patients are put into situations where they would normally feel anxious, but they are stopped from performing the compulsive behaviours that would normally accompany them. This can be done by modelling appropriate behaviour or encouraging patients. This form of therapy can be very effective, with about half of the patients showing some improvement after taking part in ERP. In one study, it was found that after receiving ERP, patients showed a significant decrease in brain activity in those brain areas that are normally active during obsessional thoughts. An advantage of behavioural therapies such as ERP is that they can improve OCD symptoms rapidly, and also they don't have any side effects, such as those found in drug treatments.

This is a reasonably effective description and evaluation of ERP therapy, but both description and evaluation lack development. This is particularly problematic in the evaluation, where there are just over 80 words ('This form of therapy can be very effective ...'). For a Grade A answer, we might expect double that amount of evaluation for the second therapy, so this student might have added a couple more evaluative points and elaborated each of the ones already made – in particular, providing supporting evidence for the effectiveness of this type of therapy.

Average answer: overall comment

This is a competent and well-informed answer, but it simply lacks detail (in the AO1) part and elaboration (in the AO2 material). Research studies are always a good source of both, so when revising it is a good idea to do your own detective work and dig out some useful material to flesh out your answers. This is equivalent to a Grade C answer.

Strong answer

Biological therapies are commonly used in the treatment of OCD. One of the problems of trying to treat OCD with drugs is that there is no specific drug treatment ☞

for OCD symptoms. However, drugs that are more usually used in the treatment of other disorders have also been used successfully in the treatment of OCD. The most common drug that has been used for OCD is antidepressants such as tricyclics and SSRIs. Antipsychotics have also been used in the most severe cases of OCD. Tricyclics work by inhibiting the reuptake of serotonin from the synaptic gap. This has the effect of reducing the symptoms of OCD. Studies of one tricyclic (clomipramine) have found that it can be effective in reducing many of the symptoms of OCD. For example, Seksel and Lindeman (2001) used clomipramine in the treatment of OCD-type symptoms in dogs and found that the symptoms were either significantly reduced or disappeared completely in 75 per cent of subjects. Geller *et al.* (2003) compared clomipramine and placebo for paediatric OCD, and provided support for the effectiveness of this drug compared to a placebo in reducing symptoms. However, the difference they found was not large, and the researchers also found some evidence of adverse effects (such as dizziness and dry mouth) in the clomipramine group. The fact that many patients do not tolerate clomipramine well casts doubt over its suitability as a treatment for OCD.

Because of the side effects of tricyclic drugs such as clomipramine, SSRIs are generally preferred as a treatment of OCD because they have fewer adverse side effects. SSRIs start to be effective in reducing the symptoms of OCD about 4 weeks after beginning treatment. This creates a problem for assessing the effectiveness of SSRIs in treating OCD because many patients stop taking the drug after a week or two because they feel they are not doing any good. SSRIs can, however, be effective in reducing symptoms of OCD. Dolberg *et al.* found that over half of those treated with SSRIs reported a significant reduction in their symptoms compared to just 1 in 20 of those who received a placebo. However, as with all drug treatments, the use of SSRIs or tricyclics only reduces the symptoms of OCD, it does not address the underlying causes of the person's obsessional thoughts or compulsive behaviour. SSRIs also have some side effects. For example, there is an increased risk of suicide in adolescents treated with this drug (Nutt 2005).

A treatment that may be used for patients who do not respond to drug treatments is psychosurgery. ☛

This answer is the exact opposite of the average answer on pp. 142–3. It also covers drug treatments, but does so in a much more detailed way. The student describes the method of action of tricyclics, although they might have made it clear exactly how the reuptake of serotonin reduces the symptoms of OCD. They make very effective use of supporting research evidence and elaborate this material by looking at the limitations of such research findings.

This is another very effective paragraph: it is mainly evaluative, so it boosts the very important AO2 content of the answer. It doesn't matter that dates aren't included for all the research studies, so long as these are used effectively to make a point about a drug's effectiveness, as they are here.

The treatment most commonly used in OCD is a bilateral cingulotomy, which targets the cingulate cortex, an area that regulates the brain circuit that is overactive in people suffering from OCD. In this operation, a surgeon burns out part of this brain area, which should result in a reduction in the symptoms of OCD, and a lifting of any feelings of depression or anxiety. This treatment can be effective for some patients. Cosgrove (2000) found that about 1 in 3 people who did not respond to drug treatments were helped by this procedure. However, patients frequently need to have more than one operation to maintain their improvement, and some patients have reported post-surgery complications such as mild cognitive deficits or even epilepsy.

In the average answer, the reference to psychosurgery was rather superficial and non-specific in terms of how the treatment was related to OCD symptoms. However, in this answer, the relevance of psychosurgery to OCD treatment is made specific and this is followed by appropriate evaluation.

More recent developments in the treatment of OCD include transcranial magnetic stimulation (TMS). TMS stimulates brain cells by placing magnets onto the surface of the skull in order to stimulate brain cells, which become either more or less active as a result of this stimulation. Specific regions of the brain can be stimulated repeatedly in order to bring about long-lasting changes in the activity of the neurons in that region. It is not clear how TMS works, but it is thought that there is an increase in the release of serotonin after treatment. The main advantage of TMS as a treatment of OCD is that it is non-invasive and totally painless. Greenberg (1997) provided evidence for the effectiveness of TMS in the treatment of OCD, finding that a single session of TMS produced a significant decrease in compulsive urges in OCD patients that lasted over 8 hours. However, other research has found no difference in improvement rates for patients receiving real TMS and those receiving 'sham' TMS (Rodriguez-Martin 2003). This suggests that the success of TMS for treatment-resistant patients is that it offers hope where there was none before.

This is a very well informed description of TMS followed by appropriate and detailed evaluation. The evaluation is particularly effective in the way that the student squeezes that little bit extra out of every point. For example, it isn't enough just to point out that there was little difference between real TMS and sham-TMS, as we are told why this might be so.

Strong answer: overall comment

This is an excellent answer to the question. The material is accurate, makes good use of research evidence to develop that all-important AO2, and elaborates all important points for maximum impact. This is typical of a high Grade A answer.

Question 2

Part (a)

Outline clinical characteristics of obsessive-compulsive disorder. [**5 marks** (2009 onwards)] [**4 marks** (2012 onwards)]

- The term 'clinical characteristics' does not have one specific meaning, so could be a brief outline of the nature of OCD (i.e. obsessions and compulsions) and/or the 'symptoms' of OCD.
- Remember that 'outline' requires descriptive (AO1) content only, so there is no need for any evaluation in this part of the question.

- As this question is only worth a few marks, you would not be expected to cover all the possible symptoms or characteristics of OCD. For 5 marks, about 150 words would probably suffice; for 4 marks (2012 exams onwards), 125 words or so would be enough.

Average answer

Obsessive-compulsive disorder is usually known as OCD. It has two main parts, obsessions and compulsions. Obsessions are intrusive thoughts, e.g. about germs or dirt, and compulsions are ritualized behaviours (such as washing the hands) that are performed to protect the person from the imagined consequences of exposure to dirt. OCD is not as rare as you might think, and a number of celebrities have the disorder. Two of the most famous are David Beckham and Natalie Appleton. David Beckham has to have all his shirts lined up in colour order, and cannot stand things not to be symmetrical, so if he finds three cans of coke in his fridge would throw one away to make them symmetrical again. Natalie Appleton is obsessed with cleaning and has a particular problem with public toilets.

This starts well enough, but then the student includes lots of irrelevant information about celebrities and their OCD. This sort of material may be interesting, but it isn't relevant and should be ignored.

Strong answer

Obsessive-compulsive disorder (OCD) has two elements. Obsessions are intrusive thoughts and impulses. Common obsessions include dirt and the possibility of contamination, and orderliness. These obsessive thoughts interrupt normal cognitive processing and cannot be dismissed without performing the compulsive behaviour. Compulsive behaviours are repeated acts that the person feels they must perform in order to ward off the anticipated consequences, e.g. repeated hand washing to avoid possible contamination. In order to be diagnosed with OCD, the individual must first acknowledge that their obsessions are a product of their own mind rather than external reality. They must also find their obsessions and compulsions excessive and unpleasant and have failed to resist at least one of these in the past. Their obsessions or compulsions should have existed for a period of at least two weeks.

This is concise and an entirely appropriate way of answering the question. The student includes a detailed outline of the nature of obsessions and compulsions, and fleshes this out with suitable examples. The symptoms described are appropriate and accurate.

Part (b)

*Explain **two or more** issues associated with the classification **and/or** diagnosis of obsessive-compulsive disorder.*
[10 marks]

- Questions that use the term 'explain' can be hard to decipher, as sometimes 'explain' can imply both AO1 and AO2, whereas sometimes (as here), it is AO2 only. Working out when a question is AO2 and when it is AO1 *and* AO2 can be tricky, but here it is simple mathematics. Part (a) is all AO1, and the skill division for part (c) is made clear with 4 marks for AO1 and 6 for AO2. So, as there are only 9 marks for AO1 *in total* (8 marks in exams from 2012 onwards), that means part (b) MUST be all AO2.

- Identifying the issues would be considered the product of analysis (and therefore AO2), and further elaboration of those issues would push the mark up into the higher mark bands.
- Reliability and validity are the usual issues, although there are others such as cultural differences in diagnosis and co-morbidity of OCD with other disorders and so on.
- Remember to cover at least two issues. Answers that cover only one issue (e.g. reliability) would not attract full marks.

Average answer

We all have thoughts about things that worry us from time to time. Sometimes, these appear overwhelming, such as trying to avoid touching a toilet door or checking that we have locked the door several times. There is a fine line between having these relatively normal thoughts and behaviours and being abnormal. This means that doctors may make an invalid diagnosis of OCD because mildly obsessional and compulsive behaviours are quite common. However, both ICD and DSM classification systems require these symptoms to be overwhelming so that should distinguish OCD behaviours from normal behaviours.

Another issue is whether diagnosis is reliable. Brown *et al.* (2001) found that the inter-rater reliability of diagnosis using a measure of OCD was reasonably high. There are also problems if OCD is misdiagnosed (e.g. as depression or generalized anxiety disorder) because this means that the treatment given may not be suitable. Another issue is the cultural bias in treatment. Research has shown that in the US, African-Americans experience OCD symptoms at the same rate as the general population, but many of the tests used to diagnose OCD are not suitable for African-Americans.

The student presents three appropriate issues (validity, reliability and cultural differences in diagnosis) in an intelligent way, although none of these are discussed in any great detail. There is also some good commentary (e.g. that classification systems require symptoms to be 'overwhelming'), but more could have been made of it. There is the basis for a very good answer here, if it were developed a little more.

Strong answer

A problem associated with a valid diagnosis of OCD is that there is a danger of interpreting normal behaviour as indicating a mental disorder. Diagnosis of OCD should only be made when thoughts and behaviours become ☞

so overwhelming that they disrupt normal life. One solution to this problem is to subdivide OCD into different types or subdivisions. A justification for subdividing OCD into different types is that these subtypes respond differently to different types of treatment. For example, Ball *et al.* (1996) found that patients who had cleaning or checking compulsions responded better to behavioural treatments than did patients with other types of compulsions.

Despite this, however, there isn't much evidence to suggest that different types of obsessions and compulsions have different causes. All forms of OCD have the same basic feature in common (the belief that something terrible will happen to them if they don't perform their ritual), which means that diagnosing different subtypes may make little difference to the validity of diagnosis.

A second issue is that diagnosis may lack reliability, as many of the symptoms of OCD are also found in other mental disorders, making misdiagnosis more likely. For example, the obsessional thoughts experienced in OCD are similar to the delusions experienced in schizophrenia. However, it is a requirement of a diagnosis of OCD that the person recognizes that the obsessional thoughts are their own and not from some external source (as is the case with schizophrenia). OCD also frequently occurs with other disorders (comorbidity) such as depression, phobias or substance abuse. For example, two-thirds of people diagnosed with OCD also have symptoms of depression, which makes it difficult to determine which disorder they should be diagnosed with and which disorder they should be treated for.

This answer covers several issues: validity (in terms of the appropriateness of subtypes of OCD), reliability of diagnosis and comorbidity. The last of these would probably count as an extension of reliability. This is accurate, logically structured as a response to the question and constantly supported by appropriate argument and evidence. Examples are entirely appropriate rather than gratuitous and add clarity to the answer.

Part (c)

*Outline and evaluate **one** psychological therapy used in the treatment of obsessive-compulsive disorder.*
[4 marks + 6 marks]

- This question requires *both* AO1 description *and* AO2 evaluation, but not in equal amounts, as the number of marks available shows (4 marks for AO1 and 6 marks for AO2). For a total of 10 marks, you should be aiming for about 250 words, but this should be split into about 100 words of AO1 and 150 words of AO2.

- Note also that the question requires only *one* psychological therapy, although variations of this therapy (e.g. different types of behavioural therapies) could count as just one therapy. Any material relating to biological treatments would not receive credit *unless* it is used as part of a critical evaluation of the psychological treatment.

Average answer

Behavioural therapy targets the compulsive behaviours that go with OCD rather than the obsessions that people with OCD experience. This might be achieved using modeling, where the therapist models the behaviour that makes the person anxious, for example handling something dirty without showing any signs of anxiety. The person with a fear of contamination will then be asked to handle the same thing after the therapist has shown them that there is nothing to worry about. A technique used in behavioural therapy is exposure and response prevention (ERP), which stops people carrying out their compulsive behaviour. For example, if the person felt a compulsion to wash their hands every time they touched a door handle because of a fear of becoming contaminated, the therapist would not let them do so. Although this is difficult at first, the patient is also taught relaxation techniques so that eventually the need to carry out compulsive behaviours disappears.

Behavioural therapies have been shown to be successful with the majority of patients, and when compulsive behaviours are reduced, obsessions also diminish. However, behavioural therapies are not effective with patients who have obsessions that are not accompanied by compulsive behaviours (e.g. sexual obsessions). There is also evidence that ERP can reduce activity in parts of the brain that causes the symptoms of OCD, which is another reason for its effectiveness.

This student has made the classic mistake of concentrating too much on the descriptive content of the answer and not enough on the more heavily rewarded evaluative aspect. No matter how good the descriptive content, it can only earn a maximum of 4 marks. The evaluative content is appropriate, but is only about half as much as might be expected for the AO2 component of the question.

Average answer: overall comment

This student's answer to Question 2 is competent, but there are some errors in planning (rather than errors in psychology), which would restrict this to Grade C level.

Strong answer

A psychological therapy used in the treatment of OCD is exposure and response prevention therapy. This works on the principle that if an individual is prevented from carrying out their ritual behaviours in situations that normally cause them anxiety, then eventually the anxiety will subside, as will the obsessions that are associated with them. To help patients refrain from carrying out their compulsive behaviours, they are taught relaxation techniques so help with any accompanying anxiety, and the therapist uses persuasion and encouragement to help the patient resist any temptation. ☛

Studies on the effectiveness of ERP treatment have found that most patients experience improvement in their OCD symptoms following this treatment. For example, Foa et al. (1985) carried out a meta-analysis of studies from different countries and found that about half of the patients showed at least a significant reduction in their symptoms. ERP has also been found to be effective in the long term. O'Sullivan and Marks (1991) reviewed nine studies that had used ERP and found that in all of these studies, the improvements after ERP treatment were maintained up to six years later. However, the success rate reported in most of these studies does not include patients who refused therapy or dropped out of treatment during the study. Keijsers et al. (1994) claimed that when these patients are included, the success rate drops considerably. ERP may not be appropriate for all patients. ERP is less effective for patients who do not exhibit overt compulsions (e.g. patients with sexual obsessions), nor those who also have moderate to severe depression.

This student has heeded the mark split for this question. The descriptive content is accurate and appropriately detailed, and the evaluative content shows an excellent critical understanding of the appropriateness and effectiveness of ERP. This is reinforced by suitable research evidence. This answer mixes strengths and limitations of ERP, which is impressive but not required for a top-mark answer, as top marks can be gained by either strengths or weaknesses alone, or by a combination of the two.

Strong answer: overall comment

This student's answer to Question 2 is excellent across all three parts, and shows evidence of excellent psychology *and* planning. This would easily be worth a Grade A.

Question 3

Part (a)

*Outline **one** psychological explanation and **one** biological explanation for obsessive-compulsive disorder.*
[9 marks (2009 onwards)] **[8 marks** (2012 onwards)]

- This part of the question is entirely AO1 description ('Outline…').
- It also requires *two* different explanations (one psychological and one biological). This requires careful planning so an 8/9-mark answer should attract about 200 words in total, which would mean about 100 words for each explanation.

- Questions like this are relatively common, so it is worth practising putting together a concise yet suitably detailed précis of *two* psychological and *two* biological explanations so you are prepared for any combination of requirements.

Average answer

There is evidence that OCD may be inherited. Family studies look at the incidence of OCD in families. One study found that children are five times more likely to develop OCD if a parent has OCD. This shows that there is a genetic risk for OCD. Grootheest et al. carried ☞

out a twin study that also showed that there was an important genetic influence in the development of OCD.

Mowrer explained OCD as a consequence of learning maladaptive fears. Neutral objects are associated with anxiety because of some unpleasant event (classical conditioning). For example, touching something that is dirty might become associated with the thought of becoming ill by contamination. The anxiety this creates is reduced by engaging in a repetitive behaviour such as hand-washing. If this works, it is repeated in the future (operant conditioning) and the repetitive behaviours become compulsions.

This answer shows a reasonable understanding of the genetic origins of OCD and of Mowrer's two-process theory. For example, the student appreciates that both classical and operant conditioning are involved. There are some minor inaccuracies: Grootheest et al. was a meta-analysis not a twin study. Neither explanation has sufficient detail and represents a rather superficial coverage of both.

Strong answer

The genetic explanation of OCD is based on information from family and twin studies.

Family studies have found that, in families with an OCD individual, the risk of developing OCD among first-degree relatives is five times greater than in families where there is no diagnosed OCD individual (Pauls et al. 1995). A twin study carried out by Lambert and Kinsley (2005) found that monozygotic twins, who are genetically identical, have a 53% concordance rate for OCD, whereas dizygotic twins, who share only half of their genes have a concordance rate of 23%. Arnold et al. (2006) found that individuals with OCD possessed a particular variant of the glutamate transporter gene (SLC1A1). This variant regulates the flow of glutamine in and out of brain cells in a way that makes it happen much quicker and makes people more susceptible to OCD.

The cognitive-behavioural explanation of OCD claims that OCD is a consequence of irrational ways of thinking being taken to an extreme. This view claims that most people experience intrusive thoughts from time to time, but are able to ignore them. However, people with OCD are unable to ignore these thoughts and blame themselves for having them. As a result, they try to neutralize these thoughts. This can be achieved by carrying out actions to bring temporary relief from the intrusive thoughts, which is reinforcing. Reinforced behaviours are then repeated and a pattern of compulsive behaviours is established. According to this explanation, the person's irrational beliefs about the world would precede their OCD symptoms.

Both explanations (genetic and cognitive-behavioural) are accurate and detailed. The outline of the genetic explanation is particularly skilled, covering family and twin studies with appropriate research detail. The student is aware of recent developments in genetic research, which would certainly impress an examiner, particularly as it fits flawlessly into the answer. The cognitive-behavioural explanation is also very competent and shows an in depth understanding of how this explanation can explain OCD.

Part (b)

Evaluate the explanations for obsessive-compulsive behaviour that you outlined in part (a). **[16 marks]**

- This part of the question is entirely AO2 ('Evaluate...').
- If part (a) should be answered in about 200 words, this second part should produce about 400 words. This is important because an examiner has separate mark allocations for each skill.
- You can include any combination of good points and bad points relating to each explanation.

- Research evidence is a useful way of building an evaluative response, but you must make it explicit by the use of phrases such as 'This is supported by...' or '...thus challenging the claim that...'. Higher marks are available for material that is elaborated, so bear that in mind when building your response.

Average answer

The genetic explanation of OCD relies on twin studies and family studies. There is evidence from these studies that support the importance of genetics. For example, Lambert and Kinsley (2005) found that identical twins were far more alike in terms of OCD than were non-identical twins. This is important because identical twins share 100% of their genes, and non-identical twins share only 50%. The fact that identical twins are more alike in terms of OCD must, therefore, mean that this is caused by a greater genetic similarity. However, there are problems with this type of study. For example, twins share very similar environments so it may be that it is the shared environment rather than genetics that is causing their symptoms. Also, in family studies, it is possible that children learn by imitating the behaviour of their parents, so if one parent has OCD, children may copy their behaviours through social learning. Another problem for a genetic explanation is that if OCD was caused solely by genetics, then there would be 100% concordance, which means that if one twin has OCD then the other identical twin (because they share 100% of their genes) would also have OCD. This isn't what has been found, so environmental factors must also be important.

Most of the evaluation for behavioural explanations is from supporting studies, which have shown that compulsive behaviours do reduce anxiety in patients who have OCD, so this is reinforcing for them. The other point of evaluation is that there are effective treatments based on behavioural explanations, which suggests that if OCD behaviours are learned, they can be unlearned. This is what happens in exposure and response prevention therapy.

Evaluation of the genetic explanation is excellent and would be typical of a Grade A answer. However, the student is let down by their rather poor evaluation of behavioural explanations. This is not unusual, as students frequently get carried away with one explanation (or in this case evaluation of that explanation) to the detriment of the other.

Average answer: overall comment

Looking at this student's responses to parts (a) and (b) combined, there is a lack detail and development for the second explanation, which suggests that perhaps the student was not prepared for a question that covered *two* explanations in equal amounts. This is equivalent to a Grade C answer.

Strong answer

A problem with family studies is that it is difficult to separate the effects of genetics from other factors in the individual's environment. For example, despite the fact that OCD behaviours are generally maladaptive, it is possible that younger family members learn these behaviours from parents or older siblings just because they spend a great deal of time with them. This would challenge the belief that the observed similarity is due solely to genetics, as individuals tend to spend more time with those with whom they are closely genetically related. Twin studies also have problems, because researchers do not have access to large numbers of twins where one twin has OCD. Instead, many studies focus on individuals with some obsessive-compulsive symptoms yet who have not been diagnosed with OCD. As most individuals display mild obsessional thinking or compulsive behaviour at some time of their life, it is difficult to reach conclusions about the origins of full-blown OCD using this subclinical sample. Even those studies that have used MZ and DZ twins that have been diagnosed with OCD fail to show 100% concordance, which should be the case if the disorder were entirely inherited. This suggests that the genetic contribution may simply be a predisposition to anxiety generally, which may or may not develop into OCD depending on childhood experiences (e.g. Adler's belief that OCD develops as a result of the inferiority complex that is a consequence of domineering parenting).

Many of the predictions of a cognitive-behavioural explanation of OCD have been supported by research findings. For example, the prediction that dysfunctional beliefs about the world should precede OCD symptoms was supported by Foa *et al.* (2002). The explanation also predicts that any event that strengthens a particular irrational belief should increase the symptoms of OCD for some people. Supporting this, Abramowitz *et al.* (2005) found that a belief in personal responsibility is strengthened after people first become parents (i.e. they develop parental responsibility) and this corresponds with the onset of OCD symptoms ☞

This is a very impressive answer. All of the material is used in a critical way, and is given an appropriate level of elaboration. The material is selected carefully to offer a searching analysis and evaluation of both explanations. Even cognitive-behavioural therapy, which is notoriously difficult to evaluate when dealing with OCD, is subject to critical examination by research evidence.

among new parents. The cognitive-behavioural explanation is also strengthened by the finding that therapies based on this approach have been shown to be successful at reducing the symptoms of OCD. For example, research (Huppert and Franklin 2005) has shown that of those who complete a course of cognitive-behavioural therapy (CBT), there is a significant improvement in 3 out of 4 cases. In fact, CBT has been found to be superior to exposure and response prevention therapy (Salkovskis 2007), which suggests that the cognitive component of the disorder is as important, if not more important, than the behaviours associated with OCD.

Strong answer: overall comment

This is accurate, appropriate and well balanced across both parts of question 3 and both AO1 and AO2. It makes excellent use of research evidence and is a clear Grade A answer.

Glossary

Affective disorder   Mental disorder characterized by dramatic changes or extremes of mood

Agency   The capacity that human beings have to make choices and to impose those choices on the world

Agonist   A chemical that works in the same way as a naturally occurring neurochemical

Agoraphobia   An extreme anxiety of being in a public place where escape is difficult (e.g. in the middle of a crowded bus) or where it would be difficult to seek help for treatment of a panic attack

Anhedonia   The inability to react to pleasure or enjoyable experiences (a symptom of schizophrenia)

Antagonist   A chemical that blocks a naturally occurring neurochemical

Atypical depression   A type of depression where the person overeats and oversleeps (as opposed to typical depression where the sufferer undereats and has difficulty sleeping)

Behavioural activation   A form of therapy that encourages patients to pursue healthy activities (individual and social) that reward them, at the same time keeping a close record of their activities and resulting mood

Bipolar disorder   A mood disorder characterized by extremes of mania and depression

Brain imaging   Non-invasive methods of studying the brain, e.g. using X-rays or radio waves to produce pictures of sections through the brain or high-definition pictures of brain structures

Catatonic behaviour   Where an individual makes characteristic movements that are repetitive or purposeless (a symptom of schizophrenia)

Classical conditioning   A form of learning where a neutral stimulus is paired with a stimulus that already produces a response, such that, over time, the neutral stimulus also produces that response

Clinical depression   A serious medical illness that negatively affects how someone feels, thinks and acts, rendering them unable to function as they used to

Cognitive error   A faulty thought process; a belief in something that is not true

Cognitive style   A term used in cognitive psychology to describe the way individuals think, perceive and remember information

Comorbidity   The presence of one or more disorders (or diseases) in addition to a primary disease or disorder

Complicated grief   A form of grief in which the bereaved gets stuck at some point and is unable to process the death of a loved one; it is often a sign of unresolved problems in the relationship between the bereaved and the deceased

Concordance rate   In a sample of twin pairs, if one twin of each pair has a particular disorder, the concordance rate refers to the number of times that the other twin also shows that disorder; in a sample of 200 pairs of twins, if 90 have the disorder, then the concordance rate is 45 per cent

Delusions of belief   Where a person thinks they have special powers or that people around them have special powers

Depression   A mood disorder characterized by sadness

Diathesis-stress model   Explanation of a psychological disorder that places importance on the interaction between the person and their environment

Discontinuation syndrome   A syndrome that can occur following the discontinuation of antidepressant treatments; common symptoms including dizziness, anxiety, irritability, panic attacks, decreased concentration and insomnia

Dopamine hypothesis   Theory suggesting that schizophrenia is caused by an overactivity of the neurotransmitter dopamine in certain parts of the brain

Double-bind hypothesis The claim that children may experience confusion, self-doubt and eventual withdrawal if they are given conflicting messages from parents who express care yet at the same time appear critical

DSM (Diagnostic and Statistical Manual of Psychiatric Disorders) A classification, definition and description of over 200 mental health disorders, used in the USA, grouping disorders in terms of their common features; the latest version is DSM-IV-TR published in 2000

Dysthymic disorder A milder but longer-lasting form of depression

Ego According to psychoanalytic theory, the part of the personality responsible for decision-making and dealing with reality

Electroconvulsive therapy (ECT) Giving a patient an electric shock, applied through electrodes on the scalp, which causes a seizure with the purpose of alleviating the symptoms of a mental disorder

Endogenous depression Depression caused by internal, biological mechanisms (as opposed to reactive depression)

Epidemiological studies Studies looking at the incidence and distribution of diseases

Expressed emotion (EE) In the context of schizophrenia, this refers to the amount of hostility and criticism that other people (often family members) direct towards the person with schizophrenia.

Extiactism The disappearance of a learned connection between a stimulus and response.

Extinction The disappearance of a learned connection between a stimulus and response

Extrapyramidal problems Extreme motor problems associated with first-generation antipsychotic drugs

Flatness of affect Where the individual seems apathetic and talks without emotion (a symptom of schizophrenia)

Gene A unit of heredity composed of DNA that may determine the characteristics of an individual

Glutamate The most common neurotransmitter in the brain

Hormone A chemical that travels in the blood and controls the actions of other cells or organs

ICD (International Classification of Diseases) A classification of physical and psychological disorders published and regularly updated by the World Health Organization; the current edition is ICD-10, published in 1992

Id According to psychoanalytic theory, the part of the personality present at birth, the mental representation of biological drives

Knight's move thinking Incoherent or irrelevant speech, where speech can be rambling and sparking off in all directions (a symptom of schizophrenia); named after the knight in chess, which doesn't move in a straight line but takes a right-angled turn

Learned helplessness A psychological state produced as a result of being exposed to uncontrollable events; observed in people who give up trying to cope because previous attempts have been frustrated and led to failure

Limbic system A set of structures in the brain, including the hippocampus, amygdala, anterior thalamic nuclei, septum and limbic cortex, which seem to support a variety of functions including emotion, behaviour and long-term memory.

Mania A state of abnormally elevated or irritable mood, arousal and/or energy levels; a feature of bipolar disorder

Meta-analysis A method of combining a number of studies on the same theme in order to detect trends in the behaviour being studied

Nature–nurture debate   The controversy about the relative contributions of genetic factors (nature) versus environmental factors (nurture) in determining a person's characteristics and abilities

Negative reinforcement   The situation where the occurrence of a behaviour is increased because it removes an unpleasant stimulus; for example, compulsive hand-washing reduces the anxiety associated with an obsessive fear of contamination

Neurotransmitters   The chemicals which allow the transmission of signals from one neuron to the next across synapses

Noradrenaline   A chemical made by some nerve cells and in the adrenal gland. It can act as both a neurotransmitter and a hormone; noradrenaline is released from the adrenal gland in response to stress and low blood pressure

Obsessive-compulsive disorder (OCD)   A mental disorder characterized by intrusive, unwelcome thoughts (obsessions) and a need to perform repetitive and ritualistic behaviour (compulsions), along with intense anxiety when these behaviours are suppressed

Operant conditioning   An explanation of learning that sees the consequences of behaviour as of vital importance to the future appearance of that behaviour. If a behaviour is followed by a desirable consequence, it becomes more frequent; if it is followed by an undesirable consequence, it becomes less frequent

Overvalued ideation   In some people with OCD, the tendency to overvalue the irrational threats (obsessions), instead considering them logical and justified

Paranoid or persecutory delusions   Where an individual believes that they are being followed by spies or other people who want to harm them (a symptom of schizophrenia)

Phobic disorders (phobias)   A type of anxiety disorder where a person experiences extreme fear out of all proportion to the actual danger posed by a particular object or situation

Positive reinforcement   A stimulus that makes a particular behaviour more likely because of the pleasant rewards it brings, e.g. being in a relationship is positively reinforced as it brings rewards such as companionship, sex and intimacy

Poverty of speech   Where an individual uses meaningless phrases, e.g. to answer questions (a symptom of schizophrenia)

Premenstrual dysphoric disorder   A depression experienced by women that has its onset in the week prior to menstruation

Proband   The original patient in a genetic study

Projective identification   A psychodynamic concept whereby one person (e.g. one without schizophrenia) projects emotions onto another person (e.g. one with schizophrenia), telling them how they should be feeling

Prospective study   An investigation where the participants are studied over an extended period of time.

Psychoactive drugs   Chemical substances that affect people psychologically, including tobacco, alcohol and recreational drugs

Psychosis (pl. psychoses)   A serious condition that affects a person's mind and causes changes to the way they think, feel and behave, with the result that they may be unable to distinguish between reality and their imagination

Psychosurgery   Any operation performed on the brain with the aim of alleviating the symptoms of mental illness

Punishment   In behaviourist terms, a stimulus that has an unpleasant effect, e.g. moving away from family and friends to search for work resulting in isolation and loneliness

Reactive depression   Depression that arises in response to external events, such as a bereavement (as opposed to endogenous depression)

Reality-monitoring deficit   A problem telling what is real from what is not (a symptom of schizophrenia)

Reductionist   An approach to behaviour that explains a complex set of facts, entities, phenomena or structures by another, simpler set (e.g. the biological explanation of schizophrenia as due solely to overactivity of the neurotransmitter dopamine in certain parts of the brain)

Reliability   In the context of classification systems, this refers to the consistency with which clinicians agree on a diagnosis for a particular set of symptoms; for a classification system to be reliable, those using it must be able to agree when a person should or should not be given a particular diagnosis

Rumination   Thinking deeply about even the simplest things

Schema   A knowledge package built up through experience that enables us to make sense of familiar situations and interpret new information

Schizoid personality disorder   A diagnosis made of people who show schizophrenic-like behaviour, but do not meet all the diagnostic criteria of schizophrenia

Schizophrenic spectrum   A view of schizophrenia that sees it as encompassing a wide range of behaviour and places less reliance on the presence of certain symptoms for certain lengths of time

Schizophrenogenic   Tending to produce or develop schizophrenia

Social phobia (social anxiety disorder)   An excessive fear of social situations, such as being asked to make a presentation

Specific phobia   Persistent and irrational fear for a particular object or situation (excluding social phobia and agoraphobia)

Suicidal ideation   A common medical term for thoughts about suicide, which may be as detailed as a formulated plan, without the suicidal act itself

Superego   According to psychodynamic theory, the part of the personality that acts as the conscience

Symbolic loss   Term used in psychodynamic theory to describe the loss of something intangible, e.g. becoming blind in adulthood

Symptoms   The clinical characteristics of a disorder or illness

Synaptic cleft   The tiny space between two nerve cells across which neurotransmitters diffuse; the small volume of the cleft allows neurotransmitter concentration to be raised and lowered rapidly

Tardive dyskinesia   An extreme motor problem characterized by repetitive and pointless movements, including lip-smacking and other facial tics

Thought broadcasting   The belief that an external force is broadcasting what an individual is thinking to others (on radio or television)

Thought insertion   The belief that an external force is making an individual think something that is distasteful or unwelcome in some way (a symptom of schizophrenia)

Thought-action fusion (TAF)   The belief that thoughts can influence the world

Unipolar disorder   A type of mood disorder where the person experiences feelings of great sadness, worthlessness and guilt, and finds the challenges of life overwhelming (see also bipolar disorder)

Urbanicity   An increasing tendency of people to live in urban rather than rural areas

Validity   In the context of a disorder, this refers to whether the condition actually exists or not

Index